From Stone to Paper

From Stone to Paper

Architecture as History in the Late Mughal Empire

Chanchal B. Dadlani

Yale University Press   New Haven and London

Published with assistance from the Annie Burr Lewis Fund.

Illustrations in this book were funded in part or in whole by a grant from the SAH/Mellon Author Awards of the Society of Architectural Historians.

yalebooks.com/art

Designed by Leslie Fitch
Set in Crimson and Source Sans type by Tina Henderson
Printed in China by 1010 Printing International Limited

Library of Congress Control Number: 2017956621
ISBN 978-0-300-23317-9

A catalogue record for this book is available from the British Library.

This paper meets the requirements of ANSI/NISO Z39.48-1992 (Permanence of Paper).

10 9 8 7 6 5 4 3 2 1

Jacket illustrations: (front) *Mausoleum of Safdar Jang* (detail of fig. 4.4); (back) Interior wall, Moti Masjid, Delhi, 1658–63
Frontispiece: Interior vaults, tomb of Safdar Jang (detail of fig. 3.9)
Page 56: Muhammad Yusuf, *A View of the Dargah or Shrine of Qutb-Sahib at Mehrauli*, c. 1845. Watercolor on paper, 17.5 × 23 in. (45 × 59 cm). British Library, London. © The British Library Board, London, Add. Or. 4308.

For my parents, and for Penny and Sanjay

CONTENTS

Acknowledgments   viii

Note on Translation and Transliteration   xi

Introduction: The Mughal Eighteenth Century   1

1   Between Experimentation and Regulation:
    The Foundations of an Eighteenth-Century Style   21

2   The Urban Culture of Mughal Delhi   57

3   "The Last Flicker in the Lamp of Mughal Architecture":
    Transforming the Imperial Capital   83

4   Codifying Mughal Architecture on Paper   113

5   Mughal Architecture Between Manuscript and Print Culture   149

Conclusion: From Historicization to Abstraction   175

Notes   180

Select Bibliography   196

Index   210

Illustration Credits   219

ACKNOWLEDGMENTS

This book would have been impossible without the vital support and unflagging generosity of many individuals and institutions, and it is a pleasure to thank them here. Gülru Necipoğlu and David Roxburgh were outstanding advisers throughout graduate school, and have remained steadfast supporters since then. My personal and intellectual debts to them are immeasurable. Ebba Koch shared her expertise on Mughal architectural history and facilitated my research in the field. Robert Travers was generous with his insights on eighteenth-century India, and understood what I was trying to do with this book before I did. Sunil Sharma offered his knowledge of Indo-Persian literature and cultural history, helped me translate texts, and encouraged me to think about artistic culture across disciplines. Tom Cummins, Emine Fetvacı, Alina Payne, Nasser Rabbat, and Jim Wescoat also made important suggestions in the early stages of my research and writing, shaping my thinking in fundamental ways. It was my privilege to study Persian with Wheeler Thackston, and he laid a solid foundation for my subsequent study of the language. I never would have pursued academia without the support of my undergraduate mentors at Columbia, and I sincerely thank Ritu Birla, Jerri Dodds, David Eng, and Stephen Murray. For sparking my love of art history, I am indebted to Jose Rodriguez and the late Beau Siegel.

I am also grateful to those who read and commented on all or part of the manuscript. Shiben Banerji, Sylvia Houghteling, Aaron Hyman, Subhashini Kaligotla, Dipti Khera, David Lubin, Megan Luke, Morna O'Neill, Yael Rice, Ünver Rüstem, Jeffrey Saletnik, Sunil Sharma, and Nancy Um read various chapters in development, and Ana Botchkareva graciously read the entire book. Gülru Necipoğlu brought incisive insights, Ebba Koch made critical suggestions, and David Roxburgh went above the call of duty, reading the manuscript under immense time pressure, his trademark green pen in hand, with crucial interventions at the ready. Nebahat Avcioğlu, Barry Flood, and Kishwar Rizvi edited and improved earlier versions of chapters 2 and 4. I would also like to thank lecture and seminar audiences at Columbia, Cornell, the Forum Transregionale Studien, the Getty Research Institute, Harvard, the Kunsthistorisches Institut, the Triangle Consortium for South Asian Studies, UC–Berkeley, UNC–Chapel Hill, UNC–Greensboro, Wake Forest University, and Yale, and audiences at the meetings of the American Council for Southern

Asian Art and the Historians of Islamic Art Association. On these occasions, feedback from Glaire Anderson, Cathy Asher, Hannah Baader, Sussan Babaie, Tim Barringer, Iftikhar Dadi, Vidya Dehejia, Vittoria DiPalma, Barry Flood, Anne Higonnet, Padma Kaimal, Holger Klein, Alka Patel, Kishwar Rizvi, Tamara Sears, Avinoam Shalem, and Nancy Um was especially vital. In addition, I benefited greatly from conversations with other Mughal scholars and Delhi enthusiasts, including Narayani Gupta, the late Yunus Jaffrey, Jerry Losty, Lucy Peck, Malini Roy, Yuthika Sharma, and Susan Stronge. It has been a privilege and pleasure to work beside my colleagues at Wake Forest University, and I would like to thank those who have discussed matters both intellectual and logistical regarding this book: Bernadine Barnes, Jay Curley, Page Laughlin, David Lubin, Morna O'Neill, John Pickel, and Laura Veneskey. Finally, thanks are certainly due to the anonymous readers who reviewed the manuscript and offered valuable suggestions for its improvement. All errors and shortcomings are, of course, my own.

I would also like to thank the archivists, curators, and librarians at the institutions where I conducted research, including Helen George and the staff at the Asia, Pacific and Africa Collections at the British Library, London; Nick Barnard and Susan Stronge in the Asian Department at the Victoria & Albert Museum, London; Marie-Paule Blasini at the Archives nationales d'outre-mer, Aix-en-Provence; the staff at the Bibliothèque nationale de France, Paris; Claus-Peter Haase and the staff at the Museum für Islamische Kunst, Berlin; Raffael Gadebusch at the Museum für Asiatische Kunst, Berlin; Veena Bhasin at the Delhi State Archives; and the staff at the National Archives of India, New Delhi.

I received substantial institutional support for this project from Wake Forest University as well as from the Department of Art History and Archaeology at Columbia University, where I was a Mellon Postdoctoral Fellow. The research for this book was supported by the Fulbright Foundation, the Andrew W. Mellon Foundation, the Aga Khan Program for Islamic Architecture at Harvard University, the Graduate School of Arts and Sciences at Harvard University, and, at Wake Forest University, the William C. Archie Fund for Faculty Excellence and the Charlotte C. Weber Faculty Award in Art. The Society of Architectural Historians' SAH/Mellon Author Award funded the image program. An earlier and shorter version of Chapter 2 was published in *Affect, Emotion, and Subjectivity in Early Modern Muslim Empires: New Studies in Ottoman, Safavid, and Mughal Art and Culture* in 2017, and has been partially reproduced here with the permission of Brill.

I am grateful to my editor at Yale University Press, Katherine Boller, whose enthusiasm and professionalism made this book possible. Thanks are due also to the rest of the team at YUP, including Sarah Henry, Heidi Downey, Laura Hensley, and Raychel Rapazza. The heroic Kendra Battle, Visual Resources Technician in the Department of Art at Wake Forest, provided invaluable assistance with the images. It was also a pleasure to work with Grae Prickett and Dylan Stein, who produced many of the maps and plans in the book.

My research and writing were made infinitely easier by the hospitality and friendship of many. In India, my research trips began and ended at the Kohli residence in Delhi, and I am forever indebted to this warm, generous, and affectionate family, especially to my lovely friends Gauri and Vidur Kohli. In London, Yani Sinanoglou and Stella Chapman have always provided me with a home away from home and a gin and tonic in the garden. Numerous friends also made the completion of this book a pleasure rather than a task. I am especially grateful to Sana Aiyar, Amna Akbar, Ladan Akbarnia, Natasha Aswani, Shiben Banerji, Sayu Bhojwani, Ana Botchkareva, Jessica Callaway, Ramsey Chamie, Nikhil Chandra, Riana Dadlani, Merih Danali, Sarika Doshi, Emine Fetvacı, Bobbi Gajwani, Yun-Yi Goh, Sarah Guerin, Sylvia Houghteling, Leah Kalm-Freeman, David Kim, Seema Rattan Kinra, Michelle Kuo, Anneka Lensen, Megan Luke, Meredith Martin, Nadia Marx, Prita Meier, Vipin Narang, Eleanor Newbigin, Zeynep Oğuz, Prue Peiffer, Jennifer Pruitt, Mina Rajagopalan, Cole Roskam, Ünver Rüstem, Rahul Sachde, Jeffrey Saletnik, Jonathan Smolin, and Suzan Yalman.

I am deeply indebted to my parents, Banu and Preeti Dadlani, my sisters, Mamta Dadlani and Gitanjali Dadlani Morris, my brother-in-law, Seth Dadlani Morris, and my niece and nephew, Sana and Shaan Dadlani Morris, who have provided constant support, much-needed perspective, and much comic relief. I am also grateful to the extended family who have always taken an interest in my work and been a source of moral support: Iman Ahmed, Stella Chapman, Wendy Darby, Andrew Sinanoglou, and Yani Sinanoglou. But my most significant debt is to my wife, Penny, a brilliant thinker, fearless travel partner, and honest critic. Her insights and unstinting support have made all the difference. And finally, I thank our beloved son, Sanjay. I will be forever grateful that he delayed the arrival of this book.

NOTE ON TRANSLATION AND TRANSLITERATION

When referencing primary sources in languages other than English, I have included citations to editions of works in their original language as well as to known English translations. Unless a translation is noted, the translations are mine.

In transliterating words from Arabic or Persian, I have followed a simplified version of the guidelines established in the *International Journal of Middle East Studies* (*IJMES*), adapted for South Asian studies. Technical terms (for example, those pertaining to architecture, literary concepts, or historical manuscript titles) are transliterated with diacritics. In all other instances, including place-names or personal names, diacritics have been omitted, with the exception of *'ayn* and *hamza*. For ease of reference, transliterated names and titles in the endnotes and bibliography appear as they do in standard online databases. When a word exists in English dictionaries (for example, "mihrab"), it is neither transliterated nor italicized.

Introduction

The Mughal Eighteenth Century

In the Delhi suburb of Mehrauli, amid low-lying apartment blocks and a network of narrow neighborhood streets, sits an abandoned Mughal palace. The Zafar Mahal (c. 1806–58), as it is known, features an imposing gateway of red sandstone and white marble, with cusped arches, floral motifs, and gracefully sloped balconies (*jharoka-yi bangla*), forms that had long been associated with the Mughal empire (1526–1858) and, more specifically, codes of imperial sovereignty (fig. 0.1). The choice to draw on an architectural language that was recognizably Mughal was a significant one. By the first decades of the nineteenth century, when the last Mughal emperors, Akbar II (r. 1806–37) and Bahadur Shah Zafar (r. 1837–58), inhabited this palatial complex, Mughal imperial authority was largely diminished. Former provinces were now independent states, emperors had been attacked or killed within the walls of the imperial palace-fortress, and the British had annexed Delhi in 1803, designating themselves "protectors" of the Mughal emperor, whose remaining authority extended no farther than Delhi itself. It was in these troubled circumstances that the Mughal emperors built the Zafar Mahal, a monument that clearly invoked the imperial past through the use of highly charged symbolic forms.

Yet the Zafar Mahal was not an isolated case of revivalism. Rather, in engaging the past to confront the present, the architects of the palace followed a pattern that had emerged over the course of the eighteenth century, the subject of this book. During the long eighteenth century, architects and patrons skillfully bridged past and present, drawing upon an arsenal of emblematic architectural forms while simultaneously responding to rapidly shifting sociopolitical currents, adapting to new modes of urbanism, and grappling with a growing interest in architectural representation. As a result, the political misfortunes of the Mughal eighteenth century coincided with—and at times resulted in—dynamism and creative transformation in the architectural sphere. Ultimately, architecture allowed the later Mughals to animate their past, refashion their identity, and stage authority, even as they experienced political loss.

This book focuses on the richness and import of eighteenth-century Mughal architectural culture—the monuments, urban spaces, building practices, and modes of theorizing and representing architecture that had currency at this time. It illuminates the critical transition from Mughal to British rule, and engages with shifts between

FIGURE 0.1
Zafar Mahal, Mehrauli, Delhi, c. 1806–58.

the early modern and the modern. I argue that it was during this period that the very
concept of a historical style identifiable as "Mughal" emerged, canonized as monuments
were built on the ground and represented on paper. As Mughal architecture was historicized and theorized, it stood at the center of dramatic political contestations between
regional Indian rulers and European colonial powers seeking to position themselves as
successors to the Mughal throne. For instance, the provincial governors (nawabs) of Awadh
in northeastern India appropriated these visual codes when they constructed the mausoleum of Safdar Jang, a monumental tomb of the type usually reserved for Mughal emperors (1753–54; fig. 0.2), with its symmetrical domed chamber topped by a bulbous white
marble dome and raised high above a wide plinth. French and British scholars, meanwhile,
sought to capture and control the legacy of the Mughals as they forged histories that
included architecture.[1] As the Mughal architectural past was contested by these competing
external powers, the Mughals themselves grew ever more self-referential. By the early
decades of the nineteenth century, the Mughals had a clear vision of their architectural
history and its significance vis-à-vis imperial authority, evident in specially commissioned
manuscripts depicting Mughal monuments from the past and in new architectural projects, such as the Zafar Mahal. What emerged over the course of the eighteenth century, in
other words, was a strongly historicist impulse in Mughal architectural culture.

To explore Mughal historicism, I interpret a rich array of built forms and urban
spaces, from the grand imperial mosques, mausolea, and palaces of north India to the

vibrant shrines and public thoroughfares of the Mughal capital at Delhi; diverse representations on paper, including building plans commissioned by European military officers, illustrated geographies in Persian and Urdu, Mughal manuscript paintings, and souvenir postcards produced for the nineteenth-century tourist market; and the depiction of Delhi and its monuments in written texts, primarily travel narratives and poetry (figs. 0.3, 0.4). Taking my cue from the Mughal conception of the monumental, which eschewed the idea of monuments as monolithic entities and instead favored expansive, multisensorial complexes, I consider the monument in space (in relation to siting and urban context) and time (in conjunction with practices of architectural representation on paper and in text).

The issue of representation intertwines the varied examples in this book and informs my approach to them. The act of representing Mughal architecture through text and image did not happen in isolation, separately from the act of building monuments in stone and mortar. Rather, Mughal architecture took shape as an idea as it was constructed on the ground and represented on the page. Thus I consider ideas embodied in the individual buildings and, just as crucially, the historical and aesthetic sensibilities monuments represent collectively (not merely in parallel). These converged with modes of representing Mughal architecture on paper, and with the idea of Delhi created in literary texts. In other words, it was not merely depictions on paper and text that produced the idea of a Mughal city and its monuments in the eighteenth century; the act of building itself was also crucial in this process of definition. A reflexive Mughal style, insistent and consistent in its self-referentiality, was just as essential in generating historicism. It was thus through

FIGURE 0.3
Artist unknown, *Gateway of the Red Fort of Delhi,* from the *Palais Indiens* (c. 1774), Faizabad. Opaque watercolor on paper, 23.2 × 35.2 in. (59 × 89.5 cm). Bibliothèque nationale de France, Paris, Od. 63, fol. 14.

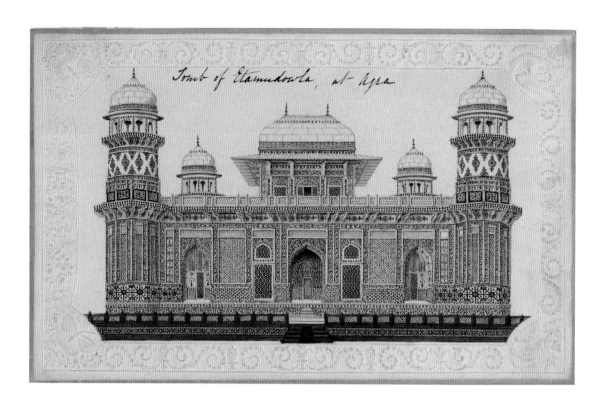

Tomb of Etamudowla, at Agra

FIGURE 0.4

Artist unknown, *Tomb of Itimad al-Daula*, c. 1820. Watercolor on paper with embossed borders, 5 × 8 in. (12.4 × 19.9 cm). Victoria and Albert Museum, London, IS.11–1964. © Victoria and Albert Museum, London.

representation enacted across multiple media and genres that historical knowledge was fashioned.

The book's temporal scope comprises a "long eighteenth century," connecting the imperial monuments of the late seventeenth century to the architectural histories circulating in the early nineteenth century and covering a span of 150 years. Many of these developments occurred in the city of Delhi, the longtime capital of the Mughal empire and the present-day capital of India, and this book approaches eighteenth-century Mughal architecture with an urbanist framework, meaning that I approach architecture from the perspective of urban users and viewers. While it addresses the historical specificities of the Mughal eighteenth century, at its most fundamental level, this is a book about the complex relationships between the codification of architectural style; its representation across media, time, and space; the production of historical narratives; and Mughal agency in these related processes.

RECASTING THE EIGHTEENTH CENTURY

To undertake this investigation, I build upon work that has emphasized sixteenth- and seventeenth-century Mughal architecture. In part, this emphasis can be traced back to the foundational scholarship of the late nineteenth and early twentieth centuries. These early histories, many of which were written by British colonial historians, set the terms of an interpretive framework that would be adopted by generations of later art historians. The standard narrative was one of efflorescence and decline, in which eighteenth-century Mughal architecture occupied a space between the corrupt and the meaningless, similar to the Rococo in Europe. The very devising of a "late" phase began as early as the Victorian period and the seminal work of James Fergusson, whose *History of Indian and Eastern Architecture* (1876) was among the first attempts in English to document and historicize the architecture of the subcontinent.[2] Fergusson designated the later seventeenth and the eighteenth centuries, the period after the first five "great Mughals" (the emperors Babur, Humayun, Akbar, Jahangir, and Shah Jahan), as one of artistic degeneration.[3] This attitude persisted in the early twentieth century, when it was incorporated into new but equally essentialist frameworks. One interpretation, for instance, asserted that the decline of Mughal architecture was tied to its "Islamicization" and departure from "Hindu" forms.[4] Another explicitly connected art historical decay to the disintegration of the empire (versus a more generalized corruption of taste), with Percy Brown writing, "After the death of Aurangzeb ['Alamgir] in 1707 the collapse of the empire was only a matter of time, and the few buildings in the Mughul [*sic*] style that were erected after this date are a melancholy proof of the decadent conditions that then ensued."[5] Despite some differences in approach, all agreed that the turn of the eighteenth century was the beginning of the demise of Mughal architecture. An early exception was Hermann Goetz, whose essay on the Qudsiyya Bagh in north Delhi proposed a transition from what he interpreted as the "Baroque" style of architecture under Shah Jahan (r. 1628–58) and 'Alamgir (r. 1658–1707) to the "gay and frivolous Rococo" exemplified by Awadhi architecture in the later eighteenth century.[6] While Goetz did not criticize the late Mughal visual idiom, he adhered to the notion of a classical phase, and partook in the essentialization of architectural and religious categories evident in the work of others. Goetz aside, in many studies of the time, the eighteenth and nineteenth centuries warranted no mention at all.[7]

Scholarship has since departed from these earlier, reductive paradigms, but for the most part it has focused on the sixteenth and seventeenth centuries. Studies have explored the Central Asian Timurid roots of Mughal architecture, the continuities between Mughal and north Indian Rajput forms, the Mughal funerary tradition, landscape history, poetic discourses on architecture, gendered spaces, and the politics of imperial and sub-imperial patronage.[8] Despite the foundational work of scholars such as Catherine Asher and Ebba Koch, these and other themes have not been fully examined in relation to the eighteenth century. One of the notable exceptions is a series of three essays by Asher, which examine eighteenth-century architecture through projects undertaken by the nobility, in the regional states, and at public spaces such as shrines.[9] Additionally, Santhi Kavuri-Bauer has considered the "afterlives" of Mughal monuments, charting a history of reception that begins with the depiction of Mughal spaces in the late eighteenth century, then concentrates on the nineteenth and twentieth centuries and the role of Mughal monuments in the formation of the British imperial and Indian national states.[10] Yet even with these important works, the overwhelming emphasis in Mughal architectural history has been the sixteenth and seventeenth centuries. Likewise, the urban history of Delhi has similarly tended to overlook the eighteenth century. Previous studies that consider the Mughals have concentrated on the seventeenth-century formation of the Mughal capital at Shahjahanabad,[11] its transformations during the consolidation of British imperial power in the nineteenth century,[12] and the comparative urbanisms of seventeenth-century Mughal Delhi and nineteenth-century British Delhi.[13] Similarly, comprehensive urban histories of Delhi tend to only mention the eighteenth century in passing.[14]

These interpretive lacunae in the architectural and urban history of the eighteenth-century Mughal empire and its capital have endured even as the period has been revised in other fields. Although a narrative of Mughal decline long persisted in historical scholarship, the eighteenth century was eventually re-theorized by scholars who compellingly argued that the period was one of decentralization, in which power and resources were redistributed across Mughal India and in which a broader range of social groups defined the political landscape.[15] While not without its critics, this fundamental reassessment was followed by studies examining the rich historical dimensions of eighteenth-century India, exploring themes related to gender, cross-cultural contact, the history of science, and intellectual history.[16]

Scholars have also illuminated the vibrant literary cultures of the period. They have explored understudied genres such as lexicography (encyclopedic in its premodern guise) and *tazkiras* (biographical dictionaries); traced shifts in the *shahrāshūb* genre in Persian and Urdu, which concentrated and commented on urban culture; and exposed the transregional, multilingual networks that linked the seemingly distinct spheres of Persian, Urdu, and Brajbhasha (the major courtly languages of eighteenth-century north India, previously considered to represent discrete cultural or religious groups).[17] These recent treatments have altered the perception that the literary, like other arts, faltered in the eighteenth century, and that the courtly languages of the sixteenth and seventeenth centuries simply died out.

Within art history, eighteenth-century Indian painting has also received increased attention. Scholars such as J. P. Losty, Malini Roy, and Yuthika Sharma have cast light on previously understudied artists from the eighteenth and nineteenth centuries. As a result, we now have knowledge of the biographies and practices of artists such as the late Mughal painter Mihr Chand, the Indian Picturesque artist Sita Ram, and the masters of topographical painting Ghulam ʿAli Khan and Mazhar ʿAli Khan.[18] Historians of British art, particularly Natasha Eaton, have contributed significantly to the study of the eighteenth-century art of South Asia by examining networks of artistic and cultural exchange between British and Indian artists, patrons, and collectors. It is through this work, for instance, that we know about the multicultural collecting communities of Faizabad and Lucknow, in which Mughal artists displaced from the imperial atelier at Delhi intersected with artists and patrons affiliated with the French and English East India Companies.[19] A number of recent exhibitions have also contributed to our renewed understanding of this period as one that was dynamic, including *Princes and Painters in Mughal Delhi: 1707–1857* (2012), organized by the Asia Society, and *India's Fabled City: The Art of Courtly Lucknow,* mounted at the Los Angeles County Museum of Art and the Musée Guimet in 2010–11.[20]

Yet for all these advances in scholarship, the study of the architectural and urban history of the late Mughal empire has lagged. This book thus makes a long overdue intervention, providing a necessary revision of a crucial chapter in Islamic and South Asian architectural history. Rather than comprehensively surveying eighteenth-century Mughal architecture, the current study provides a conceptual framework for approaching the architectural history of eighteenth-century Mughal India, complementing work that has successfully recast the Mughal eighteenth century in other disciplines. I bring the architectural history of eighteenth-century Mughal India into dialogue not only with the revisionist histories that originally reinterpreted this period but also with an ongoing interdisciplinary conversation that has revealed the Mughal eighteenth century as vibrant and generative.

Within the broader discipline of art history, this book contributes to ongoing conversations concerning the "global eighteenth century." Recent relevant works have approached the issue of globality through the lens of mobility, exploring the circulation of images, ideas, and individuals and the transmission of visual and material cultures across geographic zones.[21] These related themes of mobility, circulation, and transmission run through each chapter of the book, illuminating transregional contacts between the Mughal lands of north India, the power bases of the southern Deccan region, and the commanding provinces of eastern India, as well as cultural contact across oceans, between the courts of Mughal and Awadhi India and those of France and England. Early on, we are introduced to the family of Mughal architects who were largely responsible for transmitting a recognizably Mughal visual idiom from the imperial monuments of northern India, such as the Taj Mahal, to new centers of power in the southern region of the Deccan. This visual language took hold and adapted to dynamic urban transformations in the Mughal capital at Delhi. New ways of beholding and experiencing the city are brought to life through the travel narrative of Dargah Quli Khan. A young Persian nobleman from the Deccan, Dargah Quli recorded the delights of Delhi's urbane culture, animating the architectural spaces of the early eighteenth century in unparalleled fashion. In the mid-eighteenth century, the province of Awadh materialized its transregional connections to the Mughal center through the construction of Safdar Jang's monumental mausoleum at Delhi, mentioned above (see fig. 0.2). We also witness the circulation of images of Mughal architecture on the global stage, turning our eyes to a set of architectural studies that were taken to France by an officer of the French East India Company (see fig. 0.3), as well as a lavish manuscript that was given to the British custodian of an errant Mughal prince (fig. 0.5). In other words, the mobility of individuals and ideas contributed to the

FIGURE 0.5

Artist unknown, *Diwan-i 'Amm, Red Fort, Delhi,* c. 1815. Opaque watercolor and gold on paper, 9 × 15.5 in. (22.8 × 39.4 cm). British Library, London. © The British Library Board, Add. 20735.

vibrancy of eighteenth-century Mughal architectural culture, and to the proliferation and deployment of an architectural language that would come to be known as Mughal.

Besides studies on mobility, others have addressed period developments outside of Europe, long the primary focus of eighteenth-century studies. Within the field of Islamic art, for instance, work by Shirine Hamadeh and Ünver Rüstem has addressed the Ottoman eighteenth century, including topics such as the urban culture of Istanbul and the emergence of an Ottoman Baroque.[22] Within South Asian art history, scholars have extended the chronology of Rajput and Mughal art. Dipti Khera and Giles Tillotson have elucidated the artistic and cultural milieu at the Rajput states of Jaipur and Udaipur, which flourished during this period, while Yuthika Sharma and Malini Roy have brought to light previously understudied artists in Delhi and Awadh.[23] While many of these histories are attendant to transcultural encounters and exchanges with European artists, patrons, or objects, they simultaneously emphasize the local and the regional—be it the fountains of Istanbul or the invitation scrolls sent to Jain monks by Mewari merchants in Udaipur.[24] This study, too, sheds light on new material from Mughal India, joining the recent literature that brings the visual culture of South Asia and the early modern Islamic world into the purview of eighteenth-century studies. While some themes in the book resonate with issues long central to eighteenth-century architectural history—for example, shifts in urban perceptions and practices—I refrain from simply imposing interpretive paradigms developed for European architectural history onto the buildings and spaces of the Mughal empire, preferring instead to examine Mughal sources and buildings on their own terms. At the same time, I retain the very idea of an eighteenth century, so central to the historiography of modern Europe, both for its potential to signal the notion of transition, as well as to recuperate the Mughal eighteenth century as generative and dynamic.[25]

THE MUGHAL EIGHTEENTH CENTURY

A major tension surrounded Mughal authority in the eighteenth century. On the one hand, the Mughal emperors retained only nominal power, ceding territory and revenue rights to independent states and trading companies, losing their military capacity, and experiencing a destabilization of the socioreligious order that had legitimized their dynasty for centuries. Yet at the same time, the Mughal emperors remained on the throne, their symbolic authority intact and potent. They still observed court ceremonial and bestowed robes of honor and special titles, and numerous European officers and visitors also sought audience with the emperor (fig. 0.6). This book addresses the central role that architecture, in both visual and spatial terms, played in this process of constructing and maintaining authority.

In the sixteenth and seventeenth centuries, the Mughal empire expanded to encompass almost all of South Asia, developed a sophisticated centralized state structure, and enjoyed a premier position in global trade and diplomatic networks.[26] Subsequently, over the course of the eighteenth century, the Mughal state was decentralized as economic and military power fell into the hands of regional Indian rulers. Some destabilization came in the form of outright rebellions and challenges by the Sikhs of the Punjab, the Rajputs of the northwest, the Marathas of western India, and powerful Jat groups in the territory surrounding Delhi. These were all entities that had continually resisted Mughal authority since the seventeenth century and subsequently succeeded in defying a weakened Mughal center.[27] The eighteenth century also saw the transformation of once loyal Mughal provinces into semiautonomous states.[28] The provincial rulers retained titles such as nawab, indicating their technical subordination to the authority of the Mughal center. In the case of Awadh, coins were still struck with the name of the Mughal emperor, and his name was read during the weekly sermon (*khutba*) during Friday congregational prayers, both acts that signaled his sovereignty, as they had for centuries across Islamic lands.[29] Yet in this very province, the nawab Burhan al-Mulk Saʿadat Khan established a dynasty that would last into the nineteenth century and play a crucial role in north Indian politics, eventually forging an independent alliance with the British.[30] When Nizam al-Mulk Asaf Jah, who had also acted as Mughal prime vizier, asserted sovereignty over Hyderabad after a military victory in 1724, he met with little resistance. The nizam was technically subordinate to the Mughal center, but in reality enacted military, diplomatic, and administrative decisions on his own authority.[31] And by the 1740s, Bengal had severed administrative ties with the Mughal empire and ceased to direct the traditional revenue tribute to the emperor.[32] Thus, the material connections between the imperial center and its provinces frayed considerably in the eighteenth century, leading to a redistribution of resources and reorganization of political structures in the empire.

Simultaneously, European trading companies, most notably the English and French East India Companies, gained a greater foothold in the Indian subcontinent. These entities vied for commercial dominance in the region, negotiating trade treaties and allying

themselves with regional Indian powers. The English East India Company began as a joint stock corporation in 1600, established a settlement in Madraspatnam (later Madras, and present-day Chennai) in the 1630s, expanded territorial holdings and commercial rights over the next three centuries, and ultimately served as the foundation for British imperial India.[33] Similarly, the French East India Company (Compagnie des Indes Orientales, later Compagnie des Indes), founded in 1664 by the French finance minister Jean-Baptiste Colbert, established a strong commercial and territorial presence in the subcontinent from its base in Pondicherry in southern India.[34] The two competed fiercely with each other in the seventeenth and eighteenth centuries, their commercial conflicts often causing military skirmishes in India as the French and British simultaneously battled in other global arenas during the Seven Years' War.[35] Under the Treaty of Paris of 1763, which brought an end to the war, the French agreed to relinquish their military and territorial interests in India, while retaining some trading rights. Yet the conflicts and alliances effected by the French and British would continue, adding even more complexity to the political landscape of India throughout the eighteenth century.

As for the Mughal court in Delhi, the emperors of the eighteenth century hardly operated as sovereigns, instead functioning as mere figureheads. Unlike the long reigns that had characterized the sixteenth and seventeenth centuries, the eighteenth century saw no fewer than eleven emperors.[36] The previously inviolable authority of the Mughal emperor stood in contrast to the manipulation of "puppet" emperors by high-ranking and powerful nobles. The Mughal emperors were also personally more susceptible to attack by external forces, evinced by a successful invasion of Delhi in 1739 by the Afsharid Nadir Shah and repeated Afghan incursions in the 1750s. In order to escape the Afghan forces, the emperor Shah ʿAlam II (r. 1759–1806) spent most of the 1760s in Awadh and Allahabad under the protection of the Awadhi nawabs and the British, returning to Delhi in 1772. From this point until 1803 and the formal British imperial occupation of Delhi, Afghan, Maratha, and British forces alternately controlled the city.[37] One of the most devastating demonstrations of the weakness of the imperial throne was an attack on Shah ʿAlam by the Afghan Ghulam Qadir, who infamously blinded the emperor in 1788.

Alongside these threats to Mughal sovereignty came a shift in the Sunni-centered socioreligious order that had been cultivated by the Mughal emperors since the sixteenth century, and the related association with the Sufi Chishti order that had legitimized Mughal dynastic rule since that time.[38] The Sunni status quo stood in variance to the Twelver Shiʿism practiced among the Mughal rivals in the Deccani states.[39] The Deccan had long been connected to Iran through the Persian Gulf and Indian Ocean trade routes, and in the seventeenth century the Mughals actively sought to repress public demonstrations of Shiʿism in this region. For instance, in 1636 Shah Jahan ordered the Shiʿi-ruled Qutb-Shahi dynasty to stop including the name of the Twelve Imams and the Safavid shahs in the khutba.[40]

Even though Shiʿis held prominent Mughal administrative posts, the primacy of orthodox Sunni Islam as the state religion remained unchallenged until the early eighteenth century, when Shi'i forces began to hold greater sway in India. With the dissolution of the Safavid empire (1501–1722), greater numbers of Iranian elites migrated to north India, including administrators and military officers who joined and rose through the ranks of the Mughal bureaucracy. One example was Burhan al-Mulk, the founder of the Awadhi dynasty, who emigrated from Nishapur in 1708, joined the Mughal imperial administration, and was appointed the nawab of Awadh in 1722. Thus, Awadh, one of the most powerful of the regional states in eighteenth-century north India, was Shi'i-ruled, marking a major subversion of the Sunni primacy that had characterized the religiopolitical structure of the Mughal empire over the previous two centuries.

The Mughal empire thus experienced dramatic events and fundamental shifts over the course of the long eighteenth century. At the center of this process stood a tension: while the Mughals suffered a series of economic and military losses, their cultural authority remained largely intact, though contested by regional aspirants to the Mughal throne and foreign colonial powers alike. A deeply symbolic architectural culture lay at the heart of these negotiations, which the Mughals marshaled in the maintenance of their tenuous cultural supremacy.

ARCHITECTURE AS HISTORY

In writing the history of eighteenth-century Mughal architecture, I have not set out to offer a taxonomic, exhaustive survey. Rather, my central concern is the relationship between architectural culture and its capacity to index and constitute historical subjectivity. I use the term "history" with both flexibility and specificity—I mean history in the sense of precedent, legacy, and a consciousness of the past coupled with the act of framing it for reception in the present. Throughout the eighteenth century, the architectural sphere was a dynamic site where the Mughal past was conceived, constructed, and contested. Precedent was a departure point for artistic experimentation; forms from the past persisted and were deployed in the face of momentous social, political, and cultural change; and as the Mughals undertook the task of representing themselves to new audiences, they took a decidedly retrospective approach, turning to the architectural achievements of their predecessors to counter the losses of the present. To a certain extent, this process was not unlike the historical consciousness that the earlier Mughals had displayed, in which architecture was used to recall another time and place. For instance, the sixteenth- and seventeenth-century emperors used monumental tombs to invoke genealogical relationships between generations and with their parent dynasty, the Timurids (1370–1507).[41] Similarly, the later Mughals developed a style based on the imperial architecture of Shah Jahan: articulated in white marble, with extensively sculpted surfaces, sinuous architectonics, and a stunning array of floral and vegetal motifs, best embodied by the Taj Mahal (fig. 0.7).

Yet in the process, the later Mughals went beyond the act of simply using architecture to access history. Along the way, they historicized architecture itself. Moving beyond

FIGURE 0.7

Ustad Ahmad Lahori, Taj Mahal, Agra, 1632–48.

a historical self-consciousness based on iterative or recursive practices, they produced a conscious history in which reflexivity and recursivity were intertwined. Beginning in the late seventeenth century, and extending to the early decades of the nineteenth, the later Mughals insistently and consistently built in the style formerly associated solely with the emperor Shah Jahan, such that by the early nineteenth century, this style could be considered Mughal. This mode of producing history, developed over the course of the long eighteenth century, was distinct from the positivist architectural histories of the nineteenth century, particularly those advanced by the Archaeological Survey of India and writers such as James Fergusson and Alexander Cunningham. In this book, I resist equating the colonial study of India with the introduction of a knowledge system capable of conceptualizing Mughal architecture as a historical subject and, by extension, with the advent of modernity. Instead, what I argue is that eighteenth-century Mughal architectural culture was governed by its own reflexive impulse.

The challenge of making this argument lies in the fact that sources from the period are not typically forthcoming on questions of intentionality and agency. Mughal historians clearly expended much effort ordering and deploying the past, constructing a history of the empire that was articulated across a range of texts. These included court histories, imperial chronicles, and official and informal memoirs, all of which, to differing extents, emphasized themes of genealogy and linear chronology, as well as imperial conquest and authority. These themes can be gleaned across the wide genres of Mughal history writing, from the observations on the landscape of India offered by the first Mughal emperor, Babur (r. 1526–30), to the highly ordered and detailed chronicles produced for his illustrious descendant, Shah Jahan. Yet despite this emphasis on a sense of an ordered and specific history, when Mughal texts reference buildings or cities, they tend to rely upon standard tropes rather than historically grounded observations or assessments. Additionally, Mughal architects did not write theoretical or reflective texts devoted to architecture or urbanism, like the treatises of Italian Renaissance architects or the autobiographies of the Ottoman chief architect, Sinan.[42] Thus neither patron nor practitioner articulated their relationship to architecture in specifically textual terms, requiring me to explore the issue of historicism through close visual and spatial analysis of extant buildings and their related pictorial representations.

With this emphasis on alternative modes of constructing and conveying history, my argument relates to recent scholarship concerning the nature of history writing and knowledge production in early modern India. Scholars such as Dipesh Chakrabarty, Kumkum Chatterjee, Partha Chatterjee, Sumit Guha, Sheldon Pollock, and Sanjay Subrahmanyam (among others) have successfully dismantled the notion that European epistemic systems and modes of cultural production brought modernity and a historical sensibility to India.[43] Scholars have turned our attention to texts not typically included in standard historiographies, from myth to poetry to commemorative biographies, and mined sources to reveal new modes of expression and thought that developed in the period. Despite this powerful and fundamental scholarly reorientation, few have focused on the visual and material aspects of this phenomenon. My study adds a visual and material dimension to a conversation that has primarily taken place in historical and literary studies, and has been limited to alphabetic texts.[44] Instead of being predicated on linguistic structures, the processes of historicization I uncover in this book were elaborated in the visual and material spheres.

In this respect, this book also engages with scholars who have brought to light historically and culturally diverse modes of practicing art history. David Roxburgh, for instance, has examined the prefaces of Timurid and Safavid albums to reveal how Persian artists placed themselves in artistic genealogies, effectively forging a history of Persian art.[45] In the case of early modern Japan, as Yukio Lippit has shown, the establishment of Kano painting as a "Japanese" style involved a particular ordering and framing of the past.[46] Heather Hyde Minor has turned attention to the writings of Giovanni Battista Piranesi, who is primarily celebrated as an artist. Minor argues that Piranesi's artistic and authorial practice were inseparable and, when considered together, offer new insights into Enlightenment modes of knowledge production and historical methodology.[47] And Keith Moxey has called for a rethinking of the discipline that decenters what he deems Western or Eurocentric notions of time and history. While the latter approach risks implying that history is somehow at odds with non-Western cultures, the basic impulse, to move away from Eurocentric models of history, is one that this study also pursues.[48]

Crucial to my argument is the broad material scope of this study. Rather than survey buildings on the ground, I give equal weight to built architectural form, urban spatial organization, and architectural concepts as represented in texts and in two-dimensional representations. My narrative thus takes in a rich array of material, from intimate palace mosques, monumental funerary gardens, and vibrant shrines to expansive urban panoramas and detailed manuscript paintings meant for a variety of potential viewers, including Indian and European audiences. Equally important to this book is its geographic and temporal span. Geographically, the book centers on Delhi, focusing on its architecture and the portrayal of the city in text and image, but it also considers transregional comparisons and circulations, such as major monuments from important regional capitals, including Aurangabad and Lucknow, and the circulation of images of Mughal architecture in Europe. Temporally, although it focuses on the eighteenth century, this study begins in the latter half of the seventeenth century, when the act of codifying and enshrining a recognizably Mughal architectural language began. Similarly, the historicist impulse discernible in the eighteenth century continued and crystallized in the early nineteenth. Including seventeenth- and nineteenth-century examples allows me to explicate the transitional nature of the eighteenth century, highlighting both the seventeenth-century legacies upon which architecture capitalized and the foundations it set for the nineteenth century. By examining multiple media comprehensively and comparatively, looking retrospectively at the seventeenth century and forward to the nineteenth, and considering Delhi in a broad regional and global context, I demonstrate that a historicist mindset truly permeated the architectural culture of the Mughal eighteenth century.

As the above has made clear, I treat buildings, spaces, and two-dimensional architectural representations as both objects of analysis and vital sources. In addition, I draw on an array of written texts to illuminate the artistic, political, and cultural milieu of the period. These include state-sanctioned imperial histories; legal texts; travel narratives in English, French, Persian, and Urdu; the memoirs of administrative officials; Indo-Persian poetic texts; textual geographies in Persian, Urdu, and English; and, though they occupy a liminal position between visual and alphabetic text, building inscriptions.

My goal in drawing together these disparate sources is multifold. I aim to create as clear a picture as possible of the conditions for architectural production, looking for information about the motivations of patrons and architects. I also attempt to discern the ways that buildings and other urban spaces were used, using both textual and pictorial material. But it is a desire to understand how place and space were perceived and conceived that primarily drives my selection of sources. Again, many of my choices are informed by the absence of texts that are standard in early modern architectural histories, including treatises or a plentiful literature of description from travelers, architects, or members at court. In addition, my work in municipal and state archives in Delhi and northeastern

India yielded source material for the nineteenth century, but little that was relevant for my eighteenth-century questions.

For the earlier parts of the text, I turn to imperial histories, which are perhaps the most typically used in Mughal architectural history. They are organized chronologically, ordered by imperial regnal year and punctuated by major events such as accessions, battles, major celebrations at court such as weddings, imperial birthdays, or the observation of religious holidays, and imperial accomplishments such as the founding of the city of Shahjahanabad. By and large, references to architecture are brief or generic, but I tease out specific descriptions of the monuments under study whenever possible. I also mine a key legal text, the *Fatāwā al-ʿĀlamgīriyya*, to analyze architecture in relation to broader cultural regulations in the late seventeenth century. For the eighteenth century, imperial sources tend to be even more formulaic when it comes to the subject of architecture. More useful is the *Muraqqaʿ-yi Dihlī*, which provides an unparalleled description of urban culture in the eighteenth century. This text has been used in history and music history, but not exploited for architectural history. This narrative complements a slate of European travel narratives that are more routinely used in Mughal architectural studies, including writing by French and Italian merchants and travelers including François Bernier and Jean-Baptiste Tavernier.

To understand the culture of knowledge production, I use an equally wide array of sources. In assessing the significance of architectural representations in the late eighteenth century, for instance, I turn to the writings of the art collector, patron, and French East India Company officer Jean-Baptiste Gentil. A self-styled connoisseur and expert on India, Gentil stands out as a key voice of early French Orientalism, yet he was producing, writing, and collecting history in a way that drew on Indo-Persian manuscript culture.[49] Similarly, textual geographies from the nineteenth century reveal Indo-Persian modes of perceiving and portraying the architectural and urban history of Indian cities. The most famous of these are Sangin Beg's *Sayr al-Manāzil* (A Tour of the Sites, 1836) and Sayyid Ahmad Khan's *Āsār al-Sanādīd* (Vestiges of the Past, 1847, revised 1854). These, like other textual geographies from the period, draw upon Persianate literary forms such as the tazkira and the shahrāshūb. The tazkira, or biographical dictionary, often recounts a history of place through the portrayal of that place's inhabitants.[50] Similarly, the shahrāshūb, or "city disturber" genre of poetry, had the capacity to offer an urban ethnography.[51] These textual modes of narrating the history of place and space, which affected the nineteenth-century Persian and Urdu textual geographies, are rooted in Indo-Persian tradition. They provide a perspective on Indian architectural history that is distinct from the histories that would be produced by colonial agents such as James Fergusson, in his 1876 *History of Indian and Eastern Architecture*, and Alexander Cunningham, founder of the Archaeological Survey of India.

Although the book is organized chronologically, the thematic thrust of each chapter is distinct. In Chapter 1, I demonstrate that the architectural language that would become identified and historicized as "Mughal" was codified in the late seventeenth century,

FIGURE 0.8
Fakhr al-Masajid, Delhi, 1728–29.

setting the stage for its subsequent appropriation over the course of the eighteenth century. The space between a historically rooted mode of experimentation and an imperially propelled culture of regulation resulted in the standardization of a recently established Mughal style. I analyze select monuments such as the Moti Masjid ("Pearl Mosque") in the palace-fortress of Delhi; the Badshahi Masjid, which was the imperial Friday mosque at Lahore; and the Bibi ka Maqbara, a monumental imperial tomb in Aurangabad. The mode of experimentation current in Mughal India, as in the wider Islamicate world, measured artistic merit in relation to the artist's ability to preserve yet innovate upon established forms. As I demonstrate, such an approach strongly informed architectural practice. At the same time, the visual and material spheres were also subject to imperial restrictions, which resulted in a highly conscious regulation of architecture. This culture of regulation was essential for the standardization of architecture that was reinforced over the last decades of the seventeenth century.

This standardized, historically moored, reflexive Mughal style would stand at the center of dramatic urban shifts in the early eighteenth century, the subject of Chapter 2. Previously, in the seventeenth century, Mughal Delhi was organized around the imperial palace-fortress (the Red Fort, 1639–48), where the city's major avenues intersected. In the eighteenth century, this urban order shifted. New structures were built at different points within the walled city. While these structures challenged the spatial centrality of imperial monuments, they also reinforced the notion of an imperial style by quoting imperial precedents. Such is the case with the Fakhr al-Masajid (fig. 0.8), a small neighborhood mosque sponsored by a noblewoman that references the larger, imperial congregational mosque of Shah Jahan, the Jamiʿ Masjid (1650–56). In addition, extramural spaces beyond the core of the Mughal capital grew more prominent, particularly the shrines of legendary Sufi saints from the Chishti order. As these sites grew more popular, imperial buildings, from tombs to pleasure gardens, proliferated in their environs. In the first half of the eighteenth century, for instance, successive Mughal emperors formalized and aggrandized the shrine of Bakhtiyar Kaki through renovations in white marble, adding a gateway, processional screen, mosque, and large burial enclosure. These transformations in the urban fabric went hand in hand with changing urban practices, encapsulated by an eighteenth-century travel narrative, Dargah Quli Khan's *Muraqqaʿ-yi Dihlī*. Analyzing this key source in conjunction with the building projects of the early eighteenth century, we see how the reflexive Mughal style thus enabled and embraced new ways of fashioning and experiencing the city.

By the mid-eighteenth century, a strongly codified, symbolically charged Mughal visual language and the new spatial logic of the Mughal capital city were integrated in a landmark architectural project, the funerary complex of Safdar Jang (see fig. 0.2), the subject of Chapter 3. Safdar Jang had been the prime vizier of the Mughal emperor and governor of the powerful state of Awadh in northeastern India from 1739 to 1754. His complex revived a recognizable imperial architectural tradition, signaled by a domed mausoleum set within an elaborate funerary garden. This powerful act of appropriation positioned the Awadhi dynasty as the inheritors of the Mughal throne. Moreover, the tomb anchored a Shiʿi shrine district that grew to mirror the Sunni zone surrounding the nearby tomb of the Mughal emperor Humayun (r. 1530–40, 1555–56; tomb 1562–71). It thus provided an alternative pilgrimage center for Shiʿis in the Mughal capital, challenging the preeminence of the brand of Sunni Islam historically upheld by the Mughal emperors. In sum, the funerary complex of Safdar Jang boldly articulated new political and socioreligious orders, using the visual forms of imperial Mughal architecture and a reconfigured urban order to do so.

In the later eighteenth century, the Mughal architectural past was codified not only in the built environment, but also in architectural representations on paper. A primary example and the focus of Chapter 4 is the *Palais Indiens* (c. 1774; see fig. 0.3), a collection of twenty-six large-format architectural studies commissioned by Gentil and produced by an Indian draftsman. I situate the *Palais Indiens* within a longer tradition of European representations of Indian architecture, comparing them to English Picturesque paintings, souvenir paintings from the so-called Company School, and architectural studies drafted by British preservationists (see fig. 0.4). This comparative analysis highlights the particular work that the *Palais Indiens* did for the ongoing process of codifying not only a certain style of architecture, but also a fixed set of buildings as authoritatively Mughal. I also consider the circulation of these architectural studies between India and France and the cultural representation they enacted, revealing that Mughal architectural forms grew truly iconic in an increasingly globalized context.

In the nineteenth century, the urban image of Delhi was drawn into Mughal and British historical texts, with seventeenth-century Mughal monuments occupying a prominent position in these works, attesting to the ongoing relevance of the Mughal architectural past and the production of what would come to be seen as a Mughal "golden age." I turn attention to these texts in Chapter 5, further exploring the interconnected phenomena of appropriation and codification. Mughal manuscripts began including depictions of imperial monuments among their illustrations, while British collectors commissioned paintings of these same monuments. In addition to these examples, Persian and Urdu textual geographies highlight the central role played by architecture in constructing histories of Delhi: the *Sayr al-Manāzil* and *Āsār al-Sanādīd* map Delhi in terms of its monuments, not only describing key buildings but also recounting their histories and those of associated political and religious figures. Mughal architecture thus not only became the subject of historical study, but also emerged as the organizing principle for constructing and conveying a history of place and empire.

In the Conclusion, I reflect upon the transformation of this style from a dynastic to a supra-dynastic and ultimately globalized language, considering a subsequent and related paradox: after the eighteenth century, when Mughal architecture achieved iconic status, it slowly lost its specific historical associations. Forms that originally held currency for their Mughal referentiality became generalized, eventually standing for India at large. This fate is all the more meaningful given the eighteenth-century chapter of Mughal architectural history, when the very concept of Mughal architecture developed in historically specific terms, only to be abstracted in the later nineteenth and twentieth centuries.

CHAPTER ONE

Between Experimentation and Regulation

The Foundations of an Eighteenth-Century Style

I N THE MUGHAL PALACE-FORTRESS OF DELHI, behind a chained and padlocked door, sits an exquisite white marble mosque (fig. 1.1). Walking across the courtyard of the building and entering the open bays of its prayer hall, the viewer beholds a lavish program of sinuous curves, richly animated surfaces, and an array of floral, vegetal, and geometric motifs. The mosque is striking not only because of its sumptuous visual qualities, but also because in standard Mughal histories, its patron, ʿAlamgir (r. 1658–1707), was long cast as a religious puritan who dismissed court musicians, censored poets, dismantled the imperial

painting workshop, and single-handedly caused the death of Mughal architecture.[1] But this elegant structure, known as the Moti Masjid or "Pearl Mosque" (1658–63), tells quite a different story. In fact, the Moti Masjid embodies the dynamics of late seventeenth-century architectural culture, when a recently established, symbolically charged visual language was taken up, elaborated, and codified. This newly refashioned, notably reflexive Mughal style would ultimately become identified with the later Mughals, their successors in the Indian subcontinent, and with the very idea of Indian architecture as it circulated globally into the colonial period.

Previously, in the sixteenth and early seventeenth centuries, the Mughals had capitalized on the Persianate style of their ancestors, the Timurids of Central Asia and Iran (1370–1507). They undertook ambitious building programs that incorporated Indian architectural traditions, but expanded on Timurid visual and spatial typologies significantly. These included monumental mausolea set in elaborate funerary complexes that invoked the Gur-i Amir (c. 1400–1404), the Timurid dynastic tomb complex in Samarqand; gardens in the Persian-inspired *chahār bāgh,* or four-fold, style; and vast palaces with pavilions of stone and cloth that harkened back to the royal encampments of the peripatetic Timurid court.[2] Monuments were built primarily of red sandstone and featured bold geometric patterns or vegetal motifs. These were usually either painted directly onto building surfaces or applied as flat revetments to walls (figs. 1.2–1.4).

By the mid-seventeenth century, when the autonomy of the Mughal empire had been asserted, its claim as a universal power was articulated through a new visual style that integrated Timurid, Indian, and European visual codes, and came to serve as a stamp of Mughal identity.[3] The new visual language, characterized by white marble, naturalistic floral motifs, and sinuous architectonics, is seen in such iconic monuments as the Taj Mahal and the palace-fortresses of Agra and Delhi (figs. 1.5, 1.6). As Ebba Koch has shown, this language comprised a fixed architectural vocabulary of baluster columns; sculpted piers; cusped arches; sloped roofs, vaults, and cornices (*bangla*); pointed domes; domed kiosks (*chhatrī*); projecting eaves supported by brackets (*chhajjā*); jali, or lattice, screens; thrones with architectural framing features (jharoka); and pan-Islamic forms including *muqarnas* and *pīshtāqs* (portals composed of an arch in a rectangular frame).[4] Naturalistic, floral ornament covered the surfaces of imperial buildings. While sometimes painted, ornamental motifs were usually carved or executed in stone inlay (Italian: *pietra dura;* Persian: *parchīn kārī*) (fig. 1.7).

In the later seventeenth century, architects and patrons adapted this recently established visual language, partaking in a complex interplay between experimentation, enacted through the agency of sculptors and architects, and regulation, issued in the form of orders and proscriptions from the imperial court. For their part, artists and architects worked according to the aesthetic values current in Mughal India and in the wider Indo-Persianate world, whereby artistic merit was measured by the nature and quality of the artist's response to an existing model. In other words, there was a close interconnection between imitation and innovation, the old and the new, encapsulated in the concept of *istiqbāl.*

FIGURE 1.1
Moti Masjid, Delhi, 1658–63.

FIGURE 1.2
Mirak Mirza Ghiyas, tomb of
Humayun, Delhi, 1562–71.

FIGURE 1.3
Detail, interior vault, tomb of
Akbar, Sikandra, 1613.

FIGURE 1.4
Detail, façade, tomb of Akbar,
Sikandra, 1613.

FIGURE 1.5
Ustad Ahmad Lahori, Taj Mahal,
Agra, 1632–48.

FIGURE 1.6
Palace pavilions, Red Fort, Agra,
c. 1630.

FIGURE 1.7
Detail, pietra dura, Taj Mahal, Agra,
1632–48.

Istiqbāl implies a receptivity to and recognition of existing masterpieces, alongside a desire to refine them. In their practice, artists and architects used an established set of visual forms as a point of departure, creating dramatic sculptural effects, modifying architectural proportions, and pushing the boundaries of naturalistic representation. While the results were innovative, they relied on the visual forms of the past for scaffolding.

As for the imperial court, the reinterpreted Mughal language gained traction for multiple reasons. When ʿAlamgir took the throne in 1658, he stood to benefit from a revision of recent history: there had been a contentious war for succession, with ʿAlamgir killing his brothers and deposing his father and predecessor, Shah Jahan (r. 1628–58). These actions earned ʿAlamgir the criticism of religious and political elites alike, and in this climate, architecture that recalled the style of Shah Jahan's imperial buildings had the efficacious potential to assert continuities between the two rulers. In addition, one of the ways that ʿAlamgir responded to criticism from religious quarters was to cultivate an image of piety, one that ultimately resulted in restrictions of the visual and material spheres. Rather than leading to a flat rejection of the arts, this culture of restriction led to the regulation of artistic and architectural practices, some of which were articulated in the *Fatāwā al-ʿĀlamgīriyya* (Fatwas of ʿAlamgir) or *Fatāwā al-Hindiyya* (Fatwas of India), a legal compendium sponsored by the emperor. One such proscription restricted the use of inscriptions in mosques. In their place, a visual language with semantic potential and historical associations gained currency. Like architects, royal patrons could have reverted to earlier Indo-Islamic or Timurid codes, or fashioned a new visual language altogether. However, they instead chose to adapt the recently established Mughal style, codifying a visual language that would be co-opted in the centuries to come, its associations with "Mughalness" continuously reinforced.

ARCHITECTURE AND ISTIQBĀL

An in-depth exploration of the major imperial monuments from this period shows how deeply the concept of istiqbāl informed architectural practice. Paul Losensky has discussed this phenomenon in relation to Persian poetry, explaining that poets would, for instance, adopt the meter and rhyme of established poems to compose new "response poems."[5] As a result, poets demonstrated their knowledge of the poetic canon *and* the skill to improve upon that canon. This refined mode of imitation is distinct from *taqlīd*, a type of imitation defined by "unreflective, undeviating, and even involuntary submission to an authoritative master."[6] In Persianate painting, a similar premium was placed on productive imitative practice as early as the Timurid period. These values persisted in the Safavid and Mughal empires, where the court workshop provided the ideal setting for engaging with works from the past: artists would copy and refine selected models in order to acquire skill or to demonstrate virtuosity, forging a sense of historical tradition as they did so.[7] A similar painterly tradition informed artistic practice at the Rajput courts of north India.[8]

FIGURE 1.8

Nagina Masjid, Agra, c. 1630.

FIGURE 1.9

Plan of the Moti Masjid, Delhi, 1658–63. After Ernst Grube and George Michell, *Architecture of the Islamic World: Its History and Social Meaning* (London: Thames and Hudson, 1995), 269.

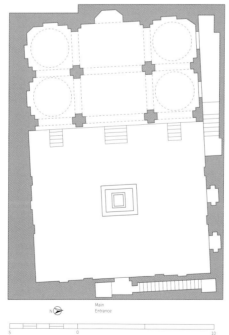

N

Main
Entrance

5   0   10

In the case of late seventeenth-century Mughal architecture, this mode of artistic practice resulted in an insistently sculptural style that was developed across the imperial sphere. As we will see, the concepts of imitation, refinement, and innovation were closely intertwined in imperial buildings, linking the projects both formally and conceptually. They share motifs and vocabularies, but more crucially, they are connected by a similar approach to the past, one that stages reflexivity across typology, geography, and time. As a result, these monuments build upon the visual codes first established in the imperial projects of Shah Jahan, reinforcing them as imperial, and ultimately historicizing them as Mughal.

Located in the palace-fortress (Red Fort) of Shahjahanabad, the Moti Masjid features an intimate courtyard and prayer hall that are slightly elevated above ground level, accessible by a small staircase. In scale, plan, and elevation, the mosque bears clear similarities with the so-called Nagina Masjid in the Red Fort of Agra (c. 1630; fig. 1.8). Both are "palace mosques" of an intimate scale, tucked into unobtrusive courtyards seemingly hidden away among the vast pavilions and gardens of their respective palaces. Both also feature a double-aisle, six-bay prayer hall, set at the end of a rectangular courtyard (fig. 1.9). The elevations, also, are similar: each mosque incorporates a façade of three cusped arches on rectangular piers, an eave that curves in the center (bangla chhajjā), and three pointed domes, aligned with the three arches of the façade. Materially, too, the mosques are connected, as both use white marble.

But the divergences between the mosques are even more striking than their similarities. The Nagina Masjid is a statement of visual austerity: its surfaces are unadorned sheaths of white marble, save for solitary bands of relief carving at the base and capital of each pier. By contrast, the Moti Masjid is an experiment in excess: it takes the plain surfaces of the Nagina Masjid and drapes them in sculpted and inlaid forms. In other words, the Nagina Masjid functions as a blank slate, the ground on which the artists and architects of the Moti Masjid experimented with ornamental forms.

The ornamental forms themselves were inspired by the nearby pavilions of the Red Fort, situated just yards from the Moti Masjid. Commissioned by Shah Jahan, the Red Fort (1639–48) displays the architectural language developed in the imperial projects of that ruler. On the one hand, we can see clear visual continuities between the palace pavilions and the Moti Masjid. For example, the curvilinear micro-arches carved along the walls of the mosque's prayer hall, enframing floral stems, echo those seen in the nearby jharoka throne of Shah Jahan (figs. 1.10, 1.11).[9] Similarly, the acanthus leaf and bulb motifs found in the capitals of the mosque's piers are comparable to those found in the lotus capitals of the baluster columns in the rest of the palace (figs. 1.12, 1.13).[10]

Yet these forms are not simply reproduced in the Moti Masjid. Rather, they are reinterpreted and systematically elaborated, conveying a sense of controlled resplendence. Whereas the stone inlay and relief carvings in the earlier buildings were relatively flat, the ornamental forms in the Moti Masjid are sculpted with greater dimensionality, using the idea of naturalistic representation to blur the line between the organic and the artificial.

FIGURE 1.12
Capital, Moti Masjid, Delhi,
1658–63.

FIGURE 1.13
Capital, palace pavilion, Red Fort,
Delhi, 1639–48.

The reinterpretation of floral ornament is most apparent in the composition of the piers, pendentives, and domes—the most structurally significant aspects of the mosque—and in the mihrab (niche indicating the direction of Mecca) and minbar (pulpit)—the most symbolically charged areas of the mosque. The transition from the piers to arches builds poetically on the concept of floral imagery: sculpted onto the sides of each capital are floral buds that grow into vines, which serve as the curvilinear lines of the cusped arches (fig. 1.14). The domes above the side aisles of the mosque are each carved with a monumental flower, while the bangla vaults are covered in vine motifs (figs. 1.15, 1.16). Placed in the pendentives are flower-filled vases, a motif first developed for the flat dados in the burial chamber of the Taj Mahal and here sculpturally manipulated to occupy the curved space of the pendentives.[11] The mihrab takes the vine motif still further, articulating it with even greater material depth than in the rest of the mosque, and the minbar is virtually alive, a

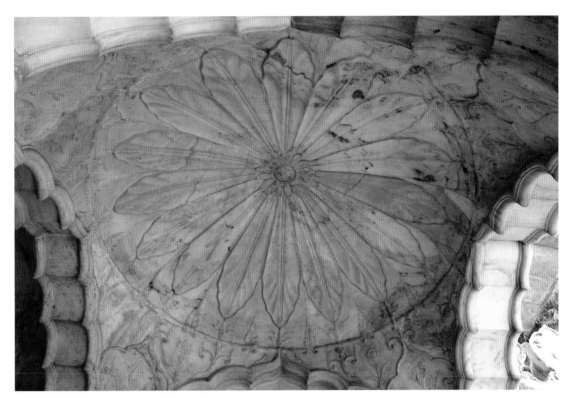

FIGURE 1.17
Mihrab, Moti Masjid, Delhi, 1658–63.

FIGURE 1.18
Minbar, Moti Masjid, Delhi, 1658–63.

FIGURE 1.19

Courtyard wall, Moti Masjid, Delhi, 1658–63.

sprawling acanthus vine supporting three steps (figs. 1.17, 1.18). Rather than rendering the minbar as a simple staircase, as is standard, the architects have once again taken an opportunity to dissolve the boundary between the natural and the built.

Although much of the building's force rests in its ornamental program, the mosque also features innovative architectonic forms. Returning to the comparison between the Nagina and Moti masjids, we see a greater attenuation of form in the later mosque, particularly in the domes and arches of the structure, the proportions of which are realized with an enhanced verticality.[12] The architectonic and ornamental converge on the rear wall of the mosque courtyard, where a signature architectonic form, the bangla, is interpreted in ornamental terms (fig. 1.19). The bangla pavilion, so identified by its sloped roof, is thought to have been inspired by a form of slope-roofed domestic architecture from the region of Bengal (after which it is named).[13] Bengal had long been one of the most important of the Mughal provinces, and this form had become extensively incorporated into Mughal architecture, with pavilions, cornices, and even the upper portion of the imperial throne featuring curved elements. Here, the concept of the bangla is taken still further, with a pavilion carved in relief as a frame around the entryway, effectively transforming a historically rich building type into a decorative motif.

FIGURE 1.20
Detail, cornice, Moti Masjid, Delhi,
1658–63.

The line between structure and ornament is manipulated in other ways. In another case, the absence of structural need is used as an opportunity for ornamental embellishment: the prominent carved brackets often found under the eaves (chhajjā) of Mughal buildings are unnecessary in the Moti Masjid, but are recalled in a series of acanthus leaves carved in relief just below the chhajjā (fig. 1.20). In all, experimentation is primarily seen in the ornamental program, but it is not restricted to ornament. Rather, the sense of experimentation (always within bounds) extends to the architectonic as well. The result is a creatively dynamic space, forged through ornamental and architectonic innovations.

The shift toward the ornamental was not only seen in the relatively private space of the Red Fort, but also embodied even in the most public of late seventeenth-century Mughal monuments, the Friday mosque of Lahore (the Badshahi Masjid, 1673–74). As with the Moti Masjid, a comparison with an earlier counterpart, the imperial Friday mosque of Delhi (the Jamiʿ Masjid, 1650–56), is instructive. Both are monumental mosques of red sandstone and white marble, with triple-domed prayer halls and towering minarets set on one end of a vast, arcaded courtyard (figs. 1.21, 1.22). In addition to their typological and material connections, each mosque was commissioned by a Mughal emperor as the primary congregational mosque of a Mughal capital (Shah Jahan sponsored the Delhi Jamiʿ Masjid, and ʿAlamgir, the Badshahi Masjid).

Where the two most notably part ways is in their ornamental programs. The Delhi mosque features plain, vertical bands of inlaid marble on its domes, and along its façade, a series of ten inscriptional panels above each arch in the courtyard-facing arcade. In addition, the spandrels of the courtyard-facing arches contain a single rosette each. Otherwise, the exterior surfaces of the façade arcade are left unadorned. By contrast, the Badshahi Masjid displays a distinctive delicacy of and play with line. The façade features niches and

FIGURE 1.21
Jamiʿ Masjid, Delhi, 1650–56.

FIGURE 1.22
Badshahi Masjid, Lahore, 1673–74.

37 BETWEEN EXPERIMENTATION AND REGULATION

FIGURE 1.23
Interior, Badshahi Masjid, Lahore, 1673–74.

FIGURE 1.24
ʿAta Allah Rashidi, Bibi ka Maqbara, Aurangabad, 1660–61.

cartouches carved in relief or inlaid in white marble against a red sandstone ground. Floral vines, carved in relief, cover the spandrels of the pīshtāq's cusped arch, and the theme continues in the interior, where floral and vegetal forms are carved in stucco along the mosque's vaults (fig. 1.23). Like the Moti Masjid, the Badshahi Masjid adapts a model from the past, but innovates upon that model, using ornament as a forum for new expression.

One final example will demonstrate how the notion of istiqbāl permeated imperial architecture from the period, affecting other building types besides mosques. The tomb of ʿAlamgir's wife, Rabiʿa Daurani (d. 1657), known as the Bibi ka Maqbara (1660–61; fig. 1.24), creatively responds to and adapts the imperial Mughal tomb tradition. A monumental, domed mausoleum in Aurangabad, the Bibi ka Maqbara is situated in the center of a Mughal chahār bāgh and thus follows a long-established plan for Mughal funerary complexes. Since the earliest years of the empire, the Mughal emperors had sponsored monumental gardens, integrating Timurid and Indian traditions of landscape architecture. For the Mughals (as for their contemporaries, the Ottomans, Safavids, and Rajputs), gardens functioned as sites of power as much as pleasure. They also carried associations with the afterlife, which, in Islamic theology, was conceptualized as a garden.[14] These meanings were deployed in imperial Mughal funerary complexes, which were repositories and generators of imperial identity and authority as well as paradisiacal resting places.

The typology of the monumental tomb, too, carried with it specific historical associations. The Mughals traced their lineage to the Timurids—in fact referring to themselves as the Timurids of India—a dynasty that itself forged a connection between dynastic identity and sepulchral architecture. Timurid princes were buried in a dynastic mausoleum, the Gur-i Amir, which was part of a multifunctional complex that also included a gateway, courtyard, madrasa, and khānqāh (Sufi convent). Through their monumentality, incorporation of extensive gardens, and placement within multifunctional complexes, the Mughal tombs of the sixteenth and seventeenth centuries show continuity with each other and with Timurid precedent. Although each of the imperial tombs is distinctive in elevation—some are domed while others are unroofed, some are polychromatic while others are monochromatic, some are primarily built of sandstone while others use marble exclusively—they are still part of a clearly articulated visual tradition.[15]

Of all the imperial Mughal tombs, the one that the Bibi ka Maqbara most closely resembles is the tomb of Mumtaz Mahal (d. 1631), the Taj Mahal (see fig. 1.5). Both feature white building materials: the Taj Mahal is built of brick faced with white marble, while the Bibi ka Maqbara is clad in white marble and stucco.[16] Both also display a prominent central dome and are set on elevated platforms with four minarets, one at each corner. And like the Taj Mahal, the Bibi ka Maqbara was built for a wife of the Mughal emperor (again, Mumtaz Mahal was married to Shah Jahan, while Rabiʿa Daurani was the wife of ʿAlamgir).[17]

Despite the formal connections between the Taj Mahal and Bibi ka Maqbara, the latter is distinguished by a shift in ornament and proportion, keeping with the theme of later seventeenth-century buildings. Whereas the surfaces of the Taj Mahal comprise relief

FIGURE 1.25
Gateway, Bibi ka Maqbara,
Aurangabad, 1660–61.

carving and pietra dura (see fig. 1.7), the ornamental program of the Bibi ka Maqbara is constituted of deeply sculpted stucco forms and multicolored painted motifs. The result is an increased dimensionality and exuberance that animate the architectural surfaces, similar to the sensibility of the Moti Masjid and Badshahi Masjid. For instance, the front façade of the complex's gateway features a two-story cusped arch with interlacing vegetal motifs densely covering its spandrels (fig. 1.25). These are accompanied by flower and vase motifs carved on the exterior and interior of the gateway, and floral sprays that are painted along its interior dados. Besides floral ornament, the gateway includes muqarnas vaulting and architectural netting, lending still more vibrancy to the composition.

Visually complex surfaces also characterize the central tomb. Echoing the gateway of the complex, the tomb's four identical façades are each articulated as a monumental pīshtāq with stacked, cusped arches on either side (fig. 1.26). Here, ornamental floral compositions dominate and define the surfaces. Tendril-like vines unfurl across the spandrels of arches, while flowers and curling leaves cascade down the vaults of the pīshtāqs. Along the walls of the vaults are floral stems and flower-and-vase compositions, framed by miniature cusped arches (fig. 1.27). In their symmetrical and idealized composition, these floral compositions evoke the carvings found on the exterior dados of the Taj Mahal (fig. 1.28), yet render them with more intricacy and density of detail.[18] Similarly, the vine tendrils in the spandrels also harken back to the multicolored vines in the spandrels of the Taj Mahal (fig. 1.29), but expand those forms so that deeply carved, interlacing vines completely take over the ground.

FIGURE 1.26
Façade, Bibi ka Maqbara,
Aurangabad, 1660–61.

FIGURE 1.27
Walls of pīshtāq vault, Bibi ka
Maqbara, Aurangabad, 1660–61.

FIGURE 1.28

Detail, exterior dado, Taj Mahal, Agra, 1632–48.

In all, the finely carved and inlaid surfaces of the Taj Mahal are here a point of departure, elaborated in the Bibi ka Maqbara with a new liveliness, complexity, and play. Forms that were formerly executed in pietra dura or carved in shallow marble relief are here more deeply carved and realized in stucco, a medium striking for its malleability. While the use of stucco has been interpreted as a sign of the Bibi ka Maqbara's inferiority to the marble-clad Taj Mahal, employing stucco facilitated the introduction of dramatic visual effects in the Bibi ka Maqbara, as the plaster could be more readily sculpted and modeled. Indeed, the architects and sculptors of the façade constantly press the boundaries of form. On either corner of the uppermost register of the pīshtāq vault, the flower and vase motif is pushed to its material limit, with the vase rendered as an empty niche. When empty, this vase-shaped niche manipulates light and shadow as it falls across the surface of the wall; it also may have held an actual vase, inviting a comparison between object and representation.

Another departure from convention can be seen in the transition from exterior to interior, which is marked by a decrease, rather than an increase, in ornament. Again, a look at the imperial monuments of Shah Jahan is instructive. In the Taj Mahal, geometric patterns on the floor increase in complexity as the viewer travels farther into the building. Similarly, while single floral stems are visible on the tomb exterior, on its interior surfaces one finds elaborately carved vases filled with multi-spray arrangements.[19] This pattern

FIGURE 1.29

Detail, exterior spandrels,
Taj Mahal, Agra, 1632–48.

holds true in other imperial spaces, such as the Red Fort. On the gateway of the palace-fortress, one finds simple carved niches. As one moves to the next space on the ceremonial axis, the imperial drum house, floral motifs are carved in relief on the structure's red sandstone walls. It is only when one reaches the inner palace precincts that one sees vibrantly colored pietra dura motifs alongside floral relief carving. In the Bibi ka Maqbara, this fundamental principle of earlier Mughal architectural practice, whereby relatively privileged spaces are marked by increasingly lavish ornament, is subverted. Upon entering the tomb, the viewer finds herself in what is essentially an octagonal viewing balcony: the grave of Rabiʿa Daurani is placed one level below. Two stories of cusped arched recesses surround the perimeter of the interior, the surfaces adorned only with simple miniature cusped arches and vault netting (fig. 1.30), in contrast to the floral ornament on conspicuous display on the tomb exterior.

As in the other imperial buildings from the period, architects also experimented with architectonic forms and proportions in the Bibi ka Maqbara, following the principles of istiqbāl. Besides the reinterpreted Mughal forms in the tomb, there are structural elements previously unseen in Mughal architecture, and more typical of the Deccan region. Laura Parodi has argued that many have failed to appreciate the Bibi ka Maqbara because they do not recognize the influence of Deccani aesthetics on this building. In this case, architects likely responded not only to Mughal precedent but to local Deccani architecture as well.[20] (Aurangabad, where the tomb is located, was the regional capital that ʿAlamgir had founded in the Deccan when he oversaw this region as Prince Aurangzeb.) The building elevation is comparable to Bijapuri examples. This is most notable in the relationship between the substructure and dome. In Bijapuri architecture, the dome dominates the building, and could have inspired the shift in proportions perceptible in the Bibi ka Maqbara. Other similarities between the Bibi ka Maqbara and Bijapuri prototypes include minarets that tower over the central tomb, and engaged corner turrets. This dialogue with Bijapuri architecture extends to the ornamental, too. The palmette motifs in the complex, particularly underneath the balconies of the minarets, also appear in Bijapuri buildings, and contrast with the floral stems and sprays usually seen in Mughal architecture.[21] The visual patterns are paralleled by textual sources, which speak to the Mughals' receptivity

FIGURE 1.30
Interior, Bibi ka Maqbara,
Aurangabad, 1660–61.

to Deccani architecture. In a letter describing a visit to Ellora, ʿAlamgir marvels at the art and architecture he encounters there.[22] That members of court were struck by the distinctive visual culture and sights of the Deccan is also evident in a lengthy description from the state-sponsored court history, the *Maʾāsir-i ʿĀlamgīrī*.[23]

Like the Moti Masjid and Badshahi Masjid, the Bibi ka Maqbara takes its place in an imperial tradition, while simultaneously departing from it in subtle but significant ways. In the case of this tomb, the artistic refinements are also influenced by local visual motifs prevalent in Deccani architecture. The incorporation of Deccani style cannot be attributed simply to the use of local architects or masons, as the architect of the building was trained in the Mughal building tradition. Instead, the Bibi ka Maqbara embodies the spirit of innovative adaptation that was prized in the Indo-Persianate cultural sphere.[24]

ARCHITECTS AND CODIFICATION

The nature of architectural training and practice facilitated this mode of historically minded experimentation. Since training involved apprenticeship, students studied with the creators of past masterpieces. Thus, as with poets and painters, a key aspect of architectural education was exposure to the past, specifically as a source of legitimate knowledge. The close networks resulting from the apprenticeship system also facilitated the circulation of architectural knowledge, from principles of engineering to the use of specific motifs. ʿAta Allah Rashidi, the architect of the Bibi ka Maqbara, serves as an excellent example of this phenomenon.[25] An inscription on the gateway of the Bibi ka Maqbara names him as the architect of the structure (fig. 1.31). He apprenticed with Ustad Ahmad Lahori, the chief

FIGURE 1.31

Inscription on door, gateway of Bibi ka Maqbara, Aurangabad, 1660–61.

architect of Shah Jahan's atelier—who also happened to be ʿAta Allah's father. The dialog-ical relationship between the Bibi ka Maqbara and the Taj Mahal—a relationship that can be characterized in terms of istiqbāl, an innovative adaptation of a model—resulted in part from the master–student relationship between the father and son architects.

Theirs was not the sole example of consequence. Rather, the closely tied networks of architects working in seventeenth-century Mughal India account, in part, for the sys-tematic connections we see across buildings from this period, as well as the creative adap-tation of prior architectural masterpieces. Ustad Ahmad's other sons were also trained in architecture or related disciplines, and together, this family of architects formed the core of an interrelated network of builders and theorists. ʿAta Allah, in addition to his work on the Bibi ka Maqbara, wrote and translated treatises on architecture and geometry, such as the *Khulasā'-i Rāz*. His brother Lutf Allah Muhandis completed several commissions for the Mughal prince Dara Shikoh (ʿAlamgir's brother and political rival) and composed a poetic work extolling his family's architectural achievements, the *Dīwān-i Muhandis*. A third brother, Nur Allah, is though to have assisted Ustad Ahmad with the Jamiʿ Masjid, possibly completing it after his father's death. Members of a third generation, Lutf Allah's sons Imam al-Din Riyazi and Khayr Allah, went on to advance knowledge in related fields, studying mathematics and geometry and writing and translating treatises on these sub-jects, including the latter's *Taqrir al-Tahrir*.[26]

Besides the professional links within this family, there were other, related partner-ships and master–student relationships. For instance, Ustad Ahmad collaborated with Ustad Hamid on the Mughal palace-fortress in Delhi, while another of his collaborators, Makramat Khan, trained ʿAta Allah in geometry, astronomy, and arithmetic. The wide-spread dissemination of and experimentation with architectural building principles and styles were thus made possible by a network of architects and theorists who were closely tied to each other through familial bonds and professional associations. This network cre-ated a framework for the controlled, historically attuned architectural experimentation we see in the late seventeenth century.

In sum, the architectural style that developed in this period was the result of a his-torically rooted architectural practice, where existing models formed the foundations of the new, and the assimilation of and refinements to the model were inextricably linked to the notion of artistic experimentation and innovation. It was through these closely con-nected processes of refinement and redefinition that architectural forms that were first developed in the 1630s and 1640s, in monuments such as the Taj Mahal and the Red Fort of Delhi, were elaborated and firmly codified in the later seventeenth century.

IMPERIAL REGULATION

The dissemination of this architectural language, marked by a visual vibrancy and a spirit of innovation, was striking given the high level of restriction at ʿAlamgir's court. It is a favorite historiographical trope that ʿAlamgir was a religious zealot who banned the arts—musical, literary, and visual. In fact, as we will see in this section, ʿAlamgir regulated, rather than rejected, the cultural, visual, and material realms. In other words, he showed not a disinterest in art, but rather a hyper-interest; the architectural language that flourished in this period did so in relation to a vigilant regulation of the sociocultural sphere. Restrictions were enacted on visual display and cultural expression in imperial spaces, with a premium placed on austerity. And yet the highly expressive architectural style of the late seventeenth century flourished, to the point that it was standardized—that is, made coherent and consistent. While the standardization resulted, in part, from the nature of artistic practice and aesthetic preferences for imitative response, as discussed earlier, another reason for these forms' persistence could be found in the political efficacy of their use.

When ʿAlamgir took the throne in 1658, he did so under fraught circumstances, engaging in a bloody war of succession with his three brothers, Dara Shikoh, Murad Bakhsh, and Shah Shujaʿ, and deposing his still-living father, Shah Jahan.[27] Some challenged the legality of ʿAlamgir's deposition and imprisonment of Shah Jahan, and there were doubts about the legitimacy of the prince's claim to the throne. This challenge was underscored when the chief *qazi* did not read the khutba (Friday sermon) in ʿAlamgir's name, and the sharif of Mecca refused diplomatic gifts sent by ʿAlamgir. In both instances, the officials claimed that the shariʿa forbade recognizing the sovereignty of someone whose father was still alive.[28]

Thus issues of propriety prevailed, affecting restrictions on visual and material display. The *Maʾāsir-i ʿĀlamgīrī* records that ʿAlamgir issued orders restricting the display of wealth, decoration, and sumptuous wares:

> On Sunday, the 18th November/2nd Shawwal, the day following the ʿId al-Fitr, the emperor sat on the throne. According to the custom of the celebrations (of coronation) betel-leaves and scents were distributed among the persons present at court. The emperor ordered the few apparel that had been used in the decoration of the coronation to be removed, and said to Bakhshi al-Mulk Safi Khan, "I abolish the celebration; return the tributary gifts (*peshkash*) sent by the Amir al-ʿUmārā, and the other grandees are not to make any presents to me. The clerks should use inkpots of porcelain and gilt stone, instead of silver ones. The amounts of *inʿām*, which were brought into the court on silver trays, should henceforth be brought on shields. Men who have no clothing that is sanctioned by the canonical law should come dressed in socks. In the *khilʿat-khānah* embroidered cloth should be used instead of stuff with gold and silver flowers worked on it. The factory of *do dāmi* (extremely fine cloth) established at Chanderi should be abolished. Erect a *kathra* (railing) of lapis lazuli set in gold, in the place of the uncanonical kathra of gold and silver. Do not plant rose-beds in any imperial garden, except in that of Āghrābād and Nurbāri. No *mansabdār* [rank-holder, or noble] above the 4-*sadi* should begin the construction of permanent houses without

permission . . . remove the gold and silver censers for burning aloe-wood which are brought into the royal residence.[29]

This highly detailed passage demonstrates the degree to which ʿAlamgir sought to restrict not only objects used at court, but the architectural activity of the nobility as well, including the way in which they constructed their houses. Other orders related to visual display in the form of personal dress were also issued, such as the orders that "men should not use in their garments cloth of gold," and that "no amir to whom a *sarpech* [turban ornament] of jewellery was granted should wear it except on Sunday; they should be content with it and should not make another themselves, and should not wear an unauthorised *sarpech*."[30]

Such regulations extended beyond visual and material display to encompass other cultural expressions, most notably music. While the standard historical narrative holds that ʿAlamgir banned music altogether, evidence suggests that the "ban" on music applied to ʿAlamgir himself, in accordance with notions of imperial decorum.[31] By way of praising ʿAlamgir, the court historian Saqi Mustaʿidd Khan reports that "in the first few years of his reign he occasionally listened to their music and had a perfect expert's knowledge of this art; yet out of extreme abstinence he [later on] totally gave up listening to music."[32] Despite this personal restraint, it was deemed appropriate for the nobility and even other members of the imperial household to play music or patronize musicians. Several musical treatises were written during this period, the nobility supported musicians, and Aʿzam Shah, ʿAlamgir's son, was himself a musician and patron.[33] (Private correspondence shows that ʿAlamgir approved of Aʿzam Shah's musical activity.)[34] The notion of an all-inclusive ban is also countered by reports that ʿAlamgir occasionally permitted the playing of music at court (usually, though not exclusively, the ceremonial band [*naubat*]). In 1669, on the occasion of his fifty-third birthday, he marked the occasion with elaborate celebrations that included a ceremonial band that played "happy strains, as formerly."[35] As late as 1689, twenty-one years after the official dismissal of court musicians, the naubat is recorded as playing "joyous tunes" on the occasion of an important military conquest (of Sambha).[36] In all, the evidence points to regulations and restrictions, rather than a wholesale rejection, of the musical arts.

Between the curbing of visual display and the broader regulation of cultural activity, it comes as no surprise that the architectural sphere, too, was subject to controls. Some of these were voiced in the *Fatāwā al-ʿĀlamgīriyya*.[37] In 1667–75, at the behest of ʿAlamgir, a group of Muslim theological scholars completed this multivolume work, collating rulings from the Hanafi school of law (one of the four major schools of Sunni legal thought, and the one that governed legal proceedings in Mughal India). The purpose of the project was to standardize legal precedents, allowing Mughal jurists to rule cases more systematically than they had before. While the *Fatāwā al-ʿĀlamgīriyya* focuses on such matters as marriage, divorce, property, and inheritance, it also offers some commentary on architecture.

A particular concern in the compendium is mosque architecture. One fatwa, for example, states that when building a mosque, a minaret is permissible only if it is truly necessary for the call to prayer to be heard. If the call to prayer can be heard without a minaret, then it is unlawful to build one.[38] Another fatwa, originating in the twelfth century, remarks upon Qurʾanic inscriptions. It proscribes that Qurʾanic inscriptions are inappropriate for the walls of mosques and mihrabs, "for fear that the inscription may fall and be stepped upon."[39]

My aim here is not to prove that architects were responding to specific prohibitions, but rather that such injunctions point to a culture of regulation. The fatwa disapproving of the use of Qurʾanic inscriptions in mosques, for instance, likely did not result from a constant fear of falling walls. Instead, it was part of a broader discourse about the sanctity of words. In 1659, as one of his first public acts after coronation, the emperor ordered that the profession of faith and the names of the four Sunni caliphs not be stamped on coins, as such coins were "constantly touched with the hands and feet of men" and "trodden upon."[40] Both of these sanctions, concerning the inscriptions and the coins, once again revolve around the idea of impropriety, versus illegality. That is, there would be no legal consequences if a Qurʾanic inscription were included in a mosque. Rather, the inclusion of such inscriptions raised the possibility of an undesirable outcome, and was thus not *recommended*.[41]

This broader discourse of regulation and propriety—manifest in the *Fatāwā al-ʿĀlamgīriyya*—likely influenced the exclusion of inscriptions from the imperially sponsored mosques of the later seventeenth century. This exclusion marked a dramatic shift in mosque architecture, and coincided with the growth of the new, ornamental style. In the most monumental imperial mosque of the time, the Badshahi Masjid, there are only two inscriptions. The longer of the two is on the exterior of the complex, over the main gateway. It praises ʿAlamgir as "victorious and valiant," underscores his genealogy by naming him as the third son of Shah Jahan, and invokes the theme of architectural patronage by describing Shah Jahan as the builder of the Taj Mahal.[42] This inscription also includes a small postscript indicating that Fidai Khan Koka, the "foster-brother" of the emperor, oversaw the project.[43] The other inscription, of the shahada (the Muslim profession of faith, "There is no God but God, and Muhammad is His Messenger"), is set in the vault of the prayer hall's entrance, completely eclipsed by carved floral sprays, cartouches, and architectural netting (fig. 1.32).

The minimal use of inscriptions provides a sharp contrast to the Jamiʿ Masjid of Delhi, which, as we have seen, was the Badshahi Masjid's most immediate precedent. The exterior inscription on the Jamiʿ Masjid, composed in Persian and placed in regular panels along the front façade, begins by extolling the virtues of Shah Jahan, the patron, at length. It goes on to celebrate the mosque, and in particular, its architectural features, in celestial terms. The inscription says that the mosque's "arches [*tāq*] [had] surpassed the upper reaches of the sky," while its vaults and domes are compared to the galaxy. After

these poetic metaphors comes an account of the inauguration of the mosque, followed by a lengthy benediction.[44] In the spandrels of the monumental pīshtāq are two roundels, which read *Yā Hādī* ("Oh Guide"), one of the 99 names of God.[45] These inscriptions run continuously along the arches, carrying the viewer along the façade of the building. Thus, the act of reading the inscriptions is intertwined with the physical encounter of the façade.

The interior of the mosque extends the inscriptional program, featuring Qurʾanic verses that are often found in mosques and tombs, and that reflect on the nature of religious architecture. Atop the mihrab arch, for instance, is a selection from Sura 39, al-Zumar ("The Troops"), that speaks of God's compassionate and forgiving nature.[46] Framing this inscription are selections from Sura 9, al-Tauba ("The Repentance"). This sura, or chapter, reflects on the distinction between mosques that are founded on piety, versus those founded on "false pretext," and the inscription emphasizes that the Delhi mosque was one "whose foundation was laid from the first day on piety."[47] This inscription also references a longer epigraphic tradition, as it was historically a popular choice for mosques.[48]

The distinction between the two imperial mosques, the Jamiʿ Masjid and Badshahi Masjid, is not simply a matter of a chance difference between two examples, but is instead reflective of a widespread shift away from inscriptions that took place in the later seventeenth century, during the reign of ʿAlamgir. Earlier in the century, inscriptions figured prominently in mosques. Two key examples are the Jamiʿ Masjid of Agra (1648) and the

Moti Masjid in the Red Fort of Agra (1653) (the latter is similarly named, but distinct from, the Moti Masjid in Delhi analyzed earlier).[49] Both feature Persian inscriptions on the exterior façade of the prayer hall, facing the courtyard. The inscriptions praise Shah Jahan, provide the construction costs and completion dates of each mosque, and include references to the status of the mosque as sacred and revered.[50] In the case of the Jamiʿ Masjid of Agra, the inscription invokes the *Bayt al-Maʾmūr*, the prototype of the Kaʿba in Mecca, located on the seventh level of heaven.[51] It also, besides eulogizing Shah Jahan, pays tribute to the piety of the mosque's patron, the Mughal princess Jahan Ara (1614–1681), who was a disciple of the Chishti order of Sufis.[52]

The inscription of the Agra Moti Masjid, meanwhile, specifically calls the mosque a Kaʿba. The inscription also comments on the beauty of the building: it praises the luster of the marble, which "dazzles" even the sun; the height of its plinth, which is "as high as the foot of the sky"; and its domes, which "embrace the roof of Paradise." Likewise its *guldastas* are "light from the bright stars," and "every golden pinnacle" is "a lamp imparting light to the heavenly luminaries; every luminous arch of it resembles the new moon in announcing the good news of the eternally happy ʿId."[53] Thus both of these mosques feature inscriptional programs that, like Shah Jahan's Jamiʿ Masjid of Delhi, are extensive, poetic, and rich in meaning.

In minimizing its inscriptions, the Badshahi Masjid passes up on the semantic potential of alphabetic text. It does not take the opportunity to extensively eulogize the emperor, or to reference the Qurʾan. Similarly, it does not compare the mosque to Paradise, the Temple of Solomon, or heavenly prototypes, as the inscriptional programs of earlier mosques had done.[54] This de-emphasis on epigraphy distinguishes the Badshahi Masjid not only from the Jamiʿ Masjid of Delhi, its most immediate precedent, and other seventeenth-century Mughal mosques, but also from the Taj Mahal, arguably the most iconic imperial monument from the reign of Shah Jahan. More than any other Mughal building, the Taj Mahal embraced the potential of epigraphy: the calligrapher, Amanat Khan, designed an inscriptional program of twenty-five Qurʾanic passages, including fourteen complete suras. The inscriptions relate to themes that are appropriate for a mausoleum set in a funerary garden: the afterlife, the Day of Judgment, and Paradise.[55]

Besides this sharp break from recent trends in Mughal epigraphy, the Badhshahi Masjid is also distinct from other Islamicate imperial architecture of the time. Looking at the wider early modern Islamic world, inscriptions also featured prominently in mosques from other regions, illustrating just how pronounced the late seventeenth-century move away from inscriptions was.[56] In the Ottoman context, imperial mosques had featured inscriptions since the fifteenth century, and the practice of including monumental Qurʾanic inscriptions in legible *thuluth* script had been standardized under the royal architect Sinan in the sixteenth century. Likewise, the Safavid imperial mosques of Isfahan, the Masjid-i Shah (1611–38) and Masjid-i Shaykh Lutfullah (1603–19), featured extensive inscriptional programs. These were executed in thuluth and Kufic script, and were drawn from both the Qurʾan and the Hadith (the "sayings" of the Prophet), as well as from poetic and historical texts.[57] In both the Ottoman and Safavid contexts, venerated calligraphers, such as the Ottoman artist Hasan Karahisari and the Safavid calligrapher ʿAli Riza al ʿAbbasi, were commissioned to design these epigraphic programs.[58]

Despite the long, rich, and much valued tradition of monumental architectural inscriptions, and the status accorded the calligraphers who designed them, the monumental Badshahi Masjid all but excludes epigraphy from its visual program. Instead, it favors a visually rich ornamental language. If this choice seems a curious one given the spirit of regulation at the time, which clearly favored austerity over excess, it was equally surprising in light of the prominent role played by mosque architecture in projecting an image of ʿAlamgir as a pious ruler.

HISTORY AND RELIGIOSITY

Monumental mosque patronage has always served as an emphatic and publicly staged expression of imperial religiosity. During the reign of ʿAlamgir, the textual record explicitly connected the emperor's piety to the patronage of new mosques:

> As it was the pious Emperor's intention to offer obligatory prayers in congregation, by the side of his retiring place, he laid the foundation of a small, elegant mosque [*masjid-i mukhtasar-i mawzūn*], with carved marble [*sang-i marmar-i munabbat*] and colored pietra dura [*parchīn kārī-yi alwān*]. It was completed in the space of five years at an expenditure of one lakh and 60,000 rupees. ʿĀqil Khan found the chronogram in the holy verse, *Innāʾl-masājid-illa falā tadʿuāmaʿ-allah* [1070 AH].[59]

The passage makes an unequivocal connection between the mosque and the "pious Emperor's intention." Furthermore, the expression "he laid the foundation" may be taken quite literally. In a later palace mosque built in the Deccan, ʿAlamgir is described as laying the foundation stones as a way of garnering spiritual worth: "The Emperor visited the mosque which was being built close to the private Audience Hall, for saying his five daily prayers and performing his constant devotional exercises, and laid a few stones with his own hands in order to accumulate spiritual merit."[60] Beyond this textual evidence, the very construction of the Moti Masjid signified a reconceptualization of daily ceremonial within the palace precincts. From this point, ʿAlamgir began offering the second daily prayer (*zuhr*), accompanied by the political and religious elite of his administration, in a space that was contiguous with the political authority represented by and enacted in the audience halls and palace pavilions of the Red Fort.[61]

Given the regulation of visual and material culture, the attention paid to the legality of inscriptions, and the centrality of mosques in cultivating the image of a pious ruler, why was a highly sumptuous visual language, fashioned in lustrous marble or deeply sculpted stucco, deemed not only permissible, but appropriate? After all, the style that architects and sculptors devised in the early projects of ʿAlamgir persisted and became standardized over the course of his reign, on both an intimate and monumental scale. The answer to this question lies in the symbolic charge of these forms, and in particular, their associations with political stability, justice, and abundance.

The architects of this period not only inherited a set of visual forms, but also a series of symbolic meanings related to these forms concerning the authority of the emperor and his successful rule.[62] The floral motifs in Shah Jahan's Red Fort and in the Taj Mahal resonated with portrayals of the emperor in textual sources that used floral imagery and poetic metaphor. Shah Jahan was described as "the spring of the flower garden of justice and generosity."[63] His reign was likened to "the spring season of the age in which the days and nights are young," and India was called "the rose garden of the earth."[64] This poetic discourse extended to the material current in the period. White marble connoted spiritual purity: the court historian Lahori wrote that white marble rose to prominence during the reign of Shah Jahan, when "sky-touching mansions of marble were built which reflect like the mirror of Alexander and are pure like the heart of spiritual persons."[65] Thus by the 1650s, the language of floral ornament carried with it strong associations of political accomplishment and a flourishing regime, while white marble connoted spiritual virtue.

These associations were exploited and advanced in the projects of the latter half of the century. Given the War of Succession and the troubled circumstances under which ʿAlamgir took the throne, maintaining continuity with the past was essential; interpreting the architectural style established during the reign of Shah Jahan was one means to achieve this end. The motifs of naturalistic ornament, systematically elaborated in ʿAlamgir's imperial visual program, reinforced the theme of political stability and asserted a connection between the reigns of Shah Jahan and ʿAlamgir.

Other visual material from the period underscores this continuity, particularly imperial painting, which provides a compelling parallel. When approaching this period, scholars of Mughal painting have often focused on the dismantling of the imperial workshop and the migration of painters to princely courts across north India.[66] While this perspective is not unreasonable, it overlooks the continuation of certain subject matter and, in particular, imperial portraiture, into the late seventeenth century. A portrait of ʿAlamgir (c. 1660; fig. 1.33), for instance, exhibits the characteristic traits of imperial portraiture developed earlier in the century. ʿAlamgir is shown in profile view, wearing lavish jewelry and resplendent, heavily embroidered robes, a gold halo encircling him. The rich surface textures and static rendering of the emperor perpetuate the existing iconography of imperial Mughal portraiture, using a visual code developed in the portraiture of Shah Jahan.[67] Two similar examples are hunting scenes featuring the emperor, *ʿAlamgir Hunting Nilgai* and *ʿAlamgir Hunting Lions*.[68] In both cases, he remains stately and iconic, rendered in the prototypical profile view, as the action of the hunt unfolds dramatically around him. Despite a substantial decrease in the production of imperially sponsored paintings during ʿAlamgir's time, imperial portraits continued to be produced, particularly in the early part

of ʿAlamgir's reign.[69] Like architecture, painting was regulated in accordance with imperial political aims, rather than abandoned altogether.

❖ ❖ ❖

By the end of the seventeenth century, the Mughal imperial style had been reimagined. Architects and sculptors participated in a historically bound mode of experimentation, taking the white marble surfaces and architectonic forms of Shah Jahan's imperial buildings in new directions. They eschewed parchīn kārī in favor of dramatized sculptural effects, articulated established architectonic forms in attenuated proportions, and diminished distinctions between the ornamental and the structural. Part of the appeal of the vibrant floral style that became standardized in the late seventeenth century was its potential to establish continuities between the early and late seventeenth centuries, and the reigns of Shah Jahan and ʿAlamgir. By using, as the basis for his own imperial style, a visual idiom associated with his imperial predecessor, ʿAlamgir formed a strong association with Shah Jahan, combatting the perception that his rule was illegitimate, illegal, and improper. Thus a strongly historicist mindset permeated both the practice of architects and preferences of patrons. Furthermore, these same imperial projects conformed to emerging notions of propriety as captured in contemporary imperial orders and in the legal opinions compiled in the *Fatāwā al-ʿĀlamgīriyya,* which had the effect of standardizing architecture—that is, producing a set of forms that were seen as acceptable. One of the most perceptible modes of such compliance was the restriction of inscriptions in mosques, which were replaced by elaborately sculpted floral and vegetal forms.

Thus, contrary to earlier interpretations, the "ornamental" style of the later seventeenth century was hardly a random exaggeration of earlier Mughal architecture, divorced from context and meaning. Within the older historiography of Mughal architecture, which positions ʿAlamgir as a religious puritan who held anti-aesthetic values, the sumptuously ornamented imperial monuments of the late seventeenth century are quite startling. But as we have seen, artistic agency and imperial expediency converged, resulting in a dynamic Mughal language that adapted, yet remained distinct from, the past. Both experimentation *and* regulation were integral to the linked processes of expanding and standardizing what would become a recognizable, reflexive Mughal style, one that would not only persist in the decades to come, but would play a crucial role in shaping new histories over the course of the Mughal eighteenth century.

CHAPTER TWO

The Urban Culture of Mughal Delhi

THE SYMBOLICALLY CHARGED, firmly codified visual language of the late seventeenth century would persist into the eighteenth, in the face of dynamic urban shifts in the Mughal capital of Shahjahanabad, in Delhi. From the moment that Shahjahanabad, or the "abode of Shah Jahan," was first inaugurated in 1648, conceptions of space in Delhi had centered on the person of the emperor (r. 1628–58) and his symbolic presence in the imperial palace-fortress, the Red Fort. The axes emanating from the main entrances of the Red Fort formed the main boulevards of the city, Chandni Chowk and Faiz Bazaar. With all roads leading to the emperor, the experience of urban space was dictated by the imperial presence and by the sense of hierarchy and limited access represented by the Red Fort.[1] But beginning in the early 1700s, this urban order shifted dramatically. Spaces outside the walled city of Shahjahanabad, and in particular Sufi shrines, grew into increasingly important centers of urban activity, identity, and growth. Delhi witnessed the construction of a new madrasa, several gardens, a series of small neighborhood mosques, and an astronomical observatory, as well as the renovation of Sufi shrines.

These transformations were intimately connected to Mughal imperial building practices, particularly the visual and spatial codes of funerary architecture. Whereas sixteenth- and seventeenth-century emperors had been buried in monumental mausolea set in extensive funerary gardens, beginning in the eighteenth century, Mughal emperors were buried in marble screen enclosures that were integrated into the precincts of dargahs, or Sufi shrines.[2] Certainly, one possible reason for this shift to smaller, less expensive building projects was the diminishing of the imperial coffers.[3] My purpose here, however, is not to explore the economic dimension of this development, bur rather to consider the implications and dynamics of this new funerary practice for eighteenth-century architectural culture. This period was also one of marked political upheaval in the old capital. Three different emperors ruled in quick succession between 1707 and 1719—one for only one year—and imperial authority was undermined by the machinations of high-ranking nobles.[4] The accession of Muhammad Shah (r. 1719–48) restored some stability to the court, although it was during his reign that Delhi was invaded and sacked in 1739 by the Afsharid Nadir Shah (r. 1736–47).[5] As imperial authority diminished, new types of spaces and buildings opened up the possibility for an encounter with the city that was less constrained by the monumental and the monolithic.

The new imperial projects also came about in relation to a newly emerging urban subjectivity, defined here as a way of being in and perceiving the city, both as a place and an idea, and discernible in literary depictions of the city. When the French merchant Jean-Baptiste Tavernier had visited Delhi in 1676, most of his attention was focused on the Red Fort. Tavernier's account of his visit to the city describes the palace-fortress and its strict ceremonial in great detail, while mentioning other parts of the city only in passing.[6] Sixty years later, when a nobleman from the Deccan named Dargah Quli Khan visited the Mughal capital, his interest was drawn by the very places and activities that Tavernier bypassed: the teeming, vibrant public spaces of the city, many of which were expanded in the building projects of the early eighteenth century. This chapter examines the early eighteenth-century architectural record in conjunction with Dargah Quli Khan's travelogue, a work known as the *Muraqqa'-yi Dihli*, showing how an architecturally revised Delhi both embraced and enabled new ways of relating to the city. It reveals that historical subjectivity and urban subjectivity converged in the early half of the eighteenth century, enabling the proliferation and visibility of the reflexive Mughal style. It was the imprinting of this style across diverse spaces and building types that truly enshrined it, making it come to unequivocally stand for the empire, versus one particular emperor.

SHRINES AND SHRINE CULTURE

Two areas that became central in the reconfiguration of greater Delhi were the neighborhoods surrounding the dargahs of the Chishti saints Nizam al-Din and Qutb Sahib Bakhtiyar Kaki (fig. 2.1). In earlier Mughal times, these spaces had been visited by the emperors, but had never been truly central in the urban order.[7] In the sixteenth century, Babur (r. 1526–30) included stops at Nizam al-Din and Bakhtiyar Kaki in his ceremonial visit to Delhi. Two generations later, Akbar (r. 1556–1605) concentrated his attention solely on the dargah of Nizam al-Din, sponsoring a monumental mausoleum for his father, Humayun (r. 1530–40; 1555–56; d. 1556), in the precincts of the shrine. Subsequently, in the seventeenth century, the tomb of Humayun itself became a pilgrimage destination for the Mughal emperors, eclipsing the Nizam al-Din dargah altogether. The shrines doubtless remained important sites of popular pilgrimage, and lower-ranking Mughal officials continued to sponsor small building projects at the Nizam al-Din dargah, but neither was a site of imperial patronage. And with the completion of the walled city of Shahjahanabad by the mid-seventeenth century, the extramural spaces of Nizam al-Din and Mehrauli became peripheral in the imperially prescribed symbolic order that emanated from the city.

This situation changed substantially in the eighteenth century. The later Mughal emperors concentrated patronage at these shrines, which were transformed into increasingly privileged central spaces in the urban order. By the mid-eighteenth century, marble burial enclosures in the precincts of Chishti shrines emerged as the preferred form for

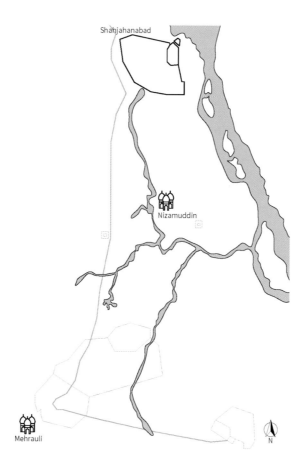

Map of Delhi highlighting
Shahjahanabad, Nizamuddin
(dargah of Nizam al-Din), and
Mehrauli (dargah of Bakhtiyar
Kaki). After Carr Stephen, *The
Archaeology and Monumental
Remains of Delhi* (Ludhiana:
Mission, 1876), pl. 1.

royal Mughal funerary architecture. This practice had its roots as early as the grave of the
emperor ʿAlamgir (r. 1658–1707), which is located in the precincts of the shrine of Zain al-
Din in Khuldabad, Aurangabad, while the form of a marble lattice screen surrounding a
burial site was seen as early as the 1640s in the Taj Mahal, where the cenotaphs of Mumtaz
Mahal and Shah Jahan are surrounded by such a screen. But this typology expanded in
the eighteenth century, so that such burial enclosures were combined with gateways, long
processional screens, and mosques. The expansion took on urban dimensions as well,
carrying the imperial presence beyond the walls of Shahjahanabad and integrating it into
more highly trafficked zones.

The dargah of Qutb Sahib Bakhtiyar Kaki (d. 1235), in Mehrauli, enjoyed a particularly notable resurgence. Though a venerated site since the medieval period, the dargah
emerged as a major center of Mughal patronage in Delhi over the course of the eighteenth
and nineteenth centuries (fig. 2.2). A disciple of Muʿin al-Din Chishti, Bakhtiyar Kaki had
been sent to Delhi in the early thirteenth century. He lived in Mehrauli on the site of the
later dargah; after his death in 1235, the site grew into a popular religious shrine during the
Sultanate period (1211–1526).[8] Prior to the eighteenth century, the shrine does not appear
to have been the focus of Mughal patronage.[9] Other than Babur's visit in 1526, there is not

Plan of Dargah (shrine) of Khwaja Kutab-ud-din
Bakhtiar Kaki at Mahrauli

1.   Grave enclosure of Nawabs of Jhajjar
2.   Main Courtyard
3.   Mosque
4.   Tombs of Akbar Shah II, Shah Alam & Bahadur Shah
5.   Pierced marble enclosure
6.   Gate
7.   Grave of Maulana Fakhr-ud-din
8.   Mosque of Khwaja Sahib
9.   Grave of Dai Ji
10. Grave of Zabita Khan
11. Grave enclosure of Nawabs of Loharu
12. Shrine wall with encaustic work
13. Graveyard of Mohtamib Khan

FIGURE 2.2

Plan of the dargah of Bakhtiyar
Kaki (14th–20th centuries) and
adjacent Zafar Mahal palace
(19th century), Delhi. After H. C.
Fanshawe, *Delhi Past and Present*
(London: J. Murray, 1902), 280.

much evidence of Mughal activity at the shrine in the sixteenth and seventeenth centuries. Patronage was instead focused on other sites, such as the tomb of Selim Chishti (d. 1572) in Fatehpur Sikri, where Akbar erected an exquisite white marble mausoleum in the precincts of his monumental Friday mosque, and the dargah of Muʿin al-Din Chishti (d. 1236) at Ajmer, which honored the order's founder.[10] However, with the building projects of the early 1700s, the Mughal emperors ushered in a sustained period of architectural development at the shrine of Bakhtiyar Kaki.

At the core of this dargah is the grave of the saint. In the spaces surrounding it other graves have been added, along with mosques and assembly halls, enclosure walls, and a series of gateways, dating from the fourteenth to nineteenth centuries.[11] These later insertions do not follow a strict sense of order or clear organizational logic; for example, graves from a particular time period are not all concentrated in one specific area, and there is no clear axiality governing the arrangement of buildings or movement through the entire space. Instead, in keeping with the spatial economy of shrines, proximity to the grave of the saint was clearly the main priority in the development of the shrine over time. This concern was reflected by the early eighteenth-century Mughal emperors, whose additions were concentrated in the area immediately surrounding the grave of Bakhtiyar Kaki.

FIGURE 2.3
Moti Masjid and burial enclosure of
Bahadur Shah, Delhi, 1709.

FIGURE 2.4
Gateway of Farrukh Siyar, dargah
of Bakhtiyar Kaki, Delhi, c. 1713–19.

One such insertion is a small mosque and burial enclosure just to the west of the dargah, sharing its exterior wall (fig. 2.3). The three-domed marble mosque, one of several known as the Moti Masjid, or Pearl Mosque, dates to 1709, during the reign of Bahadur Shah (r. 1707–12).[12] The burial enclosure houses the cenotaphs of several eighteenth- and nineteenth-century emperors, including Ahmad Shah, Shah ʿAlam II, and Akbar II. It is composed of solid marble and jali panels with cusped arch motifs, which surround a group of marble cenotaphs. The enclosure is entered through a doorway on the southern wall of the mosque courtyard.[13] The scale is intimate, the transition between mosque and tomb almost immediate, and the ensemble is unified through the materiality of marble, which, as we have seen, had clear associations with spiritual purity.[14] The result is an immersive space that balances the experience of personal devotion with the possibility of assembly and congregation.

This same sense of scale and materiality was continued in the imperial projects of the subsequent emperor, Farrukh Siyar (r. 1713–19), who commissioned two small marble gateways at the shrine, as well as a long marble screen demarcating the space around the grave of Bakhtiyar Kaki (figs. 2.4, 2.5). While the mosque and burial enclosure discussed above are technically outside of the dargah, Farrukh Siyar's additions were more directly

FIGURE 2.5

Screen of Farrukh Siyar, dargah of Bakhtiyar Kaki, Delhi, c. 1713–19.

FIGURE 2.6

Gateway and screen of Farrukh
Siyar, dargah of Bakhtiyar Kaki,
Delhi, c. 1713–19.

integrated into the area of the shrine, and had the effect of reconfiguring spatial experience within it. The extended marble screen, culminating in two gateways mediating movement into the space of the saint's grave, introduced an element of procession and axiality into the space of the shrine, formalizing entry and delineating a clear boundary between sacred and secular space (see fig. 2.2; fig. 2.6).

The first gateway is a tall, thin marble structure, the upper half of which features inscriptions, and the lower half of which features a simple pointed archway. Inscribed across the top are the names of God, the Prophet Muhammad, and the first four Sunni caliphs; underneath this is an inscription that clearly proclaims an imperial presence at the shrine:

> By the order of the emperor of the world, the king of kings Farrukh Siyar,
> to whom the nine heavens are enslaved, a beautiful screen was built around the grave of
> the master of the faithful and the pole star of the nine heavens [Bakhtiyar Kaki], exalted
> as the Qibla and sacred as the Ka'ba, around which men and angels walk.[15]

The inscription clearly proclaims the name of Farrukh Siyar on the gateway, attesting to the fact that the emperor was responsible for the marble enclosure surrounding the grave of the saint. Moreover, it underscores a new modality of articulating urban space. Rather than anchoring a city or neighborhood with a monumental building, the Mughal emperor now exalts the grave of this saint and surrounding shrine areas, folding his presence into a highly charged space of spiritual devotion and congregation.

The additions to the dargah of Bakhtiyar Kaki also mediated between the legacy of the Mughal past and the context of the present, linking urban and historical subjectivities. Given the dramatic loss of political power experienced by the Mughal center at this time, accessing alternative means of legitimacy was imperative. By building at the Bakhtiyar Kaki dargah, the Mughal emperors heightened their associations with the Chishti order, allowing imperial powers to draw on the spiritual authority afforded by such an association.[16] Yet such patronage also connected the present emperors to their collective imperial past, allowing them to appropriate the legacy of the Mughal empire itself as a source of legitimacy. The first gateway of Farrukh Siyar, for example, has been interpreted as a quotation of the forms comprising the mosque sponsored by Shah Jahan at the dargah of Mu'in al-Din Chishti at Ajmer.[17] This would visually link the patronage of Farrukh Siyar at the Bakhtiyar Kaki dargah to the patronage practices of his predecessors, and in particular Shah Jahan, at Ajmer. Here, again, urban subjectivity and the project of historicization converge.

Finally, the extensive patronage at this shrine also speaks to its importance as a site within the physical and symbolic landscape of the city. Subsequent development at the dargah suggests that it grew into an extremely popular burial site over the course of the eighteenth century and was also a center of elite patronage. This is seen, for instance, in the interment of the Mughal emperors Ahmad Shah, Shah 'Alam II, and Akbar II alongside Bahadur Shah over the course of the eighteenth century. In the nineteenth century, noble families, such as the nawabs of Loharu, even built self-contained dynastic graveyards on the outskirts of the tomb (fig. 2.7). Additionally, the nineteenth-century Mughal emperors

FIGURE 2.7
Burial enclosure of the nawabs of Loharu, dargah of Bakhtiyar Kaki, Delhi, 1802.

Burial enclosure of Muhammad
Shah, dargah of Nizam al-Din,
Delhi, 1748.

66   THE URBAN CULTURE OF MUGHAL DELHI

Akbar Shah II (r. 1806–37) and Bahadur Shah II (r. 1837–58) constructed and renovated their palace, the Zafar Mahal, to the immediate west of the shrine.

This heightened building activity suggests an increase in the use of the space over time; the shrine must have become a more frequented zone during the eighteenth century and into the nineteenth. The construction of a *majlis-khāna* (assembly hall) at the site in the eighteenth century also indicates that assemblies were held here during the period. While it is likely that such gatherings occurred at the site prior to this time, the majlis-khāna points to the formalization of such a practice. The growth in the popularity and status of this shrine, located as it was in Mehrauli, clearly emphasizes that spaces outside of the Shahjahanabad city walls became pivotal in the eighteenth century, resulting in a broader delineation of city limits and subverting the urban order that was established under Shah Jahan and that held sway in the seventeenth century.

This urban reordering was also manifest in the renovation and augmentation of another key shrine in the city, the dargah of Nizam al-Din (d. 1325). In 1748, the emperor Muhammad Shah was buried in a marble screen enclosure similar to that of Bahadur Shah (fig. 2.8). While closer to Shahjahanabad than the shrine of Bakhtiyar Kaki, the dargah of Nizam al-Din was still significant for drawing urban crowds outside of the walled precincts of the imperial capital. Like Bakhtiyar Kaki, Nizam al-Din Auliya was a Sufi of the Chishti order. While alive, his khānqāh was a vital center of religious learning and contained a *jamāʿat khāna* (residential hall) for his followers. Upon his death in 1325, Nizam al-Din was buried not far from his khānqāh; his grave serves as the core of the present dargah.[18]

Historically, the shrine had been the site of extensive building activity during the Delhi Sultanate period, particularly in the fourteenth and fifteenth centuries. During the Mughal period, the dargah of Nizam al-Din continued to be a significant site of patronage and pilgrimage, in marked contrast to the shrine of Bakhtiyar Kaki. In the sixteenth and seventeenth centuries, Mughal emperors and the nobles in their service sponsored renovations and additions to the space, from the rebuilding of the tomb over the saint's grave as a domed structure with a stone jali screen, to the construction of the domed tomb of Akbar's "foster father" and close adviser Atgah Khan (d. 1562; 1562–66), which lies just yards away from the tomb of Nizam al-Din.[19] Perhaps the most prominent Mughal project in the area of the shrine was the monumental tomb and funerary garden of Humayun, commissioned by the emperor Akbar and completed in 1562–71 by the architect Mirak Mirza Ghiyas and his son.[20]

Visiting the shrine today, one is met by the eighteenth-century burial enclosure of Muhammad Shah. With its carved gateway serving as the only point of entry to the burial site, the enclosure of Muhammad Shah is a more restricted and formalized space than that of Bahadur Shah in the dargah of Bakhtiyar Kaki. The gateway recalls the monumental pīshtāqs of imperial Mughal mausolea, from Humayun's tomb to the Taj Mahal: a cusped, vaulted arch features muqarnas niches and netting, and flower and vine motifs unfold

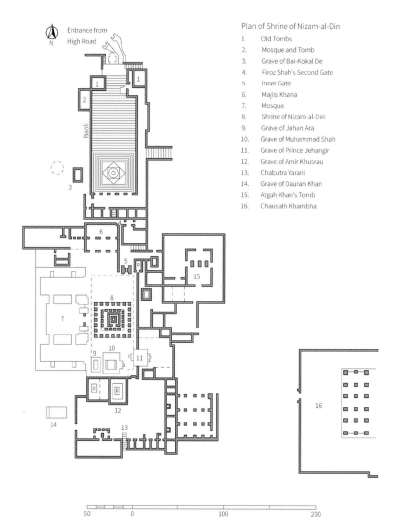

Plan of Shrine of Nizam-al-Din

1. Old Tombs
2. Mosque and Tomb
3. Grave of Bai-Kokal De
4. Firoz Shah's Second Gate
5. Inner Gate
6. Majlis Khana
7. Mosque
8. Shrine of Nizam-al-Din
9. Grave of Jahan Ara
10. Grave of Muhammad Shah
11. Grave of Prince Jehangir
12. Grave of Amir Khusrau
13. Chabutra Yarani
14. Grave of Dauran Khan
15. Atgah Khan's Tomb
16. Chausath Khambha

FIGURE 2.9

Plan of the dargah of Nizam al-Din, Delhi, 13th–20th centuries. After H. C. Fanshawe, *Delhi Past and Present* (London: J. Murray, 1902), 237.

on the spandrels. The remainder of the enclosure is composed of simple, rectangular jali panels with a carved ornamental parapet. In using these forms, the burial enclosure forms a contiguous structure with the preexisting burial enclosure of Jahan Ara (d. 1681), the daughter of Shah Jahan, which is similarly constituted of white marble jali screens and a decorative parapet.[21] These white marble structures stand out from their immediate surroundings and clearly mark an imperial presence at the shrine. In turn, visitors to the shrine would come into constant contact with the enclosures, as they are situated mere steps away from the grave of Nizam al-Din, with no structures placed in between the royal graves and that of the saint (figs. 2.9, 2.10). Therefore, the tombs of Jahan Ara, Muhammad Shah, and Nizam al-Din are part of a continuous spatial experience; to visit one grave is to visit all three.[22] Whereas the Bahadur Shah complex was a clearly demarcated, separate space adjacent to the dargah of Bakhtiyar Kaki, here Muhammad Shah's tomb is directly integrated into the Nizam al-Din shrine. This shift might indicate that the political and

social conditions prompting imperial Mughal patronage at the Delhi Chishti shrines only grew more relevant over the course of the eighteenth century, as the shrines grew ever more popular.

NEW URBAN BUILDING PROJECTS

The reinscription of Delhi was achieved through other buildings and spaces as well, many of which signified a new class of patrons. These new projects ranged from an astronomical observatory and urban gardens to small neighborhood mosques and a large madrasa. Some of these spaces, particularly the observatory and gardens, functioned to open up urban space. Others, such as the neighborhood mosques, powerfully referenced Mughal buildings from the past, casting them as models and icons.[23] Collectively, these new urban projects fundamentally changed the shape of the city and the experience of its inhabitants.

Perhaps the most unusual addition to the cityscape of Delhi was the astronomical observatory, known today as Jantar Mantar (c. 1725). Built several miles southwest of the city walls, the observatory was the work of Sawai Jai Singh II, the maharaja of Jaipur and Amer and a high-ranking mansabdār (rank-holder) in the Mughal administration.[24] Sawai Jai Singh's relationship with the Mughal administration is illustrated by his *Zīj-i Muhammad Shahī,* an astronomical text dedicated to the Mughal emperor Muhammad Shah.[25] The purpose of the observatories was to produce new astronomical tables based on data gathered in India, rather than using data taken from Central Asian or European astronomical texts.[26] The site was characterized by monumental astronomical instruments, the largest of which stretched 21.3 meters tall. With its bold, geometric forms and towering presence, the observatory made a dramatic contribution to the cityscape.[27] It was also a place of experimentation; the observatory was one of five that Sawai Jai Singh had built in major north Indian cities, the others being located in Ujjain, Varanasi, Mathura, and in Jaipur, Jai Singh's own capital city. Thus the observatory was not only unusual, but linked Delhi to a network of sites associated with new knowledge.

This period also witnessed the expansion of urban features more typical to Mughal cities, namely gardens. In the seventeenth century, the Mughal princess Jahan Ara had endowed a sprawling garden in the center of Shahjahanabad, running along the northern side of Chandni Chowk.[28] In addition, there were also other, imperial extramural gardens in greater Delhi. These included the ʿAzzabad garden west of the city gates, sponsored by Shah Jahan's wife Akbarabadi Mahal, and the gardens north of the city gates, constructed by the Mughal nobles ʿAli Mardan Khan, Jaffar Khan, and Mohsan Khan.[29] For the most part, these were large, walled gardens, following the chahār bāgh, or quadripartite, garden plan that the Mughals had imported from Central Asia and adapted to the Indian context.[30]

Building on this legacy, garden culture continued to thrive in the eighteenth century. And like the Chishti shrines, new gardens were concentrated beyond the walls of Shahjahanabad. North of the city walls, a garden complex was sponsored in the 1750s by Qudsiyya Begum, a former courtesan who had married the Mughal emperor Muhammad Shah and served as an influential queen mother during the reign of Ahmad Shah (r. 1748–54). Known as the Qudsiyya Bagh (c. 1748), the garden bordered the banks of the Yamuna River and included gateways, a mosque, and a riverfront pavilion.[31] A 1798 aquatint by Thomas and William Daniell depicts the Qudsiyya pavilion as a long, double-story structure with cusped arches, extensive relief carving, protruding jharoka balconies, and an octagonal tower at each end. This expansion of a garden landscape north of the city was mirrored by one to its south. In Mehrauli, not far from the shrine of Bakhtiyar Kaki, an expansive stepped garden had been constructed, with a multilevel waterfall at its center, which would be expanded by imperial patrons into the nineteenth century.[32]

But it is in the realm of religious architecture that we have the strongest built record for the period. As early as the 1720s a number of small mosques, all sponsored by members of the nobility or royal women, were built at various points throughout Delhi. As with much of Mughal architecture at this time, these mosques responded to past forms and models, while refashioning them to new contexts. In the seventeenth century, the main mosques in the city were the imperial Jamiʿ Masjid, sponsored by Shah Jahan and completed in 1656, as well as two mosques sponsored by two of his wives, the Fatehpuri Masjid on Chandni Chowk and the no longer extant Akbarabadi Masjid on Faiz Bazaar, sponsored by Akbarabadi Begum.[33] All of these mosques were connected to marketplaces; in the case of the Akbarabadi Masjid, both mosque and marketplace were sponsored by the same patron.[34]

In the eighteenth century, mosque patronage expanded markedly: mosques were sponsored at additional points in the city, showing the reconfiguration of urban space,

FIGURE 2.11
Fakhr al-Masajid, Delhi, 1728–29.

and showcased the patronage of an increasingly powerful elite. Chandni Chowk saw the addition of the Sunahri Masjid (Golden Mosque, 1721–22), sponsored by the amir Raushan al-Daula. On the northern border of the walled city, the noblewoman Fakhr al-Nisa commissioned the Fakhr al-Masajid (Pride of the Mosques, 1728–29). South of the Red Fort, the Mughal princess Zinat al-Nisa (the daughter of ʿAlamgir) sponsored the Zinat al-Masjid (1707). Farther afield, Qudsiyya Begum sponsored one mosque in her vast garden complex north of the city walls, and a second mosque in south Delhi, in the area of the Shiʿi Shahi Mardan shrine (c. 1750–51).[35] The geographic spread represented by these mosques reveals the re-centering of space in the city at this time. All are three-domed mosques with triple-arched façades, some featuring tall, enframing minarets. The proliferation of this building type represents the popularization of a triple-dome mosque form that, in the previous century, had become an imperial type. As this imperial type was recast in these later, smaller-scale mosques, so too was it cast as a historical precedent.

The Fakhr al-Masajid best embodies these developments (fig. 2.11). As the inscription of the mosque conveys, it was sponsored by Fakhr al-Nisa in memory of her deceased husband, Shujaʿat Khan, who had been a noble in the service of ʿAlamgir:

> The Khan, the Cherisher of Faith, Shujaʿat Khan,
> has obtained a place in Paradise.
> By the will of God and the grace of Murtaza
> Chief of the ladies and slave of Fatimah, Fakhr-i Jahan [Pride of the world],
> Built this mosque in his memory by the blessing of Mustafa.
> 1141 AH [1728–29 CE][36]

This example thus speaks to the shift whereby urban mosques, once associated primarily with royalty, were now the result of highly visible patronage by the nobility. The Fakhr al-Masajid also evinces the growth of urban activity in spaces outside of the Chandni Chowk and Faiz Bazaar areas, as it is situated in the northernmost part of the city near the Kashmiri gate, on a subsidiary road. The mosque likely facilitated commercial activity in this area: it rests atop an eight-foot-tall platform that housed shops.³⁷

But a building like the Fakhr al-Masajid also functioned as a crucial intermediary moment in the ongoing historicization of Mughal architecture. With its black and white marble domes and its use of red sandstone and white marble, the mosque clearly reproduces the key visual elements of the Jamiʿ Masjid of Delhi (see fig. 1.21). A central pīshtāq, with a cusped arch and two slim minarets, is flanked by two additional cusped arches surrounded by white marble and red sandstone frames. The alternating red and white palette is repeated in the vertical bands of marble and sandstone running down both the pīshtāq minarets and the mosque's two larger minarets. The Jamiʿ Masjid would ultimately become rendered in canonical form on paper, in the architectural studies of the eighteenth and early nineteenth centuries. But first, it was re-scaled and enshrined in stone, in mosques such as the Fakhr al-Masajid. Thus even as new building projects opened up alternative spaces in the old Mughal capital, and engaged with novel ways of being in the city, they did so in a way that not only accessed, but historicized, the past.

The same is true of other building types, such as the madrasa, a building type infrequently sponsored by the Mughals. Near the Ajmer gate, in the western part of Shahjahanabad, a madrasa was commissioned in the late seventeenth or early eighteenth century by Ghazi al-Din Khan, a nobleman and military leader who had distinguished himself in the service of ʿAlamgir.³⁸ (Ghazi al-Din's son, Nizam al-Mulk Asaf Jah I, would go on to declare the independence of Hyderabad.) It is a courtyarded building, featuring a monumental multistory gateway and elements typical of madrasas: along the perimeter of the courtyard is a series of individual rooms, appropriate for study or residence, as well as some larger rooms suited for instruction. There are, as well, aspects of the building that tie it to the architectural idiom of the Mughal eighteenth century. For instance on the western end, there is a mosque and a burial enclosure where the patron is interred. With its triple-domed elevation and its use of red sandstone and white marble, the mosque is yet another example that evokes the Jamiʿ Masjid, casting the seventeenth-century imperial mosque in the role of model or precedent. Through such persistent reflexivity, the older mosque is transformed into an icon. Similarly, the burial enclosure, a series of screens surrounding a cenotaph, is like that of ʿAlamgir and the Mughal emperors of the eighteenth century. In addition, both mosque and burial enclosure feature a floral ornamental program of the kind artists had elaborated over the course of the seventeenth century. Like other buildings from early eighteenth-century Delhi, the madrasa shows the extension of the reflexive Mughal style to buildings commissioned by the nobility as well as the imperial family, and its use in new building types.

In all, architecture sponsored by the urban elite contributed to the changing city-scape of Mughal Delhi in myriad ways. It opened up new social spaces in the city, decentering the Red Fort and Jamiʿ Masjid. Paradoxically, even as the centrality of the imperial monuments was challenged, the new projects simultaneously reinforced the visual language of Mughal imperial power, constructing new projects in the image of imperial icons. In the process, new projects reinforced the notion that Mughal imperial monuments were historical icons, and that their legacies could be mined for new purposes.

LITERARY REPRESENTATIONS OF THE CITY

An architecturally revised Delhi embraced and facilitated new ways of experiencing and perceiving the city, setting the stage for one of the most famous travel narratives from the time, the *Muraqqaʿ-yi Dihlī*. The *Muraqqaʿ* is the work of a young noble from the Deccan named Dargah Quli Khan, who visited Delhi in the late 1730s, accompanying Nizam al-Mulk Asaf Jah I of Hyderabad. He would remain until 1741, recording his observations about the city and its inhabitants.[39] The *Muraqqaʿ* profiles prominent figures in Delhi's urban life, from poets, musicians, and dancers to sufis and reciters of elegies (*marsiya khwān*) to noblemen known for their patronage of the arts. Its narrator also recounts his experiences at innumerable poetry readings (*majlis*) and musical soirees (*mahfil*), which range from the refined to the debauched. The source has been valued by ethnomusicologists because of its descriptions of various styles of musical performance, as well as its biographical notes on specific performers.[40] Historians, too, have addressed the multiple dimensions of the *Muraqqaʿ*, from its connection to larger political histories to its capacity to reveal norms concerning gender and sexuality.[41]

Yet thus far, the text has not been adequately incorporated into the architectural history of the eighteenth century, despite its potential. Certainly, with its vivid descriptions of urban life, the *Muraqqaʿ* animates the spaces and locales discussed above. But more importantly, the narrative underscores the symbiotic relationship between such physical interventions in the city's urban fabric and new urban practices. Most significantly, the encounters and experiences in the *Muraqqaʿ* are framed through visits to a range of architectural monuments and public spaces, such as dargahs, khānqāhs, mosques, bazaars, and public thoroughfares (*chowk*). Roughly half of the work is devoted to describing urban spaces and sites of assembly. What emerges from this account is a distinctly urbanistic view of the period. City life is characterized by activity in public and semipublic spaces, and established spatial hierarchies, which once favored the private zones of the imperial palace-fortress, are abandoned in favor of shifting paradigms of urban experience.

The richness and significance of the *Muraqqaʿ* result from its hybrid quality: it draws on and combines aspects of various genres to provide an animated, urbanist-minded window onto the city. As it lies between multiple genres that focus on space and place, the *Muraqqa'* stands out as an unusual text, offering information about the urban culture of the city not found in other sources. It is, first and foremost, a Persianate travel narrative (*safarnāma*), part of a large corpus of texts that attest to the circulation of people between and within India, Iran, Central Asia, the Ottoman domains, and Western Europe in the early modern period, and that have received increasing scholarly attention in recent years.[42] In the eighteenth and nineteenth centuries, the scope, orientation, and production of such travel narratives changed, as travelers moved across the globe with increasing frequency, or wrote accounts with greater regularity.[43] Linked to this development was the dramatic increase in the production of first-person narratives in the Indo-Persian world, including both travel narratives and autobiographies, which offered new, alternative viewpoints.[44]

Yet with its interest in urban depiction, the *Muraqqa'* relates to other forms of Persian literature as well, such as tazkiras. Often generically characterized as "biographical dictionaries," these are actually multidimensional texts. Besides providing biographical information about poets or saints (the most common subjects of tazkiras), these texts also shed light on social lineages and networks as well as the courtly and urban spaces occupied by these groups.[45] Echoes of this genre, in format and content, can be seen in the *Muraqqa'*. This is perhaps clearest in the latter part of the work, which comprises a catalogue of poets, musicians, and entertainers of various kinds. But the earlier part of the work also seems influenced by the logic and structure of tazkiras, though amended: the text opens with a catalogue of the major shrines of Delhi, so that the text is organized not as a list of people, but of places. In order to describe life in the city, Dargah Quli begins by describing its major spaces.

In this respect, the text engages with a third Persian literary tradition, that of the shahrāshūb poem. Translated literally as "city disturber," the shahrāshūb mode originally celebrated the beauty of a city-dweller engaged in his craft or trade, filling the space of the city with his energy and beauty. Over time, such poems increasingly focused on the qualities of the urban centers these figures occupied, so that by the seventeenth century, major cities in the eastern Islamic lands had poems dedicated to them.[46] In Islamicate India, there was a range of poems, from those that eulogized individual architectural projects, to topographical poems that provided sweeping "verbal panoramas" in verse. These praised the cities of India from the southern Deccan region to the Mughal north.[47] The vivid descriptions found in these poems are echoed by those found in the *Muraqqa'*.

The *Muraqqa'* suggests that there was a marked and fundamental transition taking place in the social and cultural order, and that the spaces of the city both enabled this shift and were transformed by it. Rather than focus on major monuments such as the Red Fort or Jami' Masjid, Dargah Quli engages in a conceptual mapping of the city that encompasses a multitude of spaces, especially those that emerged as imperial priorities in the eighteenth century. The structure of his narrative is based on his experience of the city, and the elements of religious and nonreligious congregation, recreation, entertainment, transgression, and experimentation that contributed to that experience. Throughout, it is space that enables experience. Even when profiling individuals, Dargah Quli seems unable to resist reflecting upon and representing space. His portrayal of the wealthy noble and patron Mirza Abd al-Khaliq Varasta turns into an extensive description of his haveli (mansion), his account of the poet Hazeen includes a section detailing the way in which the courtyard of his house is set up for performances.[48] In the end, Dargah Quli's chronicle of poets and patrons equally functions as a catalogue of spatial and sensory experience. These ways of thinking and writing about the city would have profound impacts on the production of histories of Delhi (discussed in Chapter 5). For the moment, however, my focus is the interconnection between urban transformations in the built environment and this key literary representation of Delhi city life.

In Dargah Quli's descriptions of architecture and space, there is a marked emphasis on shrines and shrine culture, matching the architectural concerns evinced by imperial builders. He begins the narrative by first focusing on five of the major religious centers in Delhi: a Qadam Sharif shrine, or shrine of the Holy Footprint, dedicated to Muhammad; a shrine housing the footprint of ʿAli; and then the shrines of Bakhtiyar Kaki, Nizam al-Din, and Chiragh Delhi.[49] In most of these accounts, Dargah Quli begins by first locating the site in terms of its distance either from the Red Fort or the Purana Qila (the Old Fort, of Humayun), suggesting that the imperial nucleus of Delhi remained a persistent touchstone, even as a greater cityscape grew around it. He then goes on to speak of the sanctity of the site in question, extolling Muhammad and ʿAli and eulogizing the saints buried in each of the three dargahs. The majority of his narrative, however, concentrates on describing the activities taking place at each of these shrines. Highlighting moments of high traffic, he notes the days when pilgrims converge on each of these spaces, such as the busy Thursdays at the Qadam Sharif shrine, when the path of the pilgrim is "filled with a thousand obstacles."[50]

Though he is not primarily concerned with describing the architecture of the shrines, when Dargah Quli does offer occasional remarks on architectural details or edifices that especially impress him, he tends to focus on the recent constructions of the early eighteenth century. At the dargah of Bakhtiyar Kaki, for example, he praises the jali screen commissioned by Farrukh Siyar, speaking of the "elegance" (*nazākat*) of the lattice-work and the transparency (*shafāfī*) of the marble (*sang-i marmar*).[51] That these imperial interventions stood at the center of urban growth is borne out by Dargah Quli's comments. For instance, at the shrine of Nizam al-Din, those who work at the shrine reside in its vicinity, resulting in the growth of the neighborhood. In turn, this neighborhood is supported by the heavy traffic that the shrine attracts.[52] My contention is not that imperial architecture alone prompted urban expansion, but that it was linked to it, visually and spatially.

The religious space of the shrine enabled secular and sacred activity alike. Dargah Quli reports on the activities—religious and otherwise—that take place at these spaces and in their immediate surroundings. Reflecting on the commercial aspect of these sites, he speaks of the shops and traders at the Qadamgah of ʿAli (shrine of the footprint of ʿAli) and at the dargah of Nizam al-Din.[53] In addition, his observations also suggest that visits to the shrines were linked to trips for recreation and pleasure. For example, after visiting the Bakhtiyar Kaki dargah, people would take excursions to the surrounding meadows and springs, as they would to the gardens surrounding the dargah of Nizam al-Din after pilgrimage to that site.[54] Pleasure is also afforded by musical performances, as at the dargah of Chiragh Delhi, where Dargah Quli enjoys the sounds of the *mūr chang* and *pakhawaj*.[55] When he does portray religious activity, Dargah Quli focuses on the spectacular, favoring depictions of important holidays or festivals and offering evocative images and sounds. In his relation of the ʿurs ceremonies at the dargah of Nizam al-Din, for instance, he remarks on the throng of devotees and the *qawwals* who sing through the night, which "channels the sheikhs and sufis to a state of ecstasy."[56]

Beyond the city's shrines, the Dargah Quli narrative is a testament to the myriad other public spaces that flourished in eighteenth-century Delhi, including its public boulevards, squares, and bazaars. In the narrative, these are the sites of performances and literary readings as well as spectacle and transgression. The major public avenues of Shahjahanabad are depicted as vibrant, slightly chaotic city centers where a variety of goods are available, people of different backgrounds intermingle, and striking tableaux present themselves to the casual observer moving through the streets.[57] Dargah Quli describes Chandni Chowk, the boulevard running from the Lahore Gate of the Red Fort: "Of all the marketplaces it is the most colorful, and of all the streets, the most bedecked. It is the place of recreation and house of spectacle for pleasure-seekers. In its shops are goods of all sorts, and merchandise of every kind is displayed for customers. Rarities wink from its corners and exquisite things beguile from its nooks."[58] Goods for sale in the many stores lining Chandni Chowk assault Dargah Quli's senses: as he breathes perfumes and essences from the shops of attars wafting out on to the street, he beholds glittering rubies and luminous pearls, glistening swords and daggers, exquisite glass and porcelain wares, gilded huqqas and wine cups.[59] This walk along Chandni Chowk reveals that the boulevard functions not only as a major traffic artery and commercial center, but also as a space of visual display and sensory consumption.[60] Dargah Quli does not speak of the goods for sale in terms of material acquisition, but rather lingers on the pleasure he derives from visual consumption.

But people, as much as things, attract Dargah Quli's attention. The description of Chowk Saʾadullah Khan, which extends from the eastern gateway of the Jamiʿ Masjid to the Delhi Gate of the Red Fort, suggests that not only is there an equally dizzying variety of wares available in its bazaars, as in Chandni Chowk, but that the streets also act as a theater for viewing the people of the city.[61] Dargah Quli takes in handsome young men dancing, crowds of people idly milling about, and fortune-tellers seated on wooden chairs, whom he compares to maulvis on the pulpits. This comparison alludes to the Jamiʿ Masjid steps away, and is apt given the constant blurring of the boundary between sacred and secular social spaces. His fascination with the people encountered in these public spaces is linked to poetic conventions of the time, especially the shahrāshūb mode discussed above. Moreover, the same encompassing view that brings together urban space and city dweller is found in the inscriptional record. We recall that in the gateway of Farrukh Siyar, the inscription, besides naming the emperor as the patron of the marble screen, celebrates the people who frequent the shrine. The spaces of the city, commercial vibrancy, social interaction, and visual pleasure are all inextricably linked.

Moreover, Dargah Quli does not restrict such vivid descriptions of objects and people to the city's commercial zones. Instead, there is a similarity between these and his observations of sacred spaces. His writing suggests a permeability of spatial boundaries between religious and secular zones and speaks to the reconceptualization of social spaces that characterized eighteenth-century Delhi's architectural culture. For instance, Dargah Quli's description of the six-day Basant celebrations at the various shrines of Delhi is replete with details that recall his portrayal of the chowks of Shahjahanabad. There are colorful flowers and beautiful women with porcelain bottles of perfume, the smell of ambergris fills the air, perfume is sprinkled over the pilgrims, and qawwals perform to an enraptured audience; in short, the vibrancy that characterizes the atmosphere of Chandni Chowk and Chowk Saʾadullah Khan is found once again in the shrines during Basant. Furthermore, the Basant festivities are celebrated in a different shrine for the first five days and culminate in the residences of the emperor and high-ranking nobles on the sixth day. This religious celebration crosses from sacred to secular spaces, moving from shrines to palaces and mansions.[62]

There are other instances of social practices that occur across the seemingly contained categories of sacred and secular. An explicit example of a single space that retains both a religious and recreational function is the residence of Majnun Nanak Shahi, an ascetic who is said to have Hindu and Muslim followers. While disciples visit him for ostensibly pious reasons, Dargah Quli informs the reader that this is also a popular boating spot.[63] Similarly, just as the city's shrines are the site of large congregations on specific, set days, popular musicians host standing performances in their residences, with the same regularity as religious services.[64]

At times, the lack of delineation of religious spaces, and concomitant deregulation of sanctioned behavior, slips into moments of true transgression, often invoked by the presence or absence of the *muhtasib* (censor of morals). Whereas taking an evening stroll in the gardens surrounding a shrine is viewed as an acceptable form of diversion, Dargah Quli notes the impropriety he witnesses near the grave of Bahadur Shah at the shrine of Bakhtiyar Kaki, where the amorous and the debauched fail to heed the muhtasib.[65] In another instance, Dargah Quli speaks of a residential quarter that is so crime-ridden and dangerous that even the muhtasib avoids it. And at the grave of Mir Musharraf, in a garden near the dargah of Nizam al-Din, lovers fall under the spell of flowers and fragrances so sweet that Dargah Quli claims they would intoxicate even the muhtasib.

These disruptions to decorum are matched by disturbances to the social hierarchy, a development with ramifications for urban space and its experience. In his narrative, Dargah Quli reveals a hierarchical system that underlies and governs the patronage of the arts, the attendance at specific events, and even the possession of objects, all of which are connected to the status of both patrons and artists. For instance, Baqir Tamburchi, a particularly gifted musician, is accorded importance because of his position as an imperially sponsored musician.[66] When describing the musicians Shah Nawaz Sabuche and Shah Daniyal, Dargah Quli lists their talents and makes the point that wealthy people in particular hold mahfils to hear the musicians.[67] At the eclectic mahfils held by the noble and poet Ja'far 'Ali Khan Miran, high-ranking nobles are seated in a separate section, demarcated by fine carpets, and are served special fruits and wines.[68]

But other moments in the text suggest a breakdown of social hierarchies. The courtesan Nur Bai, we are told, lives in a house full of the types of objects usually kept in the homes of nobles of high rank,[69] and the mahfils of the noble Latif Khan, a high-ranking mansabdār at the court of Muhammad Shah, are reportedly so popular that even the elite are not guaranteed admission.[70] Many times, whether discussing a mahfil or a shrine, Dargah Quli makes a point of stating that a mixed public, comprising those of high rank as well as a more general population (khāṣṣ wa 'āmm), frequent the space or event.[71] While this "public" did not encompass all social classes, Dargah Quli's narrative still indicates a broadening of social strata in attendance at any given urban space, and more importantly, a fundamental shift in the meta-ordering of the space of the city.

These destabilizations also relate to patronage. The patronage and presence of royalty at the dargah of Nizam al-Din are invoked as a sign of the shrine's importance, as Dargah Quli celebrates the space as attracting even sultans and emperors (salāṭīn wa khawāqīn).[72] At the same time, his description of this space is not driven by a history of royal patronage or attendance; rather, it is the lively spiritual and social activity associated with the shrine that is the focus of his narrative. The Muraqqa' ultimately suggests that by the eighteenth century, while imperial patronage remained significant, it was not the sole or even primary means of lending a space importance. And indeed, as evident in the new urban building projects of this period, there was a strong class of nonroyal patrons making its mark on the city.

Moreover, Dargah Quli suggests that the more open, less regimented social spaces had given rise to an experimentation with forms and the fashioning of new tastes. Performers in the imperial service are characterized by their older musical styles (*qidmān pasand*), which did not appeal to new, younger audiences.[73] Thus the spaces where social codes were more strictly observed were also the spaces where a classical style was preserved.

The transformation of the social order is made most explicit when the narrator discusses courtesans and dancers who have moved from the imperial court to the city. Both Kamal Bai and Pamna, courtesans who had formerly been attached to the court of Muhammad Shah, are said to hold performances attended by a wider population, in contrast to former times, when their company was forbidden to anyone but the emperor.[74] Dargah Quli states that since Muhammad Shah suspended mahfils at court after the invasion of Nadir Shah, these women were forced to seek employment outside of the imperial court, which they found with ease. These observations not only point to divergences between activity at court and in the wider city, they also provide an all too brief glimpse into the ways women figured into the changing social system. In his references to other imperial court performers, as in the examples cited above, Dargah Quli simply states that they were affiliated with the court and therefore held in high esteem. Here, Dargah Quli uses the language of control, commenting on the "accessibility" of these individuals.[75]

The other issue Dargah Quli raises in this passage is the invasion of Nadir Shah. While scholarship has posited this event as a major turning point in the patronage of the arts at the imperial court, in the *Muraqqaʿ* it appears to have less of an impact on the cultural life of the city. Overall, the references to Nadir Shah are scarce. At one point, Dargah Quli cites a noble who had to contribute to Muhammad Shah's tribute to Nadir Shah, with the result that his entertainment budget suffered and his mahfils grew more subdued.[76] At another moment, he alludes obliquely to the invasion. Yet his very next sentence asserts that nonetheless, singing and entertainment last from night until morning.[77]

To a certain extent, this portrayal of a vibrant urban culture, abounding with unusual sights and seemingly unparalleled opportunities for pleasure, undoubtedly reflects Dargah Quli's particular point of view. The vivid portrayal of the sights and experiences of Delhi have as much to do with Dargah Quli's fascination with the city as with what was actually there. Besides his demonstrated interest in urban life, other aspects of the narrative reflect his personal concerns. For example, Dargah Quli's Shiʿi identity might have influenced some of the narrative choices he makes: he includes the shrine of ʿAli in the opening pages of his text, inserting it between the Qadam Sharif shrine, dedicated to the Prophet Muhammad, and the three major Sufi shrines in the city. Moreover, his account of the most renowned performers in the city includes a lengthy section on marsiya khwāns, who recite in commemoration during the month of Muharram, when Shiʿis commemorate the Battle of Karbala and martyrdom of Husayn.[78] Many of his descriptions, too, are filled with details concerning music. He comments on the variety of musical styles artists perform, such as Dhruvapad, and the assorted instruments they play, from the *dholak* to the *rabāb* to the pakhawaj.[79]

Yet even though it reflects Dargah Quli's unique concerns, it is clear that by the time the text was written (1738/39–41), new patterns of spatial organization and use were firmly established in Delhi. In each of the urban snapshots and individual profiles he provides, Dargah Quli emphasizes urban activity. When writing about a dargah, he concentrates less on the visual elements of the space and more on the people he encounters and their inter- actions. In portraying individuals, he often describes them in the context of large public and semipublic gatherings, from religious festivals to performances and literary readings. The image that emerges from these pages is a city of highly populated and frequented urban spaces, spaces that allow for a multifaceted experience of urban life. Within the structural logic of the narrative, visiting a specific series of sites within Delhi is the means to accessing the people and excitement of the city. Concomitantly, buildings and spaces, though often significant because of sacred or historic associations, acquire special mean- ing when understood as spaces of congregation and interaction.

As mentioned earlier, this concern with urban spaces emerges in marked contrast to earlier travelogues documenting the city of Delhi. In his narrative of 1676, for instance, Jean-Baptiste Tavernier makes a brief mention of the long, broad boulevard he traverses to reach the imperial palace, with arcades on either side of it housing merchants carrying on their trade. The greater part of his narrative, however, is dedicated to describing the size of the palace, its organization, and the strict ceremonial that governs the life and routine of the imperial household.[80] Dargah Quli's preoccupations are entirely different; the only time he mentions the Red Fort is when describing the sights and sounds that he witnesses outside its walls. Since Dargah Quli traveled to Delhi as part of the retinue of Nizam al- Mulk Asaf Jah, his silence on the Red Fort is all the more striking. Such omissions, in favor of the type of varied urban depictions analyzed above, surely speak to the new political, religious, social, and cultural order that firmly governed life in Delhi by the time of Dargah Quli's visit. The structure of his narrative is based on a varied experience of the city, moments and elements of urban assembly, and lively social activity.

❖ ❖ ❖

Over the course of the eighteenth century, a new urban subjectivity developed in Delhi, expressed in urban space and through literary texts. Whereas the imperial Red Fort had, in the seventeenth century, once been the defining anchor of urban experience and organi- zation, this ceased to be the case in the eighteenth century. New imperial Mughal building projects, particularly at Chishti shrines, were among those that embodied changing sensi- bilities about the city and its configuration. These building interventions were on an inti- mate scale, spatially coincident with areas of lively assembly, and part of a broader shift in which small-scale architectural projects, sponsored by patrons of various status, prolifer- ated throughout and beyond Shahjahanabad. Formerly peripheral areas north and south of the walled city figured more prominently in the cityscape, its walls no longer delineating its limits. As these former boundaries dissolved, so too did hierarchies between royal patrons and the urban elite.

This shift was inescapable by the time Dargah Quli arrived in Delhi. His narrative reveals the rich range of spaces, stages, and backdrops that all played a role in shaping the visitor's perception of the city. At the same time, imperial Mughal visual codes persisted in the face of this change, showing the ongoing potency of the Mughal idiom and speaking to its potential to change and adapt. The result was that the reflexive Mughal style showed itself to be as dynamic as the period in which it was elaborated.

CHAPTER THREE

"The Last Flicker in the Lamp of Mughal Architecture"

Transforming the Imperial Capital

MUGHAL ARCHITECTURAL HISTORY provides a wealth of choice descriptions that deride the funerary complex of Safdar Jang (1753–54; fig. 3.1). In his extensive survey of Delhi's architecture, Zafar Hasan characterized it by its "promiscuous patches of white marble."[1] He also famously popularized the expression, the "last flicker in the lamp of Mughal architecture," perpetuating the decline narrative that had taken hold of "late" Mughal historiography by the early twentieth century.[2] And Reginald Heber, who wrote extensively of his travels in north India, expressed mixed feelings when he wrote of the tomb, "It is very richly inlaid with different kinds of marble, but has too much of the colour of potted meat to please me."[3]

These statements mask or miss the significance of the tomb complex of Safdar Jang, a landmark of the Mughal eighteenth century.[4] This complex combined the imperial visual

FIGURE 3.1

Tomb of Safdar Jang, Delhi, 1753–54.

language codified in the late seventeenth century with the new urban spatial order that had come to define Delhi in the decades of the early eighteenth. The resulting structure stood as a powerful appropriation—at once homage and challenge—of Mughal imperial codes. It also set the stage for the proliferation of a Mughal-inspired architectural style in other parts of north India. As this chapter demonstrates, the sense of historical referentiality that had been such an integral aspect of imperial Mughal architecture until this point was equally pressing for successor states forging their own political and architectural identities. And as in previous decades, as the Mughal past was referenced, it was increasingly historicized, this time in relation to the ongoing negotiation of Awadhi, Mughal, and Shiʿi identities.

As head of the dynasty of Awadh, Abu al-Mansur Safdar Jang (r. 1739–54) served as both the nawab of his province as well as prime vizier of the Mughal empire. The Awadhi line had been founded by Safdar Jang's father-in-law, Burhan ul-Mulk Saʿadat Khan, a Shiʿi Iranian noble who had immigrated to the Mughal empire and been awarded the governorship of Awadh in 1722. Under Saʿadat Khan, Awadh grew increasingly autonomous from the Mughal center, with the nawab controlling an independent revenue system and army. By 1764, Awadh had grown so strong that the Mughals sought its protection in the form of a military alliance against British forces. Awadh maintained its own diplomatic relations with the French and British, and in 1819, the nawab of Awadh emphatically demonstrated his independence from the Mughal imperial center by declaring himself "king" of an independent state.[5]

Additionally, the Awadhi capitals at Faizabad and Lucknow grew into important cultural centers over the course of the eighteenth century. Artists formerly based in Delhi were drawn to the new patronage and collecting networks that developed in the region, and even those who did not permanently move to Awadh traveled frequently between the Mughal center and the Awadhi provincial capitals.[6] Lucknow became associated with its own school of Urdu poetry, and distinctive art and architectural idioms were also developed in the region.[7] This shift in cultural and power dynamics occurred at a time when other territories in the Mughal empire were growing more autonomous, from the states of the Deccan to Rajasthan and Bengal.[8]

Yet when Safdar Jang succeeded to the governorship of Awadh in 1739, the dynasty still recognized the sovereignty of the Mughals.[9] When he died in Awadh in 1754, the nawab's body was temporarily kept in his home province, but ultimately sent to Delhi to be interred in a monumental mausoleum.[10] The funerary complex where he was laid to rest captures the contradictions of an upstart dynasty, forging a new identity while drawing on the authority of the past. Covered by a dome and set in a quadripartite garden (chahār bāgh), the tomb instantly recalls the funerary complexes of the early Mughal emperors, boldly aligning Safdar Jang, a nobleman and provincial governor, with the imperial tradition.[11] At the same time, the mausoleum was spatially connected to a network of Shiʿi shrines in Delhi. In anchoring a Shiʿi pilgrimage zone in the Mughal capital, the tomb challenged the tradition of Sunni Islam that the Mughal emperors had historically promoted. Besides its significance in the urban history of Delhi, the tomb played a crucial role in the spread of a Mughal-inspired style to other regions in north India, beyond the capital. In the later eighteenth century, architecture in Awadh would expand upon the heavily ornamented style expressed in the mausoleum of Safdar Jang.[12] Through this process, the Mughal visual language came to be associated with Indian royalty on a broad level, rather than signaling Mughal imperial identity exclusively.

APPROPRIATING THE IMPERIAL FUNERARY TRADITION

Entered through a monumental, elaborately painted, double-story gateway (fig. 3.2), the funerary complex of Safdar Jang is conceived as a vast chahār bāgh and enclosed by a continuous wall (fig. 3.3). In addition to the gateway and centrally placed mausoleum, the complex features a mosque, located along the front (eastern) wall of the complex, three large pavilions in the center of the remaining (northern, southern, and western) walls, and multitiered octagonal towers at the corners of the garden enclosure (figs. 3.4–3.6). The structures are executed in sandstone, marble, and stucco, and all exhibit a rich ornamental program.

FIGURE 3.2

Detail, gateway, tomb of Safdar Jang, Delhi, 1753–54.

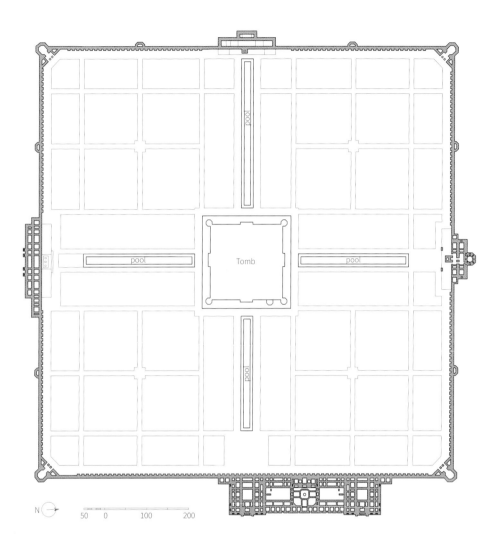

pool

pool

Tomb

pool

pool

N

50   0   100   200

FIGURE 3.3

Plan of the funerary complex of
Safdar Jang, Delhi, 1753–54.
Courtesy Ebba Koch; redrawn by
Dylan Stein.

Among the visual elements that link the complex to the Mughal imperial past are
its layout and design. In its plan, the complex responds to a long architectural tradition of
imperial Mughal mausolea. Prior examples include the tombs of the emperors Humayun
(Delhi, 1562–71), Akbar (Sikandra, 1628–38), and Jahangir (Lahore, 1637), as well as the Taj
Mahal (the mausoleum of the emperor Shah Jahan's wife, Mumtaz Mahal, Agra, 1632–48)
and the Bibi ka Maqbara (the tomb of Rabiʿa Daurani, the emperor ʿAlamgir's wife,
Aurangabad, 1660–61).[13] Following design precedents primarily associated with imperial
rulers and their wives, the central mausoleum adopts the classic Mughal "eight paradises"
(*hasht bihisht*) plan, with eight rooms surrounding a domed central chamber housing
a cenotaph.

On one level, this appropriation of Mughal architecture speaks of Awadhi allegiance
to the Mughals. Even though Mughal imperial power had diminished by this time, the
emperor's symbolic and ceremonial authority remained unchallenged in Awadh, where

FIGURE 3.4

Mosque, funerary complex of
Safdar Jang, Delhi, 1753–54.

FIGURE 3.5

Corner tower, funerary complex of
Safdar Jang, Delhi, 1753–54.

FIGURE 3.6

Garden pavilion, funerary complex
of Safdar Jang, Delhi, 1753–54.

his name was pronounced in the weekly sermon (khutba) read during Friday prayers, and coins were struck with his name.[14] In this, their first major architectural project, the Awadhi patrons incorporated a recognizably Mughal building type and site plan, and also opted for Mughal architectonic and ornamental forms. Each of the four identical façades features a monumental cusped arch, which had become a standard Mughal architectural component by the end of the seventeenth century. In addition, the central arch is surrounded by a rectangular frame (pīshtāq) and flanked by stacked cusped arches and side towers, a compositional scheme used in numerous Mughal buildings, including the tomb's immediate temporal predecessors, the Taj Mahal and Bibi ka Maqbara. Furthermore, the central vaults of each façade prominently display a projecting balcony topped by a sloped roof, a motif that combines both the classic Mughal jharoka, or "window-throne," with the bangla, or sloped or curved roof. This very combination of forms had been made iconic in the imperial palace at Delhi, where it was used in the imperial throne that stood at the center of royal ceremonial and was depicted countless times in court paintings.

The connection to the imperial Mughals is textually explicit as well, through the inscription over the eastern entrance of the building (fig. 3.7):

When that hero of the plain of bravery
departed from the transitory world

The following date of [his departure] was written
"May he be a resident of the highest paradise." 1167 [1753–54 CE][15]

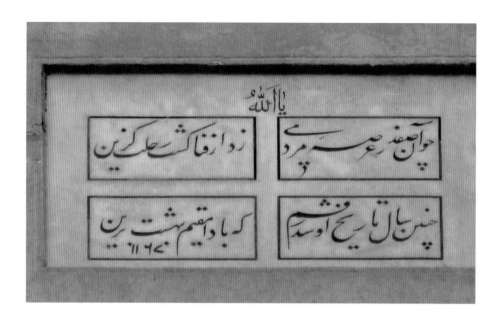

يا الله

زد ازفاكش حك كزين   چوان آصفذر عرصه مردی پر

كه باد تقيم هشت برين   چنس سال تاريخ او سدم فنشم

۱۱۶۷

FIGURE 3.7

Inscription, tomb of Safdar Jang, Delhi, 1753–54.

The inscription draws attention to the status Safdar Jang enjoyed in the imperial Mughal hierarchy. It does so by explicitly using the term "Safdar," or "hero," invoking the honorific title bestowed upon the nawab by the Mughal emperor Ahmad Shah (r. 1748–54).

Despite the image of loyalty conjured by the inscription, the tomb of Safdar Jang marks the first occasion on which a noble was interred in a monumental funerary complex of the type originally reserved for Mughal emperors, their wives, and, on rare occasion, other immediate family members. Nobles had been buried in smaller-scale funerary gardens before, as in the case of ʿAbd al-Rahim Khan-i Khanan in Delhi (d. 1627), whose tomb and garden are adjacent to the funerary complex of Humayun but are a fraction of its size. In addition, Iʿtimad al-Daula, the prime vizier and father-in-law of Jahangir (r. 1605–27), had been interred in a monumental tomb set within a chahār bāgh in Agra (1626–28). Even this mausoleum, however, represents the burial of an immediate member of the ruling royal family. Iʿtimad al-Daula was the father of Nur Jahan, who commissioned the mausoleum for her parents.[16] Thus this was the tomb of a member of the nobility who had familial connections to the imperial family. It is also appropriately smaller in scale than, for example, the nearby Taj Mahal. In contrast, the tomb of Safdar Jang marks a significant departure: it was the first instance when a member of the nobility was interred in a complex of monumental proportions, approaching the vastness of the royal complexes of the sixteenth and seventeenth centuries.

Given that it was unprecedented for someone in Safdar Jang's position to be interred in a tomb of this style and scale, these appropriations displace, as much as they reinforce, Mughal authority. By using these forms, which were strongly coded as imperial, the tomb of Safdar Jang posits the Awadhi dynasty as the inheritors of the imperial Mughal tradition. Despite his Shiʿi identity, his tomb complex does not deploy forms clearly linking Safdar Jang and the Awadhis to the predominantly Shiʿi dynasties of India's Deccan region, such as the ʿAdil Shahis of Bijapur (1490–1686), the Nizam Shahis of Ahmadnagar (1496–1636), or the Qutb Shahis of Golconda and Hyderabad (1496–1687).[17] Nor does the tomb invoke important Shiʿi sites, for instance the shrine of ʿAli in Najaf, the shrine of Husayn in Karbala, or the shrine of Imam Riza in Mashhad.[18] While later patrons and architects in Lucknow would build structures that quoted Shiʿi sites, such as the Talkatora Karbala in Lucknow (1798), with its high, cylindrical domes, at this earlier moment, they instead conspicuously highlighted Mughal associations.[19] This decision enabled a dialogue with the imperial icons of Delhi, such as the nearby tomb of Humayun and the imperial palace at Delhi, but also reached beyond this local context to invoke a longer imperial tradition, expressed in monumental mausolea from multiple Mughal imperial centers. While the Awadhi nawabs were technically deputies of the Mughals and formally recognized their sovereignty, the construction of a monumental Awadhi mausoleum in the Mughal capital asserted not only the increased power enjoyed by the nawabs by the mid-eighteenth century, but also articulated their political pretensions. Safdar Jang's tomb incorporates Safdar Jang and his dynasty into the Mughal imperial line, precisely at the moment when the Awadhis were rising to power.

Indeed, for all of its allusions and appropriations, the tomb of Safdar Jang demonstrates an equal interest in articulating difference from the imperial past. Just as Safdar Jang occupied a dual role as Mughal prime vizier and head of his own growing dynasty, so too does his monumental tomb maintain a tension between the established and the new. In part, this tension is expressed in the building's ornamental program. As we have already seen, the floral mode developed in the imperial architecture of the mid-seventeenth century, which was associated with political achievement and good governance, was taken up in the imperial monuments of the late seventeenth and early eighteenth centuries. Eventually, this visual language, rendered in white marble and pietra dura, became a clear marker of Mughal imperial identity, distinguishable from modes of ornament deployed in architectural monuments of contemporaneous Islamic courts. The Safavid monuments of Isfahan, for instance, featured tiles covered with interlacing floriated vines, while Iznik tile revetments in Ottoman architecture encompassed an ideal of "mimetic abstraction" based on novel arrangements of recognizable, semi-naturalistic flowers.[20] By the time that the tomb of Safdar Jang was built, the Mughal floral mode and the idea of the Mughal imperium were inseparable.

As with earlier adaptations, the tomb of Safdar Jang reinterprets this visual language, employing a variety of floral and geometric forms and new materials to heighten sculptural effects. With its emphasis on complex patterns and organic motifs, the building erodes boundaries between the structural and the ornamental, the built and the natural. Whereas floral motifs on mid-seventeenth-century buildings were carved relatively flatly, and incorporated precious stones and polychromy to create sumptuous surface effects, the visual program of Safdar Jang's tomb displays a greater concern with

FIGURE 3.8

Exterior vault, tomb of Safdar Jang, Delhi, 1753–54.

FIGURE 3.9

Interior vaults, tomb of Safdar Jang, Delhi, 1753–54.

FIGURE 3.10

Cenotaph of Safdar Jang, Delhi, 1753–54.

FIGURE 3.11

Cenotaphs of Shah Jahan and Mumtaz Mahal, Agra, 1658.

three-dimensionality, exploiting the potential of stucco and marble to render highly modeled sculptural forms. On each of the exterior façades, a thick, curling vine constitutes the cusped arch of a monumental, central vault culminating in a five-petal flower (fig. 3.8). The jharoka windows along the exterior are supported by brackets transformed into naturalistic acanthus leaves. Muqarnas niches and molded vault netting (*qālib kārī*) animate the exterior vaults with geometric patterns, a play with sculptural effects that continues in the interior, where deeply carved, interlacing floral vines, muqarnas, and qālib kārī motifs emphasize and articulate the curvature of vaults (fig. 3.9).

In the center of the interior chamber, a marble cenotaph, densely decorated with a double layer of acanthus leaves coming to deeply curved points (fig. 3.10), encapsulates the sculptural qualities of the tomb and offers a stark visual counterpoint to one of the most famous examples of Mughal ornament, the floral pietra dura on the cenotaph of Shah Jahan (r. 1628–58; d. 1666; fig. 3.11). While the pietra dura cenotaph presents floral motifs against an architectural ground, that of Safdar Jang dispenses with the very notion

FIGURE 3.12

Plan of the tomb of Safdar Jang, Delhi, 1753–54. Courtesy Ebba Koch; redrawn by Dylan Stein.

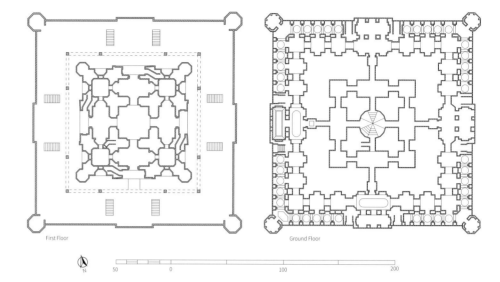

First Floor

Ground Floor

FIGURE 3.13

Plan of the tomb of Humayun, Delhi, 1562–71.

FIGURE 3.14

Plan of the Taj Mahal, Agra, 1632–48.

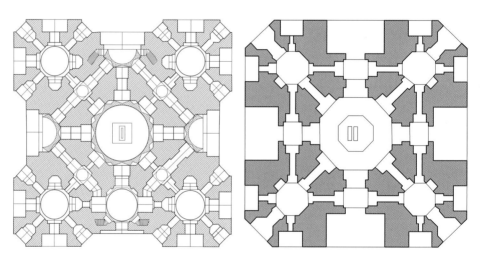

of figure and ground, the acanthus leaves appearing to grow from the marble. (This is not unlike the sculptural effects of the Moti Masjid of ʿAlamgir, taken here to an even greater extreme.) While in the rest of the building stucco is primarily used to achieve deeply sculpted visual motifs, the sculptor of the cenotaph is able to manipulate marble to this same effect. Although stucco is malleable and lends itself more readily to such extensive manipulation, marble is a harder stone, requiring a certain amount of skill to produce such striking visual effects.

The tomb is also distinctive from previous Mughal tombs because of its sophisticated vaulting technology. A two-level structure raised on a plinth, it contains over fifty-four chambers and a complex vaulting system. As with other Mughal tombs, one approaches the main level of the building via staircases incorporated into the platform. The platform itself is constituted of continuous arcades of pointed arches and projecting kiosks at each of its corners; these lead to a series of twenty vaulted chambers that follow the perimeter of the square structure (fig. 3.12).

At its core, the building follows the hasht bihisht plan. In its most basic form, the hasht bihisht is a nine-fold, cross-in-square plan that bears similarity to plan types that circulated in a variety of contexts, from the ancient Near East to Byzantium.[21] It has also been compared to the nine-fold plans of mandalas from ancient and medieval Asian art.[22] For the Mughals, however, the roots of the hasht bihisht could also be found in the palace architecture of the Aqqoyunlus in Tabriz, particularly the famed Hasht Bihisht palace of Sultan Uzun Hasan (r. 1453–78).[23] Although no longer extant, the palace is known to us through the writings of the Venetian merchant Domenico Romano, who describes it as "*astibisti,*" or hasht bihisht.[24] He explains that the palace was a two-story structure, consisting of eight rooms encircling a double-story, central domed space. The hasht bihisht plan was later used in the palace architecture of Safavid Iran in the centuries to come, with the famed Hasht Bihisht palace of Shah Sulayman at Isfahan (1669) standing out as the most noteworthy example.[25]

In the case of the Mughals, while the hasht bihisht was used in palatial settings in the sixteenth century, as in the Todar Mal Baradari and the Hada Mahal at Fatehpur Sikri (c. 1571–85), it ultimately became the preferred plan type for sepulchral architecture. The suitability of the plan related to its ability to allude to a paradisiacal afterlife. The eight rooms surrounding the central chamber in the hasht bihisht composition corresponded to the eight levels of paradise, while the nine-fold plan evoked the "nine vaults" of the sky.[26] One of the earliest elaborations of this plan type was in the tomb of Humayun (d. 1556; 1562–71). Its architect, Mirak Mirza Ghiyas, was originally from Herat and thus familiar with architectural forms and plans that circulated in the Timurid cultural milieu.[27] In the tomb of Humayun, the hasht bihisht plan of the ground floor is interpreted radially: connected to the central chamber are eight vaulted passageways. Four of these link to the iwan vaults in the center of each of the tomb's façades, while the remaining four lead to corner chambers, each of which has a radial nine-fold plan articulated in smaller scale (fig. 3.13). This plan type is also seen in the Taj Mahal, where the corner chambers are also smaller-scale renditions of a centralized, radial plan. In this case, however, the vaults leading from the corner chambers connect directly to the exterior vaults on each of the tomb's four nearly identical façades (fig. 3.14).

In the tomb of Safdar Jang, the hasht bihisht plan is elaborated with its own intricacy. A large central room is surrounded by eight smaller chambers; this layout is observed on each of the levels of Safdar Jang's tomb—that is, in the platform and in the double-story superstructure. The central chamber of the tomb is a double-story domed space with a series of eight bangla jharokas in the upper zone of transition. Four are placed in the center of each of the walls, and open to the upper level, creating a viewing gallery. The remaining four are manipulated to act as squinches spanning the upper corners of the room (fig. 3.15); this zone of transition gives way to a dome of broad muqarnas and qālib kārī receding in five scalloped tiers (fig. 3.16).

FIGURE 3.15
Interior chamber, upper zone,
tomb of Safdar Jang, Delhi,
1753–54.

FIGURE 3.16
Dome, tomb of Safdar Jang, Delhi,
1753–54.

FIGURE 3.17

Sculptural relief on interior vault, tomb of Safdar Jang, Delhi, 1753–54.

The surrounding chambers are expressed as four oblong rooms along the lateral sides of the structure and four octagonal rooms at each of its corners, a structural pattern that is repeated on the lower and upper levels. To span the space of these oblong rooms, the architects of Safdar Jang's tomb used sail vaulting.[28] Using brick, the builders created parabolic arches and pendentives between them. The resulting oval space above this composition was filled in with spiral courses of brick. Plaster was then used to face the brick structure. On the ceilings of the lower-level chambers, delicate interlacing floral motifs creep across the vaults (fig. 3.17). On the upper level of the tomb, the vaulting structure is still more intricate, and once again emphasized through ornament. The oblong rooms are constituted of multiple vaults running across space, each of which features an inset dome consisting of a central medallion of vine tendrils atop bands of muqarnas, framed by architectural netting (fig. 3.18).

Scholarship has tended to connect the tomb of Safdar Jang, with its pink sandstone and white marble and stucco, to the neighboring red sandstone and white marble tomb of Humayun. However, in its proportions and ornamental program, the tomb of Safdar Jang more readily recalls the Taj Mahal, and even more immediately, the Bibi ka Maqbara. When compared to the tomb of Humayun, the Taj Mahal features an attenuation of form and emphasis on verticality that is further exaggerated first in the Bibi ka Maqbara, and

FIGURE 3.18

Interior vaults, tomb of Safdar
Jang, Delhi, 1753–54.

then in the tomb of Safdar Jang; additionally, the dome profile grows increasingly pointed in these examples. The complex's ornamental program, featuring visually complex painted and carved stucco floral compositions, also resembles that of the Bibi ka Maqbara. Such close formal continuities not only suggest that an imperial visual vocabulary was perpetuated for political purposes, but also that an interconnected network of architects and sculptors played a central role in this process. As discussed in Chapter 1, such a network was active in the seventeenth century. For instance, the architects of the Taj Mahal and the Bibi ka Maqbara, Ustad Ahmad and ʿAta Allah, respectively, were father and son. Not only did this relationship facilitate the sharing of architectural knowledge, but the two were part of a bigger familial and professional network of interconnected practitioners and theorists, one that may have continued into the eighteenth century.[29]

Besides the innovations and refinements of ornament and architectonics, the complex also features an unusual combination of building types. The multistory gateway, for instance, was topped by a small, three-bay loggia, with delicate baluster columns and cusped arches. In the center of three of the enclosure walls is a pavilion. (In the eastern wall, this space is occupied by the complex's monumental gateway.) While exceptions to the rule exist, many earlier mausolea tended to favor gateways or towers at these points, as at Akbar's tomb at Sikandra, or at the Taj Mahal. Low-lying, single-level structures placed atop platforms, the Safdar Jang pavilions are stand-alone structures, each with multiple chambers and individualized plans (see fig. 3.3).

The function of these pavilions is unclear. Some scholars agree that these were used as lodging for the members of the Awadhi nobility during visits to the tomb and the neighboring Aliganj area.[30] This need not have served as their primary residence in Delhi, as Safdar Jang and his descendants owned property in Shahjahanabad. At the same time, other funerary complexes included structures that served as guesthouses or temporary residences, particularly during the ʿurs (annual funerary visitation and rituals).

But the pavilions call to mind other associations. In situation, with their garden prospects and the long pools that run from each structure to the central tomb, they recall Mughal palace pavilions. Comparative examples include the Sawon and Badon pavilions in the Hayat Bakhsh of the Red Fort in Delhi (1639–48), and the garden pavilions in the Shalimar Bagh of Lahore (1637–41). In front of each pavilion is a small platform, mediating between interior and exterior and serving as a vantage point for beholding and viewing the central tomb. Like the palace pavilions, and particularly those at the Delhi Red Fort, these are not self-contained units, but instead open organically onto the garden. Thus the planners of the complex integrated what were effectively palace garden pavilions in the funerary complex. The associations with pleasure and the prospects across the garden would be exploited in the nineteenth century when, under the auspices of the British Archaeological Survey of India, the site was transformed into a public park.[31]

The complex also features a small mosque along the eastern wall, elevated a story above ground level (fig. 3.19). The inclusion of this mosque combines a newly popular typology with a longer tradition of including mosques in Mughal funerary complexes. The mosque is built in the style of small neighborhood mosques that grew popular in Delhi, constructed after imperial prototypes such as the Jamiʿ Masjid and discussed in Chapter 2. A small, three-bay structure, it is built primarily of red sandstone with areas in buff sandstone and white marble, topped by three pointed domes, and opening onto a courtyard through three cusped arches. The courtyard affords a view over the gateway, the garden of the tomb complex, and the surrounding environs. Its siting undoubtedly recalls a key example from the early eighteenth-century boom in mosque architecture, the Sunahri Masjid of Raushan al-Daula in Shahjahanabad (1721–22). It, too, is elevated on an upper-level platform and overlooks Chandni Chowk, the central avenue of Shahjahanabad.

The sources reveal little about the actual functioning of the mosque, and there are no inscriptions on it. The general assumption is that it was constructed at the same time as the entire complex, but there is no confirmation for this. Zafar Hasan describes it as "an afterthought," based on the premise that mosques in Mughal tomb complexes were typically built along the western wall.[32] Regardless, what is significant is that Mughal funerary complexes did typically include mosques. The Safdar Jang mosque thus serves as yet another signal of the complex's adherence to Mughal precedent, even as it incorporates newer, eighteenth-century building trends.

On the whole, the architects and sculptors of the funerary complex of Safdar Jang turned to forms from the past, using them as the basis for new artistic expression. This approach is visible in every part of the complex, from the structural and ornamental innovations in the central tomb, to the unusual combination of building types that constitute the complex's subsidiary structures. This attitude to the visual past was not unlike that of late seventeenth-century Mughal artists and builders who, as we have already seen, engaged in a mode of imitative experimentation in such landmark structures as the Moti Masjid of Delhi, the Badshahi Masjid of Lahore, and the Bibi ka Maqbara of Aurangabad. Their artistic practice embodied the concept of istiqbāl, the concept of refining existing

FIGURE 3.19

View of mosque from gateway, funerary complex of Safdar Jang, Delhi, 1753–54.

masterpieces as the basis for artistic innovation.[33] In the mid-eighteenth century, then, not only were historic Mughal styles relevant, but so too was an artistic philosophy that embraced the past.

SHI'ISM IN THE MUGHAL CAPITAL: ENCODING URBAN SPACE

The funerary complex of Safdar Jang responded not only to architectural models from the past, but also to the new patterns of spatial organization and use that had emerged in eighteenth-century Delhi. As we saw earlier, shrines, neighborhood mosques, and other types of buildings and spaces grew into increasingly important urban centers during this period, challenging the former primacy of imperial spaces in Delhi's urban order. In light of this shift, the dialogical relationships between the tomb of Safdar Jang and other urban districts are particularly significant. For one, the tomb anchors the area known today as Aliganj, which houses a set of religious buildings all associated with Shi'ism, and sits on land that was owned by the Awadhi dynasty. The relationship between the tomb of Safdar Jang and Aliganj parallels that between the tomb of Humayun and the dargah of Nizam al-Din (fig. 3.20). Therefore the tombs of Humayun and Safdar Jang, which lie on the same axis, are related not only in terms of building and garden type, but also with respect to their relationships with the broader urban context. The area anchored by the tomb of Safdar Jang and Aliganj became an important site of Shi'i pilgrimage, possibly providing

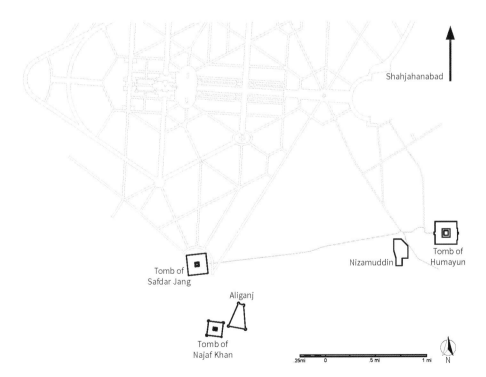

FIGURE 3.20

Map of Delhi with the tomb of Safdar Jang, Aliganj, the tomb of Humayun, and Nizamuddin.

an alternative to the Nizam al-Din dargah and its associations with the Mughal emperors and their historic promotion of Sunnism.

The urban transformations occurred as Shiʿism assumed an increasingly central role in politics and regional state formation in eighteenth-century Mughal India.[34] When Saʿadat Khan had assumed the governorship of Awadh, among his reforms was the revocation of stipends and land revenues that had been granted to Sunni scholars (*madad-i maʿāsh*) and which had supported Sunni mosques, madrasas, and khānqāhs.[35] While the Sunni elite was repressed, a Shiʿi intellectual class developed in Awadh, comprising scholars, clerics, physicians, and poets from both Iran and India.[36] A strong Shiʿi presence was also felt in the military, particularly as it grew under Safdar Jang. Besides activity in Awadh, powerful Shiʿis exerted influence in other parts of the Mughal empire. The Sayyid brothers had a strong influence on Mughal politics at the imperial center for the first two decades of the eighteenth century, effectively controlling the Mughal throne until 1720. In addition, other autonomous states besides Awadh, such as Bengal, were ruled by a Shiʿi Muslim elite, centered in Murshidabad.[37] Within the imperial Mughal family, Qudsiyya Begum, the courtesan who had married the emperor Muhammad Shah (r. 1719–48), and who was queen mother during the reign of Ahmad Shah, was Shiʿi.[38]

To understand the urban recoding enacted by the tomb of Safdar Jang, it is useful to review the urban spatial relationships between the tomb of Humayun and the Nizam al-Din dargah. As we saw in Chapter 2, the two were built in close proximity to each other. At the core of the dargah lay the tomb of Nizam al-Din Auliya (d. 1325), a Sufi of the Chishti order. Building activity was ongoing at the dargah in the centuries following its founding, speaking to the continued sanctity of Nizam al-Din and the Chishti order, and resulting in the establishment of the dargah and its environs as an important spiritual precinct. The association between Mughal royalty and the Chishti order was clear at the dargah, where members of the royal family and Mughal nobility had been buried starting in the sixteenth century.[39] The status and popularity of the shrine only increased in the early eighteenth century.

Aliganj, meanwhile, is centered around the Shahi Mardan dargah, which houses a footprint of ʿAli. Qudsiyya Begum built a complex of buildings here in the early 1750s, enclosed by an encircling wall and group of gateways. An inscription on the northern gateway informs us that Qudsiyya Begum was responsible for the enclosure walls, a majlis-khāna, a mosque, and a tank (*hauz*). The inscription also alludes to ʿAli and highlights Shiʿi tradition with the passage, "Muhammad the friend of God said, 'I am a city of learning, and ʿAli is its gateway.'" Qudsiyya Begum also oversaw the construction of a palace, garden, and mosque north of the Shahjahanabad city walls in c. 1740–50.[40] In sponsoring these buildings, Qudsiyya Begum joined a tradition wherein royal Mughal women had always been active patrons of architecture. Nur Jahan, the wife of Jahangir, was especially known for a series of Mughal caravanserais and mosques.[41] Jahan Ara, daughter of

Shah Jahan, was a prolific patron who commissioned mosques in Agra and Kashmir and gardens in Delhi.[42] While following this tradition, Qudsiyya Begum adapted it by concentrating on a building program reflecting her Shiʿi faith.[43] Safdar Jang's tomb converged with these commissions to enhance the visibility and increase the prestige of Shiʿi spaces in the Mughal capital.

The construction of Safdar Jang's tomb was soon followed by another large-scale mausoleum complex, the tomb of Najaf Khan (1782), built to the east of the Shahi Mardan complex. Najaf Khan (d. 1782) was an Iranian Shiʿi who migrated to India and was the brother-in-law of Mirza Muhsin, Safdar Jang's brother. Najaf Khan ultimately entered the service of the Mughal emperor Shah ʿAlam II (r. 1759–1806), and was promoted to the post of *Amir al-Umara* and received the title *Zulfiqar al-Daula,* an honorific that speaks directly to his Shiʿi identity ("Zulfiqar" was the name of the two-edged sword of ʿAli). The tomb stands in the midst of a large enclosure, entered through a large gateway (now damaged). While the layout of the complex brings to mind the Mughal funerary garden tradition, the form of the central structure more specifically recalls platform tombs such as that of Jahangir in Lahore (1627–37).[44] The building is a low, square structure and originally had kiosks at each of its corners (fig. 3.21). On the roof sits the cenotaph of Najaf Khan, surrounded by a low wall. In the building are two vaulted rooms, one containing the grave of Najaf Khan and his daughter Fatima, and the other containing three unmarked graves (most probably graves of other family members).

As in the gateway of the Qudsiyya Begum complex, the building features an inscriptional program replete with Shiʿi references. A marble plaque over Najaf Khan's grave reads:

> He is living who will never die
>
> This sky of crooked nature, with its back (bent) like a bow, and full of arrows, which with the arrow of misfortune does not miss the mark
>
> Shot at the most noble of Sayyids, through whom there was honor to the lineage of Safvi Sayyids, a worthy fruit of the tree of the garden of eight and four, a pure splendor of two pearls and a gem of nine shells
>
> Bakhshi al-Mulk Amir Najaf Khan, the lion-hearted and the conqueror of the countries of India with the help of (the command) "Be not afraid."
>
> A hero, if he held Zulfiqār in his hand, the king "Lāfata" would exclaim "A worthy son."
>
> May he be a companion of the Last of the Prophets (Muhammad) with his ancestor, the revealer of the secrets "If it can be revealed."
>
> The pen of ʿAli which is a twin brother of the Divine revelation, wrote the date of his death on his ashes, "This is the grave of Najaf." 1196 [1781–82 CE][45]

FIGURE 3.21
Tomb of Najaf Khan, Delhi, 1782.

Among the myriad allusions to the Shiʿi tradition are the references to the imams of Twelver Shiʿism ("the garden of eight and four"); ʿAli's sons Hasan and Husayn (the "two pearls"); and the two-edged sword of ʿAli, Zulfiqar, which also served to recall the honorific title bestowed upon Najaf Khan by the Mughal emperor (Zulfiqar al-Daula). Moreover, there is an association between the name of Najaf and the city of Najaf in Iraq, the site of the tomb of ʿAli and a center of Shiʿi pilgrimage. Such allusions are also highlighted in the inscription on the nearby grave of his daughter Fatima, appropriately named after ʿAli's wife and Muhammad's daughter.[46]

The complex of Safdar Jang thus moors a strong Shiʿi presence in the Mughal capital. As such, the Safdar Jang–Aliganj relationship mirrors that between the tomb of Humayun and the precincts surrounding the grave of Nizam al-Din. The emphasis on Shiʿi space within Delhi illuminates the changing social and cultural landscape not only of the capital but also of the empire at large. The Awadhi nawabs' active promotion of Shiʿi shrine culture stands in marked contrast to the program of Sunni orthodoxy upheld during the seventeenth century. In the eighteenth century, Sunni Islam no longer enjoyed the status of a state religion, but was instead supplanted through the very public sponsorship of architectural projects and practices that advanced Shiʿi visibility. This marked change was fostered through the influence and architectural patronage of the Awadhi nawabs, who manipulated the Mughal architectural code, ultimately transforming the political and socioreligious dynamics of the time.

THE "MUGHAL" STYLE IN NORTH INDIA

After the moment represented by the tomb of Safdar Jang, when a reinterpreted Mughal style was first associated with Awadhi architecture, this architectural mode grew to be a central component of Awadhi visual identity. The transfer of power from the Mughal center to the increasingly important regional centers and provincial capitals of north India went hand in hand with the ongoing transformation of Mughal style. Soon, a profusion of sculptural effects rendered in stucco came to signify the dynasty and region of Awadh, just as the earlier floral idiom in luxurious marble and pietra dura had been identified with Mughal imperial identity. In other words, the mausoleum of Safdar Jang signified a transitional moment in the forging of a distinctive Awadhi visual idiom. Besides drawing on the Mughal visual past as a matter of aesthetic practice, the tomb also mediated between the Mughal imperial ideal associated with floral imagery and the visual identity being fashioned in the Mughal province of Awadh. Over the course of the eighteenth century, as Awadh grew increasingly independent from the Mughal center, the image of heavily ornamented architecture became inextricably linked with the province and its ruling dynasty.

In the Awadhi context, the most characteristic and monumental of structures associated with the new ornamentalism was the Bara Imambara (or Great Imambara) complex in Lucknow (1784–91), sponsored by the nawab Asaf al-Daula, the son and successor of Shuja' al-Daula. The imambara is a feature unique to Twelver Shi'i religious complexes, providing assembly space for community rituals during the month of Muharram, when Shi'is collectively mourn the martyrdom of the Prophet Muhammad's grandson Husayn; the imambara also houses portable architectural models (ta'ziya) of important Shi'i shrines that are used in ceremonial processionals.[47] Vast in scale, the complex in Lucknow comprises two imposing gateways, a ceremonial drum house, a congregational Friday mosque, a step-well, and at its heart, an imambara of massive proportions.

The complex exhibits ornamental techniques, motifs, and approaches seen in the funerary complex of Safdar Jang. However, in relation to the tradition of interpretive response discussed earlier, it articulates an ornamental sensibility to an even greater extent. As with the Safdar Jang example, the Bara Imambara complex is unified through a lavish program of richly animated surfaces and sculpted architectonic elements. In the triple-arched gateway, for instance, the three large portal arches are nested, cusped, and lined with curling vine scrolls, and then articulated in miniature in the two stacked arcades of the gateway's upper zones (fig. 3.22). The structure's plastic quality is emphasized with four bangla balconies that project above the gateway piers, their curvilinear lines echoing the sloping banglas, pointed domes, and towering kiosks of the roofline. No surface is left unadorned, with blind and open niches running the length of the piers and large-scale floral and fish motifs placed in the spandrels and at the apex of each arch (fig. 3.23). The floral and vegetal motifs constitute sculptural interpretations of the acanthus, a component of the seventeenth-century imperial Mughal idiom, which was recast in the vaults and cenotaph of the tomb of Safdar Jang, and here interpreted with still greater expressiveness. The fish in the spandrels signify the high rank enjoyed by the Awadhis in the Mughal administration, alluding to the *mahi maratib* (Honor of the Fish).[48] These ornamental motifs, then, forge connections across temporal and geographical boundaries. They link the Awadhi monument to a broader Mughal artistic and cultural legacy, enacting an aesthetic dialogue with the past and specifically with Delhi, while simultaneously referencing Awadhi symbolic associations iconographically.

These and other links are further developed in the additional major spaces of the complex, the monumental mosque and imambara. Rooted in triple-domed pre-Mughal prototypes prevalent in India, the Friday mosque invokes the typology that

FIGURE 3.22

Gateway, Bara Imambara complex of Lucknow, c. 1784.

FIGURE 3.23

Detail, gateway, Bara Imambara
complex of Lucknow, c. 1784.

would become iconic in Mughal India, first expressed in the mid-seventeenth century
when Shah Jahan sponsored his grand congregational mosque in Shahjahanabad.[49]
The Jamiʿ Masjid of Shah Jahan comprises a rectangular hall crowned by three
domes, with two enframing minarets and a vast courtyard, built of the hallmark
Mughal building materials of red sandstone and white marble. As we have seen, it was
referenced and effectively rendered iconic by subsequent responses and quotations,
ranging from the monumental Friday mosque of Lahore (Badhshahi Masjid, 1673–74),
to the smaller-scale Fakhr al-Masajid of Delhi (1728–29). Whereas these examples were
rendered in red sandstone and white marble, underscoring their Mughal references,
the congregational mosque in the Bara Imambara complex of Lucknow features an
extensive program of stucco covering brick, showcasing the material that had by now
become a standard feature of Awadhi building. Once again, allusions to the past are
inflected by expressions of a contemporary aesthetic. The mosque also features the

cusped arches, niches, banglas, and pointed domes first introduced in the triple-arched gateway of the complex.

This architectonic and ornamental vocabulary extends to the imambara itself, on both the exterior and interior surfaces of the multilevel structure. Here, the continuity of ornamental forms is paralleled by the ongoing application of building techniques seen in earlier Mughal and Awadhi examples. Most striking are the vaulting technologies shared by the Safdar Jang and Bara Imambara complexes. The bangla vaults seen in the tomb of Safdar Jang are applied on a grander scale in the Bara Imambara, where a magnified sail vault covers the main interior hall.[50] Once again, the ongoing use of certain technologies, from vaulting to stucco techniques, in tandem with persistent ornamental vocabularies, speaks to a possible circulation of artists and architects that may have enhanced the mobility and reinvention of forms.[51]

In the following years, the Bara Imambara complex was celebrated for its grand buildings, the collection of ta'ziya, and its distinctive ornamental program. In the *Tafzihu'l Ghafilin*, Abu Talib styles the Bara Imambara the "finest" of Asaf al-Daula's buildings, saying that its gateway "dazzles the eyes" of those who behold it.[52] He describes an expansive complex, one that includes gateways, a large central courtyard and tank, the "lofty" congregational mosque, and the imambara, in addition to a hospital and travelers' quarters. He also mentions the gold and silver ta'ziya housed in the imambara, as well as glass chandeliers and gold, silver, and glass candelabras. In all, Abu Talib portrays an expansive and highly adorned space.[53] Writing about the complex in 1802, the Iranian traveler 'Abd al-Latif Shushtari explicitly praises both the architecture and ornamentation (*tazyīn*) of the imambara: "Out of great love for the Pure Imams (Peace be upon them) and utter devotion to the ceremonies of the taziyeh bearers for the lord of the martyrs [Husayn], [Asaf al-Daula] built a *taziyeh khane* [the imambara] and great mosque next to his own palace and spent large sums on the buildings and its ornament."[54]

"PICTURESQUE" LEGACIES

Although the mausoleum of Safdar Jang has been criticized as a poor imitation of older Mughal monuments, the particular aesthetic cultivated in the tomb of Safdar Jang also elicited, quite tellingly, positive responses from nineteenth-century British travelers who visited the mausoleum. Unlike their contemporary historians, whose negative characterization of the tomb was discussed at the opening of this chapter, these travelers recorded favorable impressions. These appear to be rooted in an affinity for the "Picturesque."[55] In his *Tours in Upper India*, Edward Caulfield Archer claimed that the tomb of Safdar Jang was "a grand edifice, and in extent and cost may vie with some of the first country palaces of our nobles in England, perhaps may exceed them in both respects."[56] The British political official Sir Orfeur Cavenagh describes it as a "handsome edifice,"[57] while Godfrey Mundy, who also produced sketches of numerous monuments in India, refers to it as "a very handsome and picturesque mausoleum."[58] William Howard Russell, a correspondent for the *Times of London*, also had positive impressions to relay, and invoked St. Paul's Cathedral in London when commenting on the size of the tomb: "This tomb is a grand edifice, in a grand enclosure of red stone. . . . It covers more ground than St. Paul's as far as I could judge; and it is a mausoleum of which any country might be proud."[59] Emma Roberts, well known for her multivolume *Scenes and Characteristics of Hindostan*, singles out the tomb from among Delhi's "mausoleums of great beauty and splendour."[60] Finally, Louis Rousselet, in his 1875 *L'inde des rajahs*, praised the tomb as "one of the most beautiful ornaments of this Museum of grandiose architecture [Delhi]," calling attention to the "marble dome, with a curve of extreme purity."[61]

The tomb of Safdar Jang was also one of the most frequently painted of the Delhi monuments. Although this may have been because it was on the road from central Delhi to the popularly visited Qutb Minar complex, the nearby tomb of Humayun was not as

Safdar Jung's Tomb

popular a subject of painting.[62] An 1815 watercolor of the tomb by Sita Ram was completed for Francis Rawdon-Hastings, the governor-general of India from 1813 to 1819, as part of a series of albums depicting monuments in India (fig. 3.24).[63] This depiction of the complex focuses on the garden environment, inserting trees to augment the natural landscape and emphasizing a dramatically cloudy sky. In addition, the central tomb is rendered in soft, blurred lines and recedes into the background of the painting. This atmospheric depiction of the tomb, coupled with the prominence of the garden, suggests the romantic, evocative effects associated with the Picturesque style (discussed in greater detail in Chapter 4).

While these textual and visual impressions were all recorded in the century following the construction of the tomb, it is significant that the structure speaks so eloquently to the aesthetic sensibilities of these nineteenth-century travelers and artists. These reactions indicate that the forms, proportions, and ornamental program of the tomb materialized an emerging aesthetic sensibility.

❖ ❖ ❖

Rather than employing unprecedented visual forms and types to embody the changing political order and socioreligious culture of the Mughal empire, the architects and patrons of the funerary complex of Safdar Jang instead adopted and transformed the symbolically charged forms of the imperial Mughal past. The tomb speaks to a specific, critical moment: while the imperial center had lost all tangible authority by the mid-eighteenth century, when the mausoleum was built, the signs of Mughal authority still held much currency in India. That the tomb was constructed in Delhi, the Mughal capital, and not Awadh, where the dynasty was based, points to the symbolic power of this gesture. Moreover, building the tomb in Delhi enabled the expansion of Shi'i religious sites in the Mughal capital, and the growth of the Aliganj district. The meaning and function of the funerary complex are the result of a synthesis of the defining elements of the eighteenth-century Mughal visual idiom. The sophisticated elaboration of the hasht bihisht plan and the ornamental program firmly codify the new aesthetic sensibility that had been developing since the late seventeenth century, while the relationship between the Safdar Jang complex and the nearby Shahi Mardan dargah evoked the new urban order in which shrines were transformed into increasingly important areas of urban assembly and patronage.

As with earlier examples, in the tomb of Safdar Jang the adherence to past models signals appropriation, but also results in historicization. The complex resurrects the Mughal imperial tradition of funerary tomb and garden complexes, last seen in 1660–61 in the Bibi ka Maqbara of Aurangabad. In the process, it reinforces the paradigmatic status of the hasht bihisht plan, the chahār bāgh plan, motifs such as the jharoka and bangla, and the Mughal floral mode. Its innovations, too, are based on precedents. These include a sophisticated vaulting system, a visually complex and sensuous ornamental program, and the organization of subsidiary structures that encourage the viewing of the garden landscape and make for a striking combination of Mughal typologies. Yet, even though the Awadhi architectural projects display a consistent and marked utilization of a Mughal visual vocabulary, the local changes brought about in Lucknow signal the abstraction of this vocabulary in such a way that its primary designation soon came to be "Indian," rather than "Mughal." The linked processes of historicization and abstraction would also unfold, as we will see, as Mughal monuments were represented on paper.

CHAPTER FOUR

Codifying Mughal Architecture on Paper

I N 1778, THE FRENCH ARMY OFFICER and political operative Jean-Baptiste Gentil (1726–1799) appeared at the court of Louis XVI at Versailles. Recently returned from India, where he had served the French East India Company (Compagnie des Indes Orientales, or CDIO) for twenty-six years, Gentil presented the court with a sizable collection of paintings, albums, and manuscripts, all amassed during his tenure on the subcontinent. Among these was the *Palais Indiens*, a group of architectural plans and elevations representing noteworthy Mughal and Awadhi buildings. This collection represents a watershed in the history of architectural representation in South Asia, putting north Indian monuments forward as objects of inquiry and subjects of depiction. In the process, the renderings enacted a particular historical narrative concerning Mughal architecture and cultural legacies. Previously, the built environment had served as the primary site for the representation and appropriation of cultural authority. Beginning in the eighteenth century, it was through architectural representation that various factions aspired to claim and manipulate the Mughal past. As a result, the potency of Mughal architecture became increasingly clear, its iconic status ever more firmly established.

Drawing on Indian and French representational systems, the artists of the *Palais Indiens* developed a new, heterogeneous visual language for the description of architecture. Gentil's role as patron was partly responsible for the fusing of Indian and European visual idioms, as he likely provided some of the models for these studies in the form of plans and elevations executed by military engineers working for the CDIO. At the same time, the artists of the collection incorporated conventions of architectural representation already prevalent in north India and the Islamic lands. With the integration of these myriad techniques, the *Palais Indiens* involved not only the adoption but also the transformation of multiple visual languages.

Besides developing a language for architectural representation, the *Palais Indiens* posits the architectural monument as an object of historical inquiry. While the group anticipates a longer tradition of European representations of Indian architecture—including Picturesque landscape paintings, souvenir paintings, and architectural studies drafted by British preservationists—the *Palais Indiens* contributed to the ongoing process of canon-formation in its own particular way: the visually distinctive, unified representational system developed in the studies serves to codify the Mughal architectural past, and is manipulated to suggest continuities between historical icons of Mughal architecture and the buildings of Awadh. In connecting the monuments of the Mughal emperors and the Awadhi nawabs, the *Palais Indiens* collection embodies the contestations over the Mughals' legacy that defined the political and social landscape of the time, and underscores the relevance of architectural representation in the formation of historical narratives.

THE *PALAIS INDIENS*

The *Palais Indiens* consists of plans and elevations of palaces, forts, mosques, mausolea, and garden complexes in Delhi, Agra, and Faizabad.[1] A substantial portion of the group focuses on major monuments in Delhi: three studies are dedicated to the Jami' Masjid, three to the Red Fort, and one to the mausoleum of Safdar Jang. In addition, the collection contains seven renderings of Delhi palaces and one of the city's Tripolia Gate. Beside the Delhi paintings, the *Palais Indiens* depicts the mansions and gardens of the Mughal prince Dara Shikoh in Agra. Finally, the collection also includes four structures in the Awadhi capital of Faizabad, including the palace of Shuja' al-Daula (r. 1753–75), Safdar Jang's son and successor and the reigning nawab during Gentil's tenure in Awadh. The *Palais Indiens* thus crosses temporal and geographical boundaries to draw together Mughal historical icons with the architecture of Awadh. The inclusion of Safdar Jang's tomb is particularly notable, as it highlights a major Awadhi response to imperial Mughal architectural tradition.

Executed on hand-fabricated graph paper, the paintings follow a consistent format, with a large-scale elevation or plan accompanied by an inscription providing information such as the building's owner, location, and construction materials (fig. 4.1). A standardized color palette further unifies the paintings: in all but one instance, red is used to render the elevations, with accents in gold, green, yellow, and black, while the plans are articulated in a similar palette of red and green. Buildings are never shown in use, and the paintings feature no people at all. Moreover, landscape is also absent in most of the images, and when it does appear, it is kept to a bare minimum: simple strips of blue, gray, green, and yellow signify sky, water, and riverbeds, stylized swirls indicate clouds, and abstract plant forms represent vegetation or garden plots. A sense of flatness pervades the elevations, and the few plans included in the collection are relatively spare. It is not known if Gentil

FIGURE 4.1

Artist unknown, *Riverside Façade of the Red Fort of Delhi*, from the *Palais Indiens* (c. 1774), Faizabad. Watercolor and ink on paper, 17.5 × 71 in. (45 × 181 cm). Bibliothèque nationale de France, Paris, Od. 63, fol. 3.

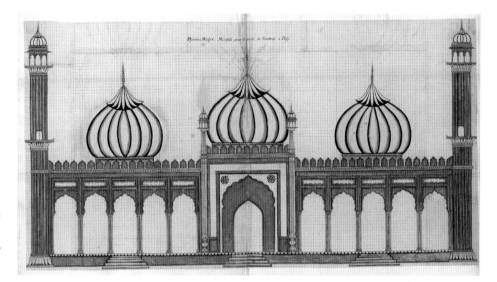

FIGURE 4.2

Artist unknown, *Jami' Masjid in Delhi,* from the *Palais Indiens* (c. 1774), Faizabad. Watercolor and ink on paper, 25 × 47.5 in. (64 × 121 cm). Bibliothèque nationale de France, Paris, Od. 63, fol. 12.

or the collection's artists were responsible for the inscriptions, but stylistically these appear to have been included when the images were first painted.

The viewer experiences the architectural studies on a monumental scale. Most of them range from approximately half a meter to one meter in height and roughly two meters in length. Though the *Palais Indiens* is always referred to and catalogued as an album, the paintings were originally produced as large-scale scrolls, requiring a viewer to unroll each of them individually. (They were bound in the early nineteenth century, and then subsequently unbound for conservation.)[2] Such a format suggests a limited audience for these paintings, in contrast, for instance, to the aquatints that would later be produced and reproduced by British Picturesque artists working in India in the 1790s and after (discussed below).

In developing the pictorial vocabulary of the *Palais Indiens,* the artists drew on and manipulated elements of Mughal architecture to produce images that are variations on a type, rather than singular, individualized depictions. For instance, the trademark Mughal building materials of red sandstone, white marble, and gold and copper sheathing inform the red, white, and gold palette of the paintings, while the architectonic and ornamental elements of the compositions are characteristic of seventeenth-century Mughal architecture: cusped arches, baluster columns, pointed domes, curved bangla roofs and cornices, shallow chhatrī domes, jali screens, pīshtāq entranceways, muqarnas vaulting, and pietra dura. Having developed this fixed set of formal features, the artists reproduce them in varying patterns to produce the different elevations. The domes of the Jami' Masjid in Delhi (1650–56; fig. 4.2), for example, are seen in miniature in the chhatrīs of the gateway of the Delhi Red Fort (1639–48; fig. 4.3); the floral frieze of the gateway, in turn, is repeated in the mausoleum of Safdar Jang (1753–54; fig. 4.4); and the domes of the Jami' Masjid and mausoleum of Safdar Jang are one and the same. A shared visual vocabulary can be seen especially in the multiple palace elevations for which the collective group is named. All of

FIGURE 4.3

Artist unknown, *Gateway of the Red Fort of Delhi,* from the *Palais Indiens* (c. 1774), Faizabad. Watercolor and ink on paper, 23.2 × 35.2 in. (59 × 89.5 cm). Bibliothèque nationale de France, Paris, Od. 63, fol. 14.

FIGURE 4.4

Artist unknown, *Mausoleum of Safdar Jang,* from the *Palais Indiens* (c. 1774), Faizabad. Opaque watercolor on paper, 29 × 36.8 in. (73.5 × 93.5 cm). Victoria and Albert Museum, London, AL 3858. © Victoria and Albert Museum, London.

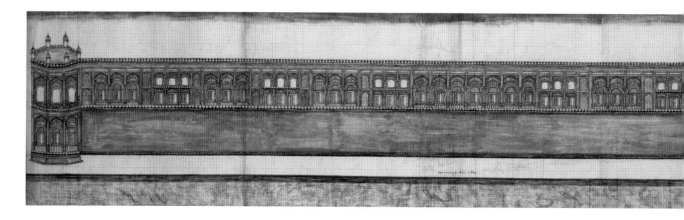

FIGURE 4.5

Artist unknown, *Façade of a Delhi Palace,* from the *Palais Indiens* (c. 1774), Faizabad. Opaque watercolor on paper, 20 × 94.5 in. (51 × 240 cm). Bibliothèque nationale de France, Paris, Od. 63, fol. 13.

these paintings are long, horizontally oriented panoramas of riverside façades, composed of different combinations of the elements identified above.

The paintings' modular architectural morphology is underscored by their articulation on graph paper. In the elevations, architectonic elements such as walls, columns, towers, stringcourses, and cornices correspond to the rows and columns marked on the paper. In the *Façade of a Delhi Palace,* for example, rows of squares are filled in with alternating colors and patterns to render elements such as a plinth, a foundation wall, intermediate stringcourses, friezes, eaves, and a cornice (fig. 4.5). The areas between are filled in with single- and double-story arcades, repeated in regularly alternating patterns to create a unified façade.

Like the elevations, the plans rely on units of graph paper to articulate information about the monuments. A set of conventions, including red lines to indicate walls and

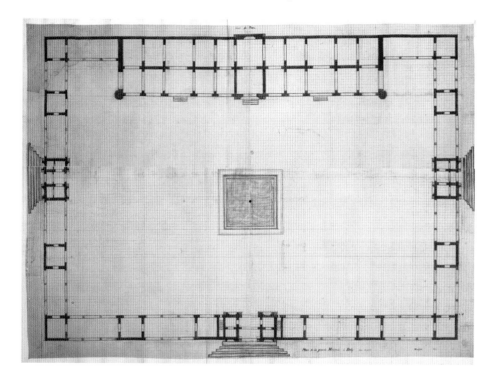

FIGURE 4.6

Artist unknown, *Plan of the Jami' Masjid of Delhi,* from the *Palais Indiens* (c. 1774), Faizabad. Opaque watercolor on paper, 16.5 × 53 and 22 × 53 in. (42 × 135 and 56 × 135 cm). Bibliothèque nationale de France, Paris, Od. 63, fols. 8–9.

single green squares for columns, depict structural units. These elements are then integrated in order to illustrate the overall organization of a building. The plan of the Jamiʿ Masjid in Delhi, for example, employs these conventions to graphically represent a series of monumental gateways and rooms surrounding a central courtyard (fig. 4.6). Although this plan is spare, it conveys the defining aspects of the building, such as symmetry and regularity, and its most notable features, including its monumental gateway.

TOWARD A LANGUAGE OF ARCHITECTURAL DEPICTION

Prior to the *Palais Indiens,* architecture had seldom served as the primary subject matter in Mughal and Rajput painting (the styles most current in north India in the seventeenth and eighteenth centuries).[3] For one, architectural representation did not emerge as a distinct genre in the classical Mughal painting canon of the sixteenth and seventeenth centuries, as did portraiture and studies of flora and fauna.[4] When architecture appeared in manuscript and single-page painting, it often functioned as pictorial background, providing a generic setting for courtly scenes or lending geographical specificity to historical ones. This is true of even the most specific of architectural depictions from earlier Mughal painting, such as a painting of the tomb of Akbar in Sikandra, which appears in the background of *Jahangir Receives a Prisoner* (c. 1618–20; fig. 4.7).[5] The tomb of Akbar occupies the uppermost register of the painting, an oblique view rendered with some perspective. The site is identifiable through its distinctive multicolored gateway, topped by four white minarets, and a multilevel red sandstone tomb crowned by a white marble pavilion. In the same zone of the painting is another, unidentified multilevel building. Both recede into a hazy horizon point, suggesting the techniques of atmospheric perspective. Another example is a c. 1635 painting from the *Pādshāhnāma,* the imperial chronicle of the Mughal emperor Shah Jahan (r. 1627–58). The painting features a sizable rendering of the fortress of Daulatabad during a siege (fig. 4.8), but the architectural monument is not the sole focus of the painting.[6] Ebba Koch has suggested that European paintings served as models for techniques of architectural representation in the *Pādshāhnāma,* pointing to angled bird's-eye city views, for instance (though these were modified and adapted by Mughal artists).[7] But even with the incorporation of such techniques, in these cases as in others, architectural representation is linked to textual narrative. In the seventeenth-century Mughal context, the architectural rendering did not function independently.

In other genres of Indian painting besides manuscript painting, such as city plans and single-folio topographical painting, there are later examples of architectural elevations. In a map of Agra from after 1722, now in the Jaipur City Palace Museum, a series of garden plots along the Yamuna River are represented in plan, while individual buildings within these zones are rendered in elevation (fig. 4.9). Emphasizing structures in the city that required repair, and containing extensive notes on building and area measurements, the map serves as a renovation and construction aid.[8] An eighteenth-century plan of the tomb

OVERLEAF:

FIGURE 4.7

Artist unknown, *Jahangir Receives a Prisoner,* from the *Jahangirnāma* (c. 1618–20). Opaque watercolor on paper, 11.4 × 8.6 in. (29 × 22 cm). Chester Beatty Library, Dublin, In 34.5. © The Trustees of the Chester Beatty Library, Dublin.

FIGURE 4.8

Murar, *The Siege of Daulatabad,* from the *Pādshāhnāma* (c. 1635). Opaque pigment and gold on paper, 23 × 14.5 in. (58.6 × 36.8 cm). Royal Collection Picture Library, Windsor, RCIN 10052025, fol. 144r. Royal Collection Trust/© Her Majesty Queen Elizabeth II 2017.

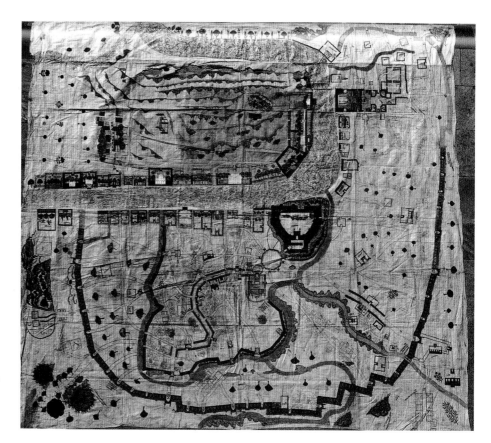

FIGURE 4.9

Artist unknown, *Map of Agra,* after 1722. Pigment on cloth, 115 × 107.8 in. (292 × 274 cm). City Palace Museum, Jaipur. Courtesy of the Maharaja Sawai Man Singh II Museum Trust, City Palace, Jaipur.

and garden of Iʿtimad al-Daula, Agra, is also conceived as a multi-perspectival painting and contains elevations of the complex's central structure (fig. 4.10).[9] These images suggest that in topographical paintings and site plans, there were conventions for rendering elevations, even if these did not give rise to a distinctive genre before the eighteenth century.

Despite the absence, before the eighteenth century, of a critical mass of architectural elevations, there is evidence of a tradition of gridded plans dating to at least the sixteenth century, a tradition that the *Palais Indiens* adopts and transforms. Such plans were widespread in the post-Timurid eastern Islamic world, with Ottoman, Iranian, and Central Asian examples dating from the sixteenth to eighteenth centuries extant today.[10] In the Ottoman context, plans were executed on a "blind" grid, in which lines were incised rather than drawn. Ottoman plans indicate standard conventions for representing architectonic features, such as thick red lines for walls (not unlike the *Palais Indiens* plans), interlocking lines for lattice windows, circles for domes, and semicircles for arches.[11] In these plans, the individual squares corresponded to cubits; since building materials were standardized in the Ottoman empire and builders were paid on a per-cubit basis, the plans facilitated the calculation of construction costs.[12] Similarly, Uzbek plans from Central Asia also show modular buildings rendered on gridded plans, pointing to the prevalence of this system of representing architecture. Again, each square of the plan represents a cubit, and as with the Ottoman plans, builders could calculate the amount that would be necessary for a particular project. The modularity of such plans also corresponded to the modularity of the resultant structures.[13]

Although there are no surviving Mughal plans, there is pictorial and textual evidence for a history of similar architectural plans in Mughal India, where standardized modular planning governed architectural design.[14] Indeed, the use of gridded plans had become a well-established aspect of architectural practice in Mughal India by the time the *Palais Indiens* was painted, and cannot necessarily be explained by the influence of Europeans, as has sometimes been assumed.[15] A well-known manuscript painting from the *Bāburnāma* (c. 1580), the memoirs of the first Mughal emperor, Babur (r. 1526–30), attests to this tradition.

In the painting, a group of men are assembled in a garden, its walls lined by lush fruit trees (fig. 4.11). The centerpiece of the garden is an elevated flowerbed, divided into four parts by intersecting water channels, one of which is shown emptying into a square pool (this is the Mughal chahār bāgh garden type).[16] To the right, in a resplendent yellow coat, is the Mughal emperor Babur, accompanied by a small retinue. Along the left of the painting are a group of gardeners, some holding spades. Most notable are the two figures near the center of the composition. One, likely a building supervisor, holds a red board with a modular grid etched on it. The other is a gardener or builder who pulls a string across the axis of the garden, conveying a correspondence between the built space and plan.[17] Here we see the clear use of a grid in the elaboration of a modularly planned space: it occupies a central position in the planning and execution of one of the most paradigmatic of Mughal landscape types, the walled, four-part garden.

Besides such illustrations, Mughal textual sources also reference architectural plans (ṭarḥ, ṭarāḥ, and naqsha) in various contexts. The *Pādshāhnāma* and *ʾAmal-i Ṣāliḥ*, chronicles of the reign of the Mughal emperor Shah Jahan, report that the emperor ordered plans of

FIGURE 4.10
Artist unknown, *Plan of the Funerary Complex of Itimad al-Daula,* 18th century. Watercolor and ink on paper, dimensions unknown. City Palace Museum, Jaipur. Courtesy of the Maharaja Sawai Man Singh II Museum Trust, City Palace, Jaipur.

buildings he liked, and also approved plans before construction was to begin on his major building projects.[18] On multiple occasions, Shah Jahan's successor, ʿAlamgir (r. 1658–1707), ordered plans of noblemen's houses, and the *Kalimāt-i Taiyabāt,* a collection of imperial decrees, describes ʿAlamgir's consultation of a plan as he prepared to attack a fort in the Deccan.[19] Over the course of the seventeenth century, drawing architectural plans grew into a specialized task assigned to chief or master architects (*ustād miʿmār*), who were differentiated in rank, responsibility, and pay from engineers and technical supervisors (*muhandis*), as well as from masons (*bannāʾ*).[20] Given this evidence, it is clear that there was a Mughal tradition of gridded plans that was firmly in place by the eighteenth century.

There are, moreover, gridded plans from eighteenth-century Rajput India that exhibit a striking visual similarity to those in the *Palais Indiens*.[21] These, too, are painted on hand-fabricated graph paper, with walls and supports similarly articulated in simple lines of red and green. Despite the stylistic echoes between the *Palais Indiens* and Jaipur plans, however, they serve markedly different functions. A plan of the palace at Amber, just outside Jaipur, exemplifies the Rajput plans; these all bear concrete relationships to the processes of construction and renovation (fig. 4.12).[22] While the *Palais Indiens* plans are economical with detail, the Amber plan contains extensive pictorial and textual information. Individual building features are far more clearly articulated; the layouts of gardens, for example, are rendered as detailed patterns, rather than as stylized green squares. In addition, each of the rooms is labeled either with the name of its occupant or its function, and building renovations are also recorded on the plan. Related examples from Jaipur demonstrate the same detailed and process-oriented approach, serving as progress reports on completed and proposed renovations on the fort of Jaigarh and Man Mandir in Benares.[23] Another set of three plans from Jaipur appears to have been used during the construction of the Ganesh Pol, the monumental gateway in the Amber Fort outside of Jaipur. These include two plans showing two different stages in the construction history of the gateway, and an elevation that was used to calculate the gradient of the Ganesh Pol ramp.[24] The *Palais Indiens* plans, by contrast, serve as idealized records of built structures. Thus, while the *Palais Indiens* draws on techniques of architectural representation firmly established in India since at least the seventeenth century, it also signifies a divergence from the earlier tradition, serving a commemorative rather than technical function.

In this respect, the *Palais Indiens* paintings engage with modes of representation seen in architectural studies prepared by French military engineers working in the subcontinent. Within the French context, the practice of producing archival copies of architectural studies and maps was formalized by Louis XVI in 1776, when he ordered visual records of the French colonies to be deposited at Versailles.[25] The *Palais Indiens*, too, was submitted to Versailles by Gentil after his return to France in 1778, pointing to its similarly

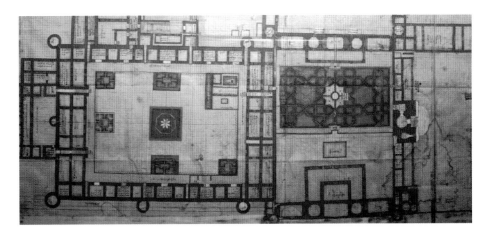

FIGURE 4.12

Artist unknown, *Plan of Amber Fort,* 18th century. Opaque pigment and ink on paper, dimensions unknown. Jaigarh Fort Museum, Jaipur. Courtesy of the Maharaja Sawai Man Singh II Museum Trust, City Palace, Jaipur.

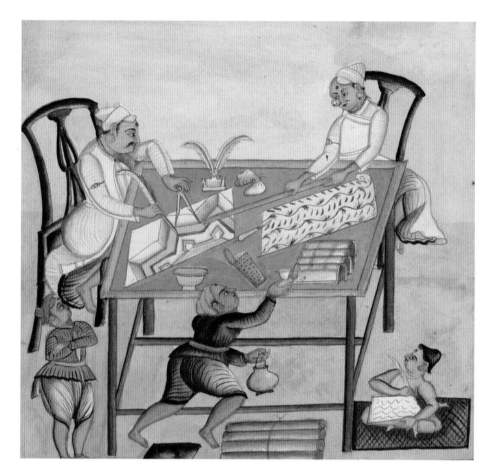

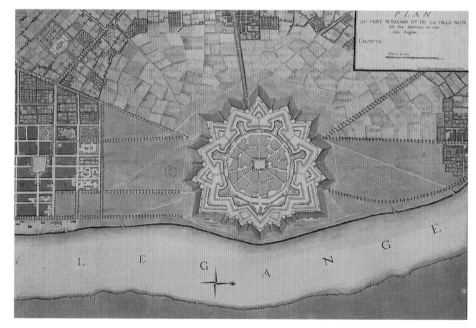

commemorative function, linked of course to the larger enterprise of knowledge collecting and empire building. Yet while both the CDIO studies and the *Palais Indiens* served as records of French expansion and interest in India, in the latter case, artists working in Faizabad drew on both Indian and French representational conventions to produce their architectural renderings.

Given Gentil's background as a French military officer and governmental representative, it is likely that he had access to CDIO studies or was familiar with their conventions. Surviving pictorial evidence of the CDIO's documentary activities includes maps, plans, and views of European and Indian cities from the eighteenth century, including the French-founded towns of Pondicherry, Mahé, and Chandernagore; the growing British colonial centers in Calcutta and Madras; the Dutch outposts at Negapatnam, Cochin, and Colombo; and regional Indian capitals and strongholds, such as Tanjore.[26] In addition to maps and plans of entire cities, there are also architectural studies of major French governmental, commercial, and military buildings: the Governor's Palace and *blanchisserie* in Pondicherry, the French magazine at Mahé, and the Loge at Chandernagore. A significant portion of the material is dedicated to documenting the architecture of other European colonial powers, such as the British-built Fort William in Calcutta, as well as the Indian forts at Daulatabad and Arcot.

Indian artists were well aware of the drafting techniques represented by this corpus of works, as shown in a 1785 painting in the Victoria and Albert Museum (V&A), London, in which two Indian draftsmen work on a watercolor ground plan of a *trace italienne,* the iconic star-shaped fortification that grew popular in Europe from the sixteenth to the eighteenth century (fig. 4.13). In the Indian context, the plan most immediately recalls plans of Fort William, held by the British in Calcutta. (A plan of this fort is included in the archives of the CDIO, and includes a title and notation in French [fig. 4.14]). The painting depicts a collaborative studio: two men sit at a table with drafting tools, including a straight-edged rule, compass, quills, and a pouncing bag. Their special status is conveyed by their white robes and gold jewelry. Beside the table, seated on the floor, is a scribe, holding a quill and a large sheaf of paper covered with writing. They are accompanied by two attendants, one of whom brings them tea. On the table is a group of bound manuscripts and a single sheet with an abstracted vine motif, and on the floor there is a bundle of scrolls.

The scene suggests that there was a system in place for producing architectural renderings, and that Indian draftsmen were at the center of it. Once European drafting conventions had been brought to the subcontinent by architects and engineers working for the East India trading companies, Indian artists incorporated these into their repertoire of techniques. This was not dissimilar from the way in which Mughal artists had incorporated European representational techniques into their painting practice beginning in the late sixteenth and early seventeenth centuries. When European prints and books had arrived at the Mughal court with the Jesuit missions in the late 1500s,

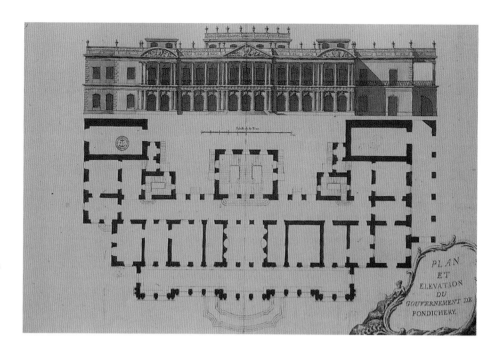

FIGURE 4.15

Dumont, *Plan and Elevation of the Governor's Palace in Pondicherry*, 1755. Watercolor and ink on paper, 24 × 37.8 in. (61 × 96 cm). Archives nationales d'outre-mer (ANOM, France), Aix-en-Provence. FR ANOM 81A.

FIGURE 4.16

Artist unknown, *Façade of the Palace of Dara Shikoh in Agra*, from the *Palais Indiens* (c. 1774), Faizabad. Opaque watercolor on paper, 26 × 84 in. (66.4 × 214 cm). Victoria and Albert Museum, London, AL 1761. © Victoria and Albert Museum, London.

FIGURE 4.17

Artist unknown, *Plan of the Palace and Garden of Dara Shikoh in Agra*, from the *Palais Indiens* (c. 1774), Faizabad. Opaque watercolor on paper, 59.5 × 24 and 59.5 × 28 in. (151 × 61 and 151 × 72 cm). Bibliothèque nationale de France, Paris, Od. 63, fols. 17–18.

the artists of the imperial workshop set about integrating Christian imagery and European pictorial devices, such as modeling and naturalism, into their repertoire. Two centuries later, Indian artists did the same with drafting techniques aimed at rendering architecture.[27]

A comparison between a 1755 study of the Governor's Palace in Pondicherry (fig. 4.15) and a pair of paintings from the *Palais Indiens* sheds light on the assimilation of French drafting conventions. Inscribed *"Plan et Elevation du Gouvernement de Pondichery,"* the French study features a front elevation and ground-floor plan. It is rendered on unlined paper, in contrast to the graph paper used in the *Palais Indiens.* But what is significant here is the correspondence between plan and elevation. Features such as the projecting central façade and receding, niched wings of the building are clearly delineated in the plan. Similarly, a plan and an elevation of the palace of the Mughal prince Dara Shikoh from the *Palais Indiens* are drawn in correlation to each other (figs. 4.16, 4.17). In the elevation, three large octagonal towers frame two prominent bangla pavilions, with smaller subsidiary pavilions and chambers interspersed. The plan includes not only the building's major features, such as the three towers, but also every column, doorway, and window of the façade. The pillared towers are indicated by red octagons surrounded by squares, while the columns of the bangla and subsidiary pavilions are articulated as series of green squares. Red-filled squares signify the walls of the intervening rooms. Despite Indian traditions of drawn plans, there are no known examples of correlated plans and elevations earlier than this.

Collectively, then, the Mughal, Rajput, and French body of material represents a rich deposit of drafting techniques that circulated throughout the Indian subcontinent in

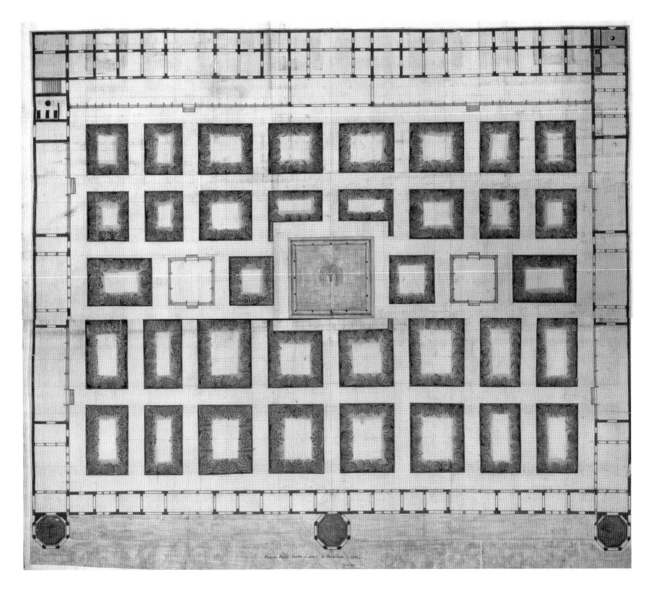

the late eighteenth century. In drawing on these multiple systems of visual representation, the *Palais Indiens* collection evinces a rich visual heterogeneity. The plans in the collection, with their execution on hand-fabricated graph paper and use of a set visual language for rendering architectonic features, adapt north Indian representational techniques. Simultaneously, the elevations show a level of detailed execution associated with Mughal and Rajput painting. Finally, the overall format of a coordinated plan and elevation reflects the conventions of French architectural studies.

The visual heterogeneity of the *Palais Indiens* raises questions about artistic agency. Although very little is known about the artists involved in the *Palais Indiens* commission, evidence suggests that at least one artist or architect based in Awadh executed some of the paintings. Gentil employed manuscript painters in the region for his numerous commissions, and three artists in particular are mentioned in his writings—Mohan Singh, Mihr Chand, and Nevasi Lal.[28] Certainly, the mastery of Mughal and Rajput painting techniques evident in these studies suggests the hand of an experienced and well-established artist. Mohan Singh and Nevasi Lal had migrated to Awadh after the dissolution of the imperial atelier in Delhi, and Mohan Singh was the son of Govardhan II, a painter who had been in the service of the Mughal emperor Muhammad Shah (r. 1719–48).[29] In addition, the amalgamation of Mughal, Rajput, and French painting and drafting techniques was well within the practice of this group of artists, who were experienced in the Mughal tradition of absorbing and transforming global painting styles.[30] Though their identities remain unknown, the new language of architectural depiction that these artists crystallized was inextricably linked to the formation of historical knowledge. As we will see, the *Palais Indiens* posited the monument as an object of historical inquiry and, in the process, "wrote" a historical narrative that underscored the potency of the Mughal past and its relevance to the eighteenth-century present.

REPRESENTING ARCHITECTURE, WRITING HISTORY

The *Palais Indiens* collection is characterized by a methodical compositional system, suggesting that the monuments in question have been carefully surveyed and systematically reproduced, rather than invented or imagined. In addition, textual glosses imply that the paintings are based on on-the-spot observation. An inscription along the lower edge of one of the paintings, for instance, states that the structure is built of red stone, inlaid with white and black marble and sits under domes of white marble.[31] Moreover, the legibility afforded by the paintings' monumental scale means that the viewer can easily comprehend how the paintings are composed and, by extension, how the structures are built.

While such pictorial strategies imply fidelity to an original, closer analysis reveals the ways in which the artists take representational license, not only by reusing standardized architectural elements but also, and most notably, with respect to the depiction of ornament. The artists of the *Palais Indiens* imbue the buildings with a lavish ornamental

FIGURE 4.18
Gateway of the Red Fort, Delhi,
c. 1639–48.

sensibility. In the painting of the monumental marble and sandstone gateway of the Red Fort, inscribed *"Porte du Fort où est le Palais de l'Empéreur"* (see fig. 4.3), an exquisite ornamental program is rendered with a wealth of detail, including a rich chevron pattern on the engaged minarets, intricate muqarnas netting in the central vault, extensive incised relief on the metal door, a jewel-toned floral frieze running across the pīshtāq, carved cartouches running the length of the side towers, and, at the capital and base of these towers, floral motifs and vegetal scrolls that virtually curl off the page. While striking, the sensuous decoration is curious given that many of these ornamental features are absent from the actual gateway. Instead, the gateway is a relatively austere building featuring a continuous sandstone façade with limited panels of ornamental relief (fig. 4.18).

In fact, elements from at least two other Mughal-era monuments—the gateway of the Taj Mahal (fig. 4.19) and the tomb of Safdar Jang (fig. 4.20)—appear in the painting. The profile and proportions of the painted building, as well as the inclusion of ornamental motifs such as floral pietra dura, evoke the Taj Mahal gateway without precisely replicating the full architectural and ornamental program of that building. For instance, the elaborate pietra dura work is not reproduced in the spandrels of the central arch, but rather in horizontal friezes. Furthermore, the building's extensive inscription and the stacked, pointed side arches of its façade do not appear in the painting at all. While the side towers are visually distinct from those of the Taj Mahal gateway, they closely resemble the side towers of the tomb of Safdar Jang, with their alternating panels of quatrefoils and cartouches (fig. 4.21).

The amalgamation of these forms exemplifies the inventiveness and license that marks the *Palais Indiens,* as well as demonstrating its interest in the depiction of ornament.

FIGURE 4.19
Gateway of the Taj Mahal, Agra,
c. 1632–48.

FIGURE 4.20
Tomb of Safdar Jang, Delhi,
1753–54.

FIGURE 4.21
Corner tower, tomb of Safdar Jang,
Delhi, 1753–54.

In describing this group of structures, the artists concentrate on developing a consistent visual vocabulary and systematic method for the representation of architecture. What emerges is a coherent set of built forms, unified in style and palette. But the *Palais Indiens* paintings "effect," rather than "reflect," reality, curiously implying methodical, on-the-spot observation of buildings while actually offering subjective portrayals that draw on a heavily ornamental aesthetic, describing the buildings of the seventeenth century in a style current to the eighteenth.

The visual continuities developed in the collection ultimately suggest historical continuities. More specifically, by emphasizing elaborately carved surfaces, the studies underscore the visual connections between Mughal and Awadhi architecture. As we saw in Chapter 3, the Mughal style of the eighteenth century is exemplified by the mausoleum of Safdar Jang, which was based on Mughal sepulchral prototypes but featured elements that would also come to define the architecture of Awadh in the late eighteenth and nineteenth centuries. Its surfaces are replete with lavish floral and geometric designs, similar to the compositions in the *Palais Indiens*. Another key example of later Awadhi architecture that features a similar sensibility is the Bara Imambara complex of Asaf al-Duala (1784–91). The deployment of an ornate ornamental program in this structure represents the persistence and further development of the eighteenth-century architectural style that moved between Mughal Delhi and Awadh. In the buildings of the Bara Imambara complex, like the tomb of Safdar Jang and the Mughal monuments of the late seventeenth and early eighteenth centuries, interior and exterior spaces are richly animated with an array of curvilinear shapes, floral motifs, and complex geometric patterns, demonstrating how the ornamental forms articulated in the *Palais Indiens* were integral to the ongoing development and expression of a shared Mughal–Awadhi architectural identity.

This inclination to connect a chronologically, geographically, and stylistically disparate group of architectural monuments encapsulates the cultural and power dynamics of late eighteenth-century Mughal India, when the potency of Mughal architectural codes and symbolic practices was keenly felt by successor states and colonial powers seeking to solidify their legitimacy and authority in the subcontinent. The *Palais Indiens* demonstrates how architectural representation could occupy a central position in these negotiations, allowing various parties to harness the historical legacy represented by seventeenth-century Mughal buildings.

The interpretive potential of the *Palais Indiens* becomes even more compelling when it is considered in the context of the Gentil collection, the manuscripts and albums amassed by Gentil during his tenure in India. The other works in the Gentil collection document and appropriate Mughal historical legacies, contributing to the officer's goals of acquiring authority on and over India. Although the collection comprised texts on law, religion, lexicography, poetry, calligraphy, and numismatics, and included Sanskrit, Persian, and Arabic manuscripts, the majority of Gentil's literary activity related to Mughal and Awadhi history.[32] These new works combined Indian primary sources, which were translated by Gentil with the help of Indian scholars and translators, with his own observations and analysis; they were also often illustrated by the artists he employed in his studio.[33] These included a history of the Mughal emperors; an atlas of the Mughal empire, based on the sixteenth-century *Āʾīn-i Akbarī* (Institutes of Akbar, composed by the emperor Akbar's prime vizier, Abu al-Fazl); and the so-called *Gentil Album,* a hybrid history-ethnography of the Mughal and Awadhi courts and myriad cultures and religions of India, also loosely based on the *Āʾīn-i Akbarī.*[34] Since these works were the result of extensive collaboration, and often relied on Mughal primary sources, they likely embodied widespread cultural perceptions, rather than reflecting Gentil's individual perspective. In other words, we can regard the *Palais Indiens* and related objects not as idiosyncratic to Gentil, but emblematic of the cultural currents that defined eighteenth-century north India.

The importance accorded to architectural representation is attested not only by the *Palais Indiens,* but also by a series of city plans of Shahjahanabad now in the V&A.[35] A group of large, minutely detailed, extensively labeled watercolors combine to form a monumental plan of the Red Fort and the two main avenues leading from it, Chandni Chowk and Faiz Bazaar (fig. 4.22). Multilingual textual glosses, in Persian and French, provide the names of mosques, bathhouses, squares, and mansions (havelis); the plans also contain survey information in Latin.[36] Evidence suggests that at the very least, Gentil acquired, if he did not commission, the plans and was responsible for their transfer to Europe, as they are included in an eighteenth-century catalogue of works in the Gentil collection.[37] Like the *Palais Indiens*, these renderings concentrate on architecture as a primary focus of representation and object of historical interest.

The *Palais Indiens* also suggests that Mughal architecture could allow individuals, as well as political states, to claim the cultural authority associated with Mughal identity. In considering his collection, it is tempting to cast Gentil as an outsider attempting to capture the unfamiliar. However, the space that he occupied at the Awadhi court was complex and layered. Rather than merely recounting Indian history as a series of distantly observed events, Gentil uses visual and textual narratives to present it as an ongoing process in which he actively participates. In 1764, Shuja' al-Daula entrusted Gentil with the task of brokering a peace settlement with the English after the defeat of allied Mughal and Awadhi forces at Buxar.[38] The meeting during which the treaty was ratified is depicted in the *Gentil Album*, and included in his memoirs, in which Gentil boasts of the praise and recognition Shuja' bestowed upon him after he procured agreeable terms for negotiation: "This prince, pleased with the opening of this negotiation and wanting to place me in the position of negotiating as an equal with the two Indian lords, who were at the head of the English (delegation), bestowed upon me all the titles that an Indian grandee can possess, calling me *Rafioudoulah, Nazemdjenk, Bahadour, Tadbir-oul-Moulouk* [*sic*]."[39] Here, Gentil emphasizes the crucial role he played in these negotiations, and uses the occasion to introduce his Persianate titles "Uplifter of the State" (*rafi' al-daula*), "Leader in War" (*nizam-i jang*), "the Valiant" (*bahadur*), and "Counsel of Kings" (*tadbir al-muluk*). His ability to act as a broker with the English translated into a capacity to earn the respect usually accorded to "Indian lords" (*seigneurs Indiens*). Gentil adopted his Persianate titles fully, and a seal bearing them is found on many of his albums and manuscripts. The close friendship between Gentil and Shuja' al-Daula is emphasized throughout the memoirs, which are dedicated to the nawab.

Besides this political alliance with Shuja' al-Daula—who was not only nawab of Awadh but also vizier of the Mughal empire—Gentil claimed another connection to the Mughal dynasty, through his wife, Thérèse Velho. Velho's grandmother Juliana, a native of Goa, had been entrusted with the education of the Mughal prince Shah 'Alam I (later the emperor Bahadur Shah I, r. 1707–12) and eventually provided him with political counsel, thus occupying a prominent position in Mughal government.[40] So valuable was her advice, Gentil reports, that Bahadur Shah I awarded Juliana gifts equal to 900,000 rupees, four villages producing 50,000 rupees in annual revenue, and the Palace of Dara Shikoh.[41] This extraordinary account of Juliana's role in Mughal history concludes by quoting Bahadur Shah I as saying, "If this woman were a man, I would make her vizier."[42] Gentil

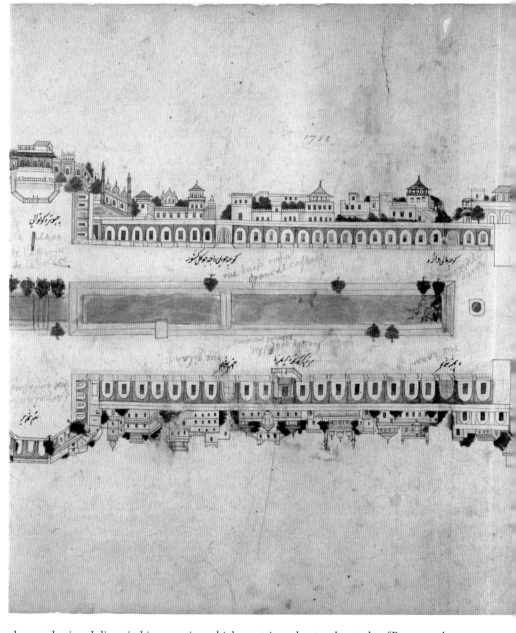

also emphasizes Juliana in his memoirs, which contain a chapter devoted to "Renowned Women of India." Gentil places Juliana alongside sovereigns and leaders such as the Sultanate princess Razia, the royal Mughal women Nur Jahan and Jahanara, and the legendary Begum Samru, who went from courtesan to head of a mercenary army and ruler of the Indian principality of Sardhana.[43] In other words, Gentil creates an illustrious history for his wife's ancestor, highlighting her Mughal connections. By including narratives of Juliana in his historical works, Gentil integrates his wife, through her lineage, into Mughal history, and by extension, inserts himself into that history. This personal connection might account for the plans and elevations of Dara Shikoh's Delhi palace in the *Palais Indiens*.

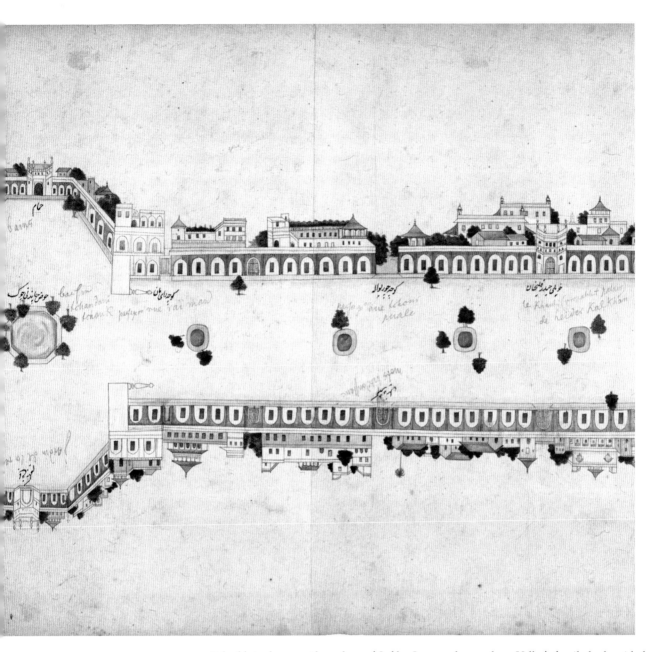

It had later become the palace of Safdar Jang, and was where Velho's family had resided while in Delhi.

Architectural representation, then, opened up possibilities for states and individuals alike to create and claim Mughal identity. The images in this group suggest that the historical legacy of Mughal Delhi, and in particular its architectural signs of political and cultural power, remained relevant in a broader Indian historical imagination, ready to be claimed by a power like Awadh. Similarly, for Gentil, the representation of Mughal architecture was linked to a broader project of self-fashioning, enabling and reinforcing Gentil's professional and personal claims to authority.

SITUATING THE *PALAIS INDIENS*

The *Palais Indiens* were completed at a time when Mughal architecture began to receive the increased attention of artists and scholars. Starting in the late eighteenth century, there was a proliferation of Rajput plans and elevations of Mughal buildings. In the 1780s and 1790s, British landscape painters in India who were working in the Picturesque style dedicated attention to the subcontinent's monumental architecture. Soon after, a new genre of painting developed in the subcontinent, the so-called "Company School," which documented India's architecture among its flora, fauna, and "natives." This preoccupation with representing Indian architecture would intensify in the nineteenth century, particularly as European trade and colonial ambitions increased and the new technologies of photography came to the fore. While these distinct visual traditions hardly constituted a unified category of representation, they did share a sustained interest in the depiction of architecture. Though the *Palais Indiens* shared this same preoccupation, it stands out for its relatively early date, preceding most of these art historical developments by at least a decade.

As we saw earlier, over the course of the eighteenth century, Rajput artists and architects cultivated a style of architectural representation characterized by the use of gridded paper, a fixed set of conventions such as thick red lines for walls, and a system of notation that specified the use and function of spaces within a plan. Not only were Rajput buildings represented in this manner, but so too were Mughal monuments. A late eighteenth-century plan of the Red Fort details its myriad spaces, from its monumental gateway to its central axis and its many courtyards, gardens, and pavilions, all bound in the elongated octagonal walls that surrounded the complex. The plan is carefully labeled in Devanagari, each label conveying the name or function of the particular space.[44] Rajput artists also produced elevations of Mughal spaces. A rendering of Akbar's tomb in Fatehpur Sikri combines both plan and elevation, portraying the walls and quadrilateral layout of the chahār bāgh–type garden, as well as the individual structures that compose the complex.[45] The four quadrants of the garden are shown to be lushly planted, with a pool at the center of each quadrant. The complex's gateways and its centrally positioned, multilevel tomb, including the freestanding pavilion on the topmost level, are all on axis with each other, with the main axis of the complex punctuated by a series of pools and fountains. Overall, whether rendering buildings in plan or elevation, the Rajput depictions tend to emphasize architectural systems, spatial logic, and spatial experience.[46]

The Picturesque tradition represented another approach to architecture altogether. The most famous of the British Picturesque painters to depict Mughal architecture were William Hodges and the uncle and nephew team Thomas and William Daniell. Hodges traveled and worked in India from 1780 to 1783, under the auspices of British Governor-General Warren Hastings and the English East India Company. During his three tours of India, he surveyed British-controlled territory; the city of Benares and aspects of "Hindu culture"; and Mughal cities and monuments.[47] Besides the paintings, drawings, and prints that resulted from these travels, Hodges also wrote an account that accompanied his *Select*

Views in India (1786), and a separate account, *Travels in India* (1793), in which he claimed to present a history of India through his depictions of its landscape and architecture.[48] Hodges was soon followed by Thomas Daniell and William Daniell, who arrived in India in 1786 and spent the next eight years working in the subcontinent, returning to England in 1794. The Daniells began their travels by using Hodges's *Select Views in India* as a guide, but went on to explore the temples of western India with the British artist James Wales, who was based in Bombay.[49] They subsequently published a magisterial multivolume collection of engravings, entitled *Oriental Scenery* (1795–1807), as well as *Antiquities of India* (1803), which focused on the western Indian temple sites they had toured with Wales.[50]

Although Hodges and the Daniells produced their own distinctive styles, their work did have in common the aesthetic values associated with the Picturesque, current in late eighteenth-century England. Their compositions were characterized by wild landscapes, decaying ruins, and a rejection of eighteenth-century Neoclassical convention.[51] Architectural monuments served as crucial elements of these romantic scenes, alongside overgrown vegetation and "natives" in "traditional" dress. In an etching of Hodges's *View of the Gateway of the Tomb of Akbar at Sikandra* (1786), the gateway of the mausoleum of the Mughal emperor Akbar (r. 1556–1605) is rendered in the distance, patches of its core rubble masonry visible through gaps in the building's exterior facing (fig. 4.23). A craggy, rock-strewn landscape extends before the gateway, and in the shadowy foreground we see a structure standing in partial ruin. Space recedes dramatically, and the gateway is manipulated to tower majestically over its surroundings.

FIGURE 4.23
John Browne, after William Hodges, *View of the Gateway of the Tomb of Akbar at Sikandra*, 1786. Etching, 18 × 24.5 in. (46.5 × 62.2 cm). British Library, London. © The British Library Board, P2327.

In the Daniells' *The Taje Mahal, at Agra* (1801), the mausoleum of the Mughal empress Mumtaz Mahal (d. 1631) is rendered through similar pictorial conventions, placed as the centerpiece of a sweeping prospect (fig. 4.24). The luminous marble tomb is viewed in the distance, raised on its red sandstone plinth across the Yamuna River, underneath a gray, cloud-filled sky. On the closer riverbank, which is enveloped in shadow, people walk and gather on the sand, trailed by an elephant and camel. Farther along, directly across from the Taj Mahal, are a decaying viewing tower and a collapsed pavilion. Vegetation grows from both structures, which are riddled with cracks and missing bricks. As these examples illustrate, in the work of Hodges and the Daniells, Mughal monuments were cast in terms of grandiosity and decay, signs of an imperial power that had once been great but had fallen into decline. Through the pictorial logic of these images, India was presented as a site that was primed to be resuscitated by the British.[52]

Mughal architecture also figured prominently in another group of paintings associated with British imperial interests, classified as "Company Painting." Originally conceived as a coherent category in Mildred Archer's 1972 catalogue, *Company Drawings in the India Office Library,* this classification was elaborated and reinforced in Archer's later *Company Paintings: Indian Paintings of the British Period.*[53] Archer defined this group of objects as art produced by Indian artists for European patrons affiliated with the English East India Company. By and large, Company Painting has been discussed in terms of the taste and influence of European patrons, with little attention paid to the role played by individual Indian artists in forging new pictorial languages or bringing fresh subject matter to light.[54] Of late, scholars such as Yuthika Sharma have redressed this problem by examining the biographies and agency of artists typically classified as Company Painters, and by showing

FIGURE 4.24

Thomas and William Daniell, *The Taje Mahale, at Agra,* 1801. Colored aquatint, 17 × 23.5 in. (43.1 × 59.7 cm). British Library, London. © The British Library Board, P395.

continuities between art produced for Mughal and European patrons (this point will be elaborated below).[55] Nevertheless, the terms "Company Painting" and "Company School" are still in wide use. As the term "Company Painting" still requires interrogation, I use it purposefully here, so that we might inflect this category further.

Among the standard subject matter of Company Painting are flora and fauna, indigenous populations, and local customs. Along with cartography, the depiction of such subjects has long been the stock-in-trade of imperial expansion; the British empire in India was no exception.[56] In the context of Company Painting, architecture became the subject of ethnographic and scientific inquiry, rendered through pictorial devices that suggest that the buildings have been carefully observed and painstakingly reproduced. The *Tomb of Selim Chishti* (c. 1820) is one such example (fig. 4.25). Painted by an unnamed artist, it shows the mausoleum of the Sufi saint Selim Chishti (d. 1572), who famously prophesied that a son and heir would be born to the emperor Akbar. The watercolor portrays a central, pointed dome resting atop a cubic structure with a carved cornice, deep eaves (chhajjā), and a series of latticework jali screens. The building has been rendered in a simple white, conveying the luminous marble of the structure and the delicacy of its screened façade. The artist depicts the architectonic and ornamental program with great care, from the intricate, variegated geometric patterns of the screened walls and platform, to the carved chevrons on the portico columns and graceful brackets supporting the eaves. He also manipulates perspective so that the lines of the staircase and the eaves in the composition converge on the central axis of the structure—where the tomb of the saint is

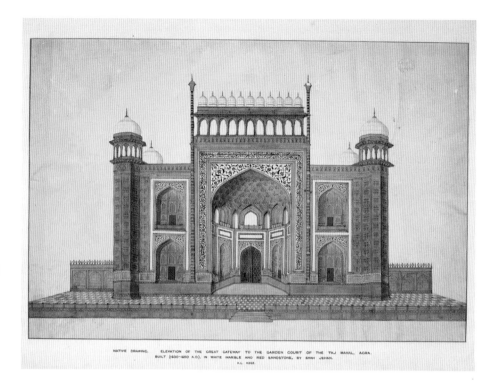

located—while its lattice and carved panels remain perfectly flat. This spatial manipulation allows the viewer to take in as many of the tomb's elements and details as possible.

Despite this wealth of information, what is missing from the composition is any physical context. There are some red brick tiles before the structure, but its surroundings remain unknown. In reality, the mausoleum was situated in the courtyard of a vast red sandstone mosque, its white marble causing it to stand out dramatically from its red sandstone environs. This information is lost in the painting, which transforms the building from a contextualized space into a scientific, objectified specimen.

Other Company Paintings depict architecture in a similar vein, showing how widespread these conventions were. In the *Gateway of the Taj Mahal* (c. 1820; fig. 4.26) and the *Tomb of Itimad al-Daula* (c. 1820; fig. 4.27), the artists convey ornament in great detail.[57] The Taj Mahal gateway, for instance, is shown with the elegant pietra dura that covers its spandrels, while the mausoleum (1622–28) of the nobleman I'timad al-Daula (d. 1622), who was a high-ranking noble, the father of Nur Jahan, and father-in-law to the emperor Jahangir (r. 1605–27), is draped with multicolored stone inlay. Like the *Tomb of Selim Chishti,* both structures are also rendered in a soft palette and executed in watercolor, and in each, perspectival space is similarly manipulated to display a multiplicity of building surfaces.

Even though these examples—which are representative of a much larger corpus— share pictorial devices, they functioned quite differently from each other. The representation of the Taj Mahal gateway was painted on a relatively large scale (48.5 by 70.8 centimeters) and was part of a group made for a British inspector of public buildings, who was responsible for the upkeep and restoration of monuments.[58] In contrast, the *Tomb of Itimad al-Daula,* also part of a set, was slightly larger than postcard-size (12.4 by 19.9 centimeters), included embossed borders, and was acquired as a souvenir.[59] Thus, the established conventions of Company School paintings were used to a variety of ends.

There are, too, examples of eighteenth-century architectural representation that do not fall neatly into these categories. A prime example is a set of depictions (c. 1785) commissioned by Antoine Polier, the Swiss engineer, collector, and longtime officer of the English East India Company.[60] These formed an album of sixteen folios, with Arabic, Urdu, and Persian text on the verso and the paintings on the recto. Two depict the primary imperial monuments of Delhi, the Jamiʿ Masjid and the Red Fort; one illustrates a royal polo match; and one comprises a series of portrait medallions of members of the Timurid and Mughal royal house. The remaining twelve show palace courtyards, gardens, or landscapes.[61] While the album (now disassembled) stands out for its visualization of idealized garden settings, landscapes, and architectural vistas, the two architectural depictions are similarly remarkable for their rendering of idealized space: both emphasize the symmetry, regularity, and axiality of these buildings, often at the expense of accuracy, representing the ideals of Mughal architecture rather than the buildings themselves. In this respect, these two works related to the mode of idealization at work in the *Palais Indiens.* This

point is especially significant since Gentil and Polier knew each other well, worked with the same group of artists, and had access to each other's collections.[62]

Scholars have approached this body of material in a multitude of ways. Their analyses, which have explored themes such as artistic agency, painterly virtuosity, subjectivity, and imperial expansion, have enriched our understanding of what it meant to depict Mughal architecture in the late eighteenth and early nineteenth centuries. By delineating recent critical approaches, my aim in the remainder of this section is to highlight the unique qualities and strategies I see working in the *Palais Indiens,* particularly its relationship to the project of historicization.

Mughal architectural representations first received sustained scholarly attention when Mildred Archer conceptualized the genre of Company Painting. Archer showed that architectural depictions of Mughal buildings were executed in a variety of media and formats, from conservation studies done by engineers to postcards and painted ivory boxes.[63] In her formulation, however, architectural depiction was solely the product of British agency, resulting from scholarly fascination, imperially driven efforts at scientific documentation, or a brisk tourist industry. Scholars have since moved away from the formulations offered by Archer to offer a wider array of interpretations.

One of the major contributions of recent scholarship has been to shed light on the role played by individual artists in the production of images of Mughal architecture. For instance, J. P. Losty has charted a history of topographical painting in Delhi, one that is not restricted to architectural representation but that also encompasses panoramas, urban views, and landscape paintings from the 1750s to the 1850s. His analysis has revealed much about painterly approach and virtuosity, including how artists handled techniques such as linear perspective, and has emphasized the biographies of individual masters of topographical painting including Ghulam 'Ali Khan, Mirza Shah Rukh Beg, and Mazhar 'Ali Khan.[64] Yuthika Sharma, too, has excavated these individual artist biographies to underscore the central role of artistic agency in the production of topographical paintings. Her artist-centered approach has destabilized the notion that Mughal court painting and Company Painting were distinct realms, calling into question the very constitution of the category of Company Painting and the assumptions about European agency that it carries.[65]

Scholars have also explored the sociopolitical dimensions of architectural representation. Sharma, for instance, focuses on Mughal authority in the period following the Mughal emperor Shah 'Alam II's return to Delhi in 1772.[66] She argues that topographical painting was explicitly used to highlight the associations between the Mughal empire and Shahjahanabad, and to assert the notion that the city was a seat of power for the weakened Mughal emperor.[67] Santhi Kavuri-Bauer, meanwhile, offers a Lacanian reading of the representation of Mughal monuments in the Picturesque paintings of William Hodges. She posits that the ruined Mughal buildings and landscapes in Hodges's paintings were meant to symbolize the "lack" of adequate Mughal governance, setting the stage for British intervention. Moreover, she connects the themes of loss present in Hodges's architectural depictions to a wider eighteenth-century prevalence of nostalgia, citing the shahrāshūb poetry of Mir, which lamented the loss or dissolution of the city.[68]

In some ways, the *Palais Indiens* anticipates these later examples, which it predates by at least a decade. The question of agency is particularly relevant for the *Palais Indiens,* as well as the broader Gentil collection, as the "Gentil" material resulted from a production context in which patron, artists, and writers collaborated to produce objects, each playing a role in the conceptualization and making of the objects in question.[69] Similarly, the issues of imperial identity, expansion, and loss, explored by Sharma and Kavuri-Bauer, also come to bear on the architectural representations in the *Palais Indiens.*

Yet the *Palais Indiens,* I argue, represents a distinctive moment in the longer history of the depiction of Indian architecture, embodying its own pictorial conventions and approach. In landscape paintings by Hodges and the Daniells, architecture was but one compositional component of fuller landscape scenes. As discussed above, their body of artworks exhibited connections with notions of the Picturesque developed in Europe, and intersected with British imperial concerns. Later Company School paintings, in which architecture grew into a distinct genre of representation, more compellingly echo the *Palais Indiens,* but were different in execution and import.[70] Even the *Polier Album,* which includes idealized depictions of the Red Fort and Jamiʿ Masjid, is distinctive. As Raffael Gadebusch has shown, although the group does include two depictions of specific monuments, the aim of the painter and patron seems less to document or portray actual buildings, and more to convey idealized garden settings.[71] The *Palais Indiens* stands out in that it made a specific historical argument, underscoring connections between the Mughal architecture of the past and the new architectural style that was popularized in the eighteenth century, especially in the monuments of Awadh. As we have seen, by presenting a select group of seventeenth-century Mughal monuments alongside later Awadhi examples, the creator(s) of the *Palais Indiens* contested, claimed, and reinforced Mughal architectural identity all at the same time. My contention is that these processes were not separate or coincident, but were instead closely intertwined.

MUGHAL ARCHITECTURE GOES GLOBAL

Gentil returned to France in 1778, ready to offer French audiences the mechanisms to encounter and comprehend India. As the *Palais Indiens* traveled from India to France, Mughal architecture began to circulate and be consumed on a global scale. Upon his return to France, Gentil submitted most of his collection to the Royal Library (Bibliothèque du Roi) at Versailles; the collection would ultimately form the core of the Oriental Manuscripts Department of the Bibliothèque nationale de France (BnF). In this context, the *Palais Indiens* was poised to speak to multiple audiences: the royal court at Versailles; the group of early French Orientalists who were pursuing the study of Indian languages and cultures; and a print-consuming public. Mughal architecture, as represented by the *Palais Indiens,* would grow both iconic and abstracted as it helped to enact a set of cultural mediations aimed at these diverse audiences.

The first audience for the collection was the royal court at Versailles. The *Palais Indiens* was a suitable response to the directive earlier issued, by Louis XVI, that colonial representatives acquire maps and plans of French and rival holdings in territories abroad. Although most of the resulting objects were completed by engineers and architects working for the French East India Company, the *Palais Indiens* showed a similar focus on the architecture of newly acquired or desirable territory. The larger Gentil collection was also of special interest to scholars who were in the process of establishing the field of Oriental studies in France. For instance, Louis-Mathieu Langlès, the first keeper of Oriental Manuscripts for the Royal Library (and hence the first keeper of Oriental Manuscripts for the BnF), remarked on its significance for the study of India, as did the head of the Cabinet des Estampes (the later Department of Prints and Photographs).[72] Similarly, they noted the importance of the Indian paintings and drawings acquired by Gentil. In addition, the collection was also connected to Abraham Anquetil-Duperron, the famed French scholar who had lived and worked in India between 1754 and 1762 and was renowned for his translation of ancient Indian and Iranian texts, namely the Sanskrit *Upanishads* (translated from a Persian version) and the Zoroastrian *Zend Avesta.*[73]

Besides these royal and scholarly audiences, the Gentil collection appealed to a popular and commercial audience. For one, the collection was considered a useful repository of Indian motifs and designs. Over a decade after the Gentil materials entered the French collections, it was referenced during consultations for the design of a Sèvres porcelain service. The service was commissioned in honor of the embassy of Tipu Sultan, the south Indian ruler of Mysore who sent three ambassadors to Versailles in 1788, and some thought that the Gentil collection could inspire appropriate visual motifs.[74] In addition, there was a more widespread interest in the depiction of Indian and other cultures, exemplified by the success of Jean-Frédéric Bernard and Bernard Picart's *Religious Ceremonies and Customs of All the Peoples of the World* (1723–43).[75]

Yet, amid all this interest, the *Palais Indiens* experienced a curious and unfortunate fate: it failed to attract the attention that the broader Gentil collection did. There are no reports of architects or historians studying or utilizing the *Palais Indiens.* Scholars did not refer to the studies as they did to the texts in the collection; Langlès, for instance, had reportedly mentioned specific manuscripts in the Gentil collection by title when he attested to its overall value. The *Palais Indiens* also did not seem to register on an image-focused audience in the way that other paintings and drawings in the Gentil corpus did. Nor were the architectural studies reproduced, as were the Picturesque scenes created by Hodges and the Daniells, or collected by a wider public, as were the Company School depictions of architecture. Even the generic name given to the collection—"Indian Palaces"—shows that the range of building types that it depicted was lost on its new audiences. The same fate appears to have awaited studies of Mughal monuments in the collections of other French officials, recently included in a survey published by Jean-Marie Lafont. The Motigny and de Boigne papers, for instance, include watercolor paintings of the Taj Mahal, Jami‛ Masjid, Red Fort, and Humayun's tomb, but little is yet known about their circulation or audience in France.[76] Ultimately, then, the architectural forms depicted in the *Palais Indiens,* originally potent for their specific Mughal referentiality, became generalized. The studies came to stand for Indian architecture at large, and the historicization of architecture originally achieved by the *Palais Indiens* very soon gave way to its abstraction and designification.

❖ ❖ ❖

The *Palais Indiens* is among the earliest known representations dedicated to the portrayal of Indian architecture, and more specifically, remains one of the earliest systematic depictions of Mughal architecture on record.[77] The artists of these studies developed a visual language to convey fundamental architectonic and ornamental information about a group of select buildings from north India, drawing on Mughal, Rajput, and French representational systems for representing architectural space and structure. Through these studies, the Mughal architectural past was both enshrined and connected to the political and social realities of the eighteenth-century present. In the process of claiming the Mughal past as their own, successor states such as Awadh and individual agents such as Gentil codified and constructed a notion of Mughal-ness that could be represented by and claimed through architecture. Even as foreign and regional powers gained political and economic strength during this period and challenged Mughal sovereignty, Mughal cultural authority remained a persistent force, its legacy contested and claimed not only through architectural projects on the ground, but through architectural representations on paper.

In the decades immediately following the completion of the *Palais Indiens,* architecture would attract the attention of artists, scholars, government officials, and tourists, especially those affiliated with the English East India Company. In the 1780s and 1790s, Mughal monuments featured prominently in the romanticized landscapes painted by British artists such as William Hodges and Thomas and William Daniell. Mughal architecture was also among the favorite subjects of artists working in the representational mode associated with Company School painting. While the *Palais Indiens* did not have a traceable influence on these later examples, the collection anticipates the interest in Indian architecture that would emerge in the late eighteenth century and gain impetus in the nineteenth. Yet it is also distinctive not only by virtue of the historical perceptions and political aspirations it embodies, but also for the crucial role it played in putting a set of Mughal buildings forth as a coherent canon of architecture. Ultimately, when the collection traveled to France, its historical specificity was lost. Yet, as we will see, Mughal architectural representation remained a compelling visual force in India in the decades to come, playing an even more crucial role in the formation of historical narratives.

CHAPTER FIVE

Mughal Architecture Between Manuscript and Print Culture

In 1815, the Mughal emperor Akbar II (r. 1806–37) gifted J. T. Roberdean, a British magistrate stationed in north India, a lavishly illustrated 'Amal-i Ṣāliḥ, a classic historical work written in Persian that narrated the reign of Shah Jahan (r. 1628–58), Akbar II's ancestor. Though many editions of the manuscript had been commissioned since it was first composed in 1659 by the court historian Muhammad Salih Kanbo, the 1815 version given to Roberdean stands out for a series of striking architectural renderings included amid its illustrations.[1] The 'Amal-i Ṣāliḥ was the first imperially sponsored Mughal manuscript to include folios devoted to the representation of architecture. Traditionally, Mughal manuscript paintings constituted a well-grounded tradition of repeated themes and fixed genres. These included portraits of royalty and nobility, in which individuals were singled out and often portrayed in their most opulent regalia; frenzied battle scenes, which were usually intended to highlight the glory of the Mughal victor; or depictions of court ceremonial that were filled with countless bodies, obediently lined up in the entourage of the ruler. The 1815 'Amal-i Ṣāliḥ introduced the architectural monument into this repertoire of subject matter, with all of its fixed conventions.

As we learned in Chapter 4, the late eighteenth century witnessed the development of various genres of architectural depiction in India. Given the range of representational modes circulating in the subcontinent, and the wider project of refashioning Mughal imperial identity, the inclusion of architectural paintings in the 'Amal-i Ṣāliḥ cannot be interpreted as a simple mimicry of European artistic practice. Instead, the 'Amal-i Ṣāliḥ adapted a new visual trend—the architectural representation—into an existing framework from the Mughal context: the illustrated manuscript. Moreover, the depictions of architecture in this manuscript exhibit distinctive qualities and were specifically used to render historical textual narratives accessible to varied audiences. Ultimately, by linking the paintings to a Mughal historical text, the manuscript creators rendered the text legible— and made the past accessible and deeply connected to the present—to multilingual and multicultural nineteenth-century audiences.

This chapter accounts for this unprecedented development and considers its long-lasting implications. In introducing architectural representations into the 'Amal-i Ṣāliḥ, the manuscript creators underscored the notion that there was a canon of Mughal architecture with strong historical symbolic associations. Incorporating these portrayals allowed Akbar II to draw on the political achievements of the Mughal past, particularly the reign of Shah Jahan, as embodied in its architectural monuments. By comparing the nineteenth-century version of the *ʿAmal-i Ṣāliḥ* with earlier Shah Jahan chronicles, I demonstrate that the nineteenth-century manuscript deployed images to amplify textual descriptions of architecture, offering a visual narrative that was replete with symbols of imperial authority and that offered a complement to strictly textual narratives.

In part, my purpose in analyzing issues of visuality and textuality is to examine how the Mughals conceptualized and presented their cultural past in the final decades of their political loss. In the later eighteenth century, until the formal British occupation of Delhi, the city was alternately controlled by Afghan, Maratha, and British forces.[2] Finally, in 1803, British forces took over Delhi and designated themselves custodians of the imperial Mughal family. It was in the face of this most recent political challenge that Akbar II commissioned the *ʿAmal-i Ṣāliḥ*, an object that reveals how the Mughals perceived themselves and attempted to assert their imperial status, however tenuous it may have been at that time. In the manuscript, the Mughal monuments of Delhi, still occupied and used by the royal family, are presented as symbols of an illustrious and politically successful past. Through the architectural depictions, Akbar II highlighted the city of Delhi as part of his dynastic past, and thus, as a foundation for his cultural authority. This process involved the representation of what had become a canon of classical Mughal monuments, and their integration into a visual narrative that could speak to multiple audiences. Historicism and cultural authority went hand in hand.

This interpretation of the *ʿAmal-i Ṣāliḥ* underscores how architectural representation had the potential to achieve two interlinked aims: to structure historical narrative and to constitute historical thinking. As a manuscript featuring renderings of architectural monuments, the *ʿAmal-i Ṣāliḥ* played a significant role in asserting the relevance of symbolically charged visual languages in the social construction of imperial authority in nineteenth-century Mughal India. In addition, the manuscript allows us to understand the centrality of architecture in the construction and circulation of Mughal historical narratives at this time, and urges us to think about the pictorial as a viable language of architectural history. Scholars tend to think about the practice of architectural history in South Asia in relation to British colonial writers such as James Fergusson and his multivolume *History of Indian and Eastern Architecture,* or Alexander Cunningham and the Archaeological Survey of India, associating the birth of Indian architectural history with the survey, classification, and documentation methods of nineteenth-century positivism, even as they critique the development of such historical approaches. Instead, the *ʿAmal-i Ṣāliḥ* and related works provide an alternative framework for considering architectural history as a concept and practice in South Asia.

Over the course of the nineteenth century, architectural depictions were increasingly used to lend meaning and order to literary texts. Among the most notable examples were Sangin Beg's *Sayr al-Manāzil* (A tour of the sites, 1836) and Sayyid Ahmad Khan's *Āsār al-Sanādīd* (Vestiges of the past, 1847, revised 1854). In grouping these narratives together and evaluating them in relation to each other, I call into question established historiographies of Indian architectural history, which typically trace its beginnings to the antiquarianism exhibited by organizations such as the Asiatic Research Society, or to the survey and documentary practices of the Archaeological Survey of India. Instead, the *'Amal-i Ṣāliḥ* evinces the historicism and reflexivity that had marked Mughal architectural culture since the late seventeenth century, and that was now making itself evident in architectural representations on the pages of an imperial manuscript from the early nineteenth century.

IMAGE AND TEXT IN THE *'AMAL-I ṢĀLIḤ*

The theme of dynastic history arises early in the progression of the narrative of the *'Amal-i Ṣāliḥ*. Although it begins with the birth of Shah Jahan, the manuscript quickly moves back in time to offer an account of Shah Jahan's predecessors, from the fourteenth-century Mughal progenitor Timur (r. 1370–1405) to the seventeenth-century emperor Jahangir (r. 1605–27), Shah Jahan's father and immediate predecessor. It is only after this point that the text provides a regular accounting of the life and reign of Shah Jahan. The act of connecting past and present had long characterized Mughal illustrated histories. Beginning with the manuscripts of the sixteenth century, when the dynasty was born, Mughal emperors had commissioned copies of their predecessors' memoirs and court chronicles.[3] The *Akbarnāma*, for instance, begins as far back as Adam.

This historicist impulse was clearly evident in painting, with the Mughals commissioning illustrated genealogies and multigenerational portraits. Such images had circulated in the eastern Islamic lands as early as the Timurid period. Genealogical charts with medallion portraits of Timur and his descendants were included in illustrated manuscripts such as the *Ẓafarnāma* of Sharaf al-Din 'Ali Yazdi, which feted Timur's life and accomplishments, and Ulugh Beg's *Ulūs-i arba'a-yi Chingīzī* (The four Chingizid nations).[4] These were similar to a genealogy commissioned by the Timurid prince Khalil Sultan and a jade tomb inscription at the Timurid dynastic mausoleum, the Gur-i Amir.[5] This tradition was directly referenced in Mughal genealogies that followed the same compositional scheme. In a Mughal pictorial genealogy from the 1620s, the emperor Jahangir is shown seated in a portrait medallion, surrounded by portrait medallions of various scales with likenesses of his descendants (fig. 5.1). The connection between this and the Timurid pictorial genealogies is made explicit: beneath the Mughal genealogical chart is a similarly composed one with Timur in the central portrait medallion. The Timurid practice of genealogical portraiture was taken up not only by the Mughals but also by the Ottomans, showing just how widespread this imperial practice was. In the Ottoman case, serial portraits of the Ottoman sultans were produced in the sixteenth and seventeenth centuries. The artists of these works developed a standard iconography whereby individual sultans were

recognizable through certain attributes—such as pose or dress—if not through physiognomic likeness.[6] In both the Ottoman and Mughal case, genealogy, dynastic history, and imperial legitimacy were closely interconnected.[7]

But whereas earlier Mughal emperors—and their predecessors and counterparts in the Timurid and Ottoman empires—had used imperial portraits and textual narratives to delineate continuities between past and present, Akbar II employed architectural representation in the ʿAmal-i Ṣāliḥ to elucidate this same theme. It is telling that it was specifically the reign of Shah Jahan that Akbar II invoked as he attempted to assert imperial status. Not only did Shah Jahan's era signify a high point in the political history of the empire, but Shah Jahan was also the founder of the imperial capital at Delhi and its impressive monuments, including the palace where Akbar II resided and the imperial congregational mosque. Akbar II's occupation of the capital city permitted him access to the trappings, if not the power, of imperial rule.

Just as significantly, it was the imperial architecture of Shah Jahan that formed the basis of the reflexive Mughal style that developed in the late seventeenth and the eighteenth centuries. As we have seen, this style was achieved through a process of imitative response to the architectural models established during Shah Jahan's reign, one that was enacted across a broad range of building types, from mosques and madrasas to shrines and tombs. As this expansive visual culture drew upon the mid-seventeenth-century architectural monuments, and structures such as the Taj Mahal, the Red Fort of Delhi, and the Jamiʿ Masjid served as models, they grew truly iconic. The ʿAmal-i Ṣāliḥ indexes not only the monuments themselves but their subsequent historicization.

The manuscript includes several full-page architectural depictions that evince a striking stylistic consistency. As J. P. Losty has noted, these lie along the processional route of Chandni Chowk.[8] Of note are the imperial buildings: the first gateway of the Red Fort, the Naqqar Khana (second gateway and drum house), the Diwan-i ʿAmm (hall of public audience), and the Jamiʿ Masjid, all executed primarily in a palette of red and white, evoking the trademark Mughal building materials of red sandstone and white marble (figs. 5.2–5.5), just as the Palais Indiens had. In all of the examples, the monuments dominate the pictorial field and are similarly framed: they are centered on the folios, with arcades and walls extending beyond the limits of the frame. People are absent from the compositions, and landscape is kept to a minimum, with only the inclusion of vegetation or a sunset to complement the buildings. The result, as in the Palais Indiens, is a unified group of buildings, bound by palette and composition.

Besides the pictorial attention given to architecture, the consistent approach to representing ornament and space is especially noteworthy. The renderings are not studied, detailed compositions that faithfully reproduce architectural details with precision. Although the patterned textiles that furnished these spaces, including awnings and carpets, are included in the portrayals, the overall emphasis is on the major contours and defining features of the structures, particularly the strong horizontals that define the stretches of

FIGURE 5.2

Artist unknown, *Gateway of the Red Fort, Delhi,* c. 1815. Opaque watercolor and gold on paper, 9 × 15.5 in. (22.8 × 39.4 cm). British Library, London. © The British Library Board, Add. 20735, fol. 368.

FIGURE 5.3

Artist unknown, *Naqqar Khane, Red Fort, Delhi,* c. 1815. Opaque watercolor and gold on paper, 9 × 15.5 in. (22.8 × 39.4 cm). British Library, London. © The British Library Board, Add. 20735, fol. 369.

FIGURE 5.4

Artist unknown, *Diwan-i ʿAmm, Red Fort, Delhi,* c. 1815. Opaque water-color and gold on paper, 9 × 15.5 in. (22.8 × 39.4 cm). British Library, London. © The British Library Board, Add. 20735, fol. 370.

FIGURE 5.5

Artist unknown, *Jami' Masjid, Delhi*, c. 1815. Opaque watercolor and gold on paper, 15.5 × 9 in. (39.4 × 22.8 cm). British Library, London. © The British Library Board, Add. 20735, fol. 373.

walls and rooflines of the buildings treated. Similarly, the artists are not concerned with conveying spatial systems or rendering three-dimensional space. While some elements of the buildings are rendered in perspective, such as the steps of the Jami' Masjid (see fig. 5.5), with its staircase that narrows as it recedes into space, for the most part spaces are collapsed and surfaces flattened. Through these representational techniques, the buildings are effectively transformed from lived spaces, used in the present, into static icons of the past.

This approach to architecture marked a clear departure from Mughal manuscript tradition, demonstrated by a comparison with the seventeenth-century Windsor *Pādshāhnāma*.[9] In the folios of this manuscript, architecture is recognizable and specific. In the painting *Shah Jahan Receiving His Three Eldest Sons,* the audience hall of the Red Fort in Agra provides the setting for a scene at court (fig. 5.6). Architectural elements such as the distinctive, elevated imperial jharoka throne and the paintings in the throne hall lend

specificity to the scene, and to many others in the same manuscript.[10] Special attention is devoted to the projecting capitals at the top of the columns, which extend in multiple directions, and to the motifs on the walls that represent detailed, if not quite naturalistic, renderings of plants and flowers. A few others, such as *The Siege of Daulatabad,* examined in Chapter 4, surrender much pictorial space to the depiction of architecture, yet foreground narrative action enacted by the individuals in the composition (see fig. 4.8). Indeed, human activity and architectural space are closely intertwined in the *Pādshāhnāma.*

By contrast, architecture plays a much more prominent role in the ʿAmal-i Ṣāliḥ paintings, even when the depicted buildings are technically in the background. Two examples in particular illustrate this point: these are the depictions of Shah Jahan in front of the riverfront façade of the Red Fort, and the funeral of Shah Jahan. Both of these paintings seem to belong to the more standard genres of royal portraiture and historical narrative than to the architectural scenes discussed above. The comparative seventeenth-century manuscript paintings we have examined feature Shah Jahan in an imperial setting, such as the jharoka of the hall of public audience. In these examples, the compositions are usually so full of individuals that architectural details are often obscured, and the decorative details of the buildings clamor for attention among a sea of faces and bodies. By contrast, the later, nineteenth-century *'Amal-i Ṣāliḥ* paintings emphasize the architectural setting, asserting that the buildings themselves are worthy of depiction. Again, it should be noted that this independent treatment of buildings is entirely unprecedented in Mughal manuscript painting.

In the image of Shah Jahan and the Red Fort, the palace-fortress's marble pavilions stretch across the folio; on the opposite side of the riverbank, in a different zone of the painting altogether, is Shah Jahan on horseback, with attendants (fig. 5.7).[11] Here, the Red Fort does not serve as mere backdrop. Instead, we see two iconic portraits working in tandem—one of an emperor, and one of the imperial seat of power that he built. Their independence from each other is underlined by the fact that there is no overlap between the portrait and the building's reach. In the funeral scene, the identification between emperor and building is even stronger, as is the monument's potential to stand for the royal body.[12] In this double-page composition, Shah Jahan's casket is being carried atop a bier, covered by a canopy. The funerary ensemble is resplendent: a white casket is covered with a dense floral motif (like the emperor's marble cenotaph in the Taj Mahal, covered with floral motifs in pietra dura), and the canopy is gold and blue. Included in the procession are pallbearers, individuals holding the canopy, and a figure leading the now riderless imperial steed. Behind the funerary procession is a lush hillock with a grove of trees, and beyond this landscape, in the distance but clearly articulated and rendered with precision, is the Taj Mahal. The eye is led directly from the cenotaph to the tomb, with various diagonal lines leading the gaze of the viewer from right to left. Whereas the imperial body is not visible, his most famous imperial commission looms over the composition, metonymically standing in for the emperor (fig. 5.8).

When presented to Roberdean, the *'Amal-i Ṣāliḥ* volume was accompanied by another, companion volume chronicling the reign of Shah Jahan, a *Pādshāhnāma* of Lahori, which included nine paintings and served as a useful counterpart to the *'Amal-i Ṣāliḥ*. A comparison to the Lahori volume allows us to see the uniqueness of the *'Amal-i Ṣāliḥ*, with its unprecedented architectural paintings. The *Pādshāhnāma* volume illustrates major events in the life of the emperor, such as his birth, the festivities held during his accession to the throne, and the wedding of his son Dara Shikoh.[13] Overall, the choice and range of subject matters in this companion volume are much more in keeping with the conventions of sixteenth- and seventeenth-century Mughal manuscripts. *The Birth of Shah Jahan*, for instance, follows the compositional patterns seen in earlier birth scenes, with the infant Shah Jahan surrounded by his mother, female family members, and other women of the imperial zenana, or harem. Similarly, the celebrations at the time of Shah Jahan's accession

are presented in a familiar double-page composition: in the right half of the composition, Shah Jahan sits on a platform throne (*takht*), surrounded by attendants. The left half of the composition features an assembly of musicians providing entertainment for the emperor and court. And in the *Wedding of Dara Shikoh*, the prince processes atop a horse, fireworks illuminating the night sky behind him. This image relates not only to the text, but also to other paintings of the same event, which include similar details and follow the same compositional form.[14]

Thus on the one hand, the nineteenth-century volumes adhere to established visual strategies, using familiar compositions and referencing well-known figures and historical episodes. At the same time, the manuscript creators innovatively introduce the new subject matter of architectural representation into the format of the illustrated manuscript, putting forward a new set of intentions and representational preoccupations. While the number of these dedicated architectural depictions might seem relatively low (there are six in total), the number is proportional in relation to the entire pictorial program of the manuscript. More importantly, however, the very significance of including the architectural folios cannot be overstated. The relevance of this new iconographic system is attested by later illustrated histories that continue this pattern. Illustrated copies of the Shah Jahan chronicles continued to be commissioned well into the 1840s, with architecture as a persistent and prominent feature.[15] An *'Amal-i Ṣāliḥ* from the 1830s, for instance, includes representations of the Taj Mahal, Red Fort, and Jamiʿ Masjid among its eleven illustrations.[16] In this later version, the style of depiction in the 1815 *'Amal-i Ṣāliḥ* has been elaborated to include more landscape elements and a few figures, and the paintings also feature perspectival spatial representation.[17] Yet despite these differences, the focus on architecture, and the decision to include these paintings among the more conventionally themed manuscript illustrations, unmistakably follows the precedent of the 1815 manuscript.

That architecture came to stand for the imperial body is also evident in a lithographed manuscript from 1851, produced during the reign of Bahadur Shah Zafar (r. 1837–58), the last Mughal emperor.[18] Although this is a print work, lithographed and painted manuscripts can be seen on a continuum at this time, when scribes were still producing books even as the press was beginning to take up a new role in India.[19] In addition, the manuscript states that the portraits were reproductions of painted works, and the first portrait, of Timur, is illuminated.[20] The work was compiled for Bahadur Shah Zafar by Muhammad Fakhr al-Din Husain and Hakim Ahsan Ullah Khan, with the artists Ghulam ʿAli Khan and Babar ʿAli Khan. It comprises an exhaustive list of the Mughal emperors and their Timurid predecessors.[21] Thus, like the genealogical portraits discussed earlier, the object asserts a continuity between the original Timurid dynasty and their self-designated successors, the Timurids of India, or Mughals. Alongside chronological tables containing the birth, death, and regnal dates of each ruler are included not only their portraits, but also representations of their tombs. Indeed, the images of the imperial tombs precede the imperial portraits: the domed tomb of Humayun introduces the section on the emperor, the Taj Mahal the section on Shah Jahan. For ʿAlamgir I (r. 1658–1707; d. 1707), there is his open-air grave at Khuldabad, and in the case of Muhammad Shah (r. 1719–48; d. 1748), his burial enclosure at the shrine of Nizam al-Din. The style of the black-and-white lithographed manuscript is spare, emphasizing the iconographic role played by the imperial mausolea. It was this very potential that the ʿAmal-i Ṣāliḥ tapped into and actualized. In the following section, we will consider the import of such a visual system for multicultural and multilingual audiences.

READING PERSIAN, READING PICTURES

The grouping together of the ʿAmal-i Ṣāliḥ paintings suggests that the buildings featured in them were considered a coherent set of monuments. Moreover, they constitute a discrete visual narrative situated within a textual narrative. In this way they are distinct from other paintings in the manuscript, which depict courtly or battle scenes and which are scattered throughout the text, and that assimilate more readily to the character of the stories that are oriented around social activities. Furthermore, while the other scenes are oriented vertically, the architectural renderings are oriented horizontally, requiring the reader to turn the manuscript and engage with these images—or, put another way, requiring the reader to become a viewer (fig. 5.9). This physical disruption, and the associated need for reorientation of the book in hand, draws increased attention to the architectural paintings, highlighting their cohesion as a group and their distinctiveness from the rest of the manuscript. While the architectural portrayals are not the only illustrations in the text, the experience of viewing these paintings sets them apart. For the non-Persian reader, there is a visual text that is so distinct from the literary, that one can in effect "read" this part of the manuscript even if one does not engage with alphabetic text. Architectural representation thus becomes a comprehensible language, while also representing a break in the manuscript's progression.

In representing these buildings, the ʿAmal-i Ṣāliḥ emphasized bold architectural forms over the elaborate ornamental programs of the structures. We have already seen how under Shah Jahan's patronage in the seventeenth century, imperial architecture was characterized by a new ornamental vocabulary that emphasized floral motifs, and that this vocabulary had specific symbolic associations with political power. This theme was developed simultaneously in both the literary and visual spheres; garden metaphors, articulated explicitly in textual form, inspired visual parallels in palatial and funerary architecture associated with the emperor.[22] For example, Shah Jahan's imperial thrones in the palace-fortresses of Agra and Delhi were covered with intricately carved floral motifs, as was his cenotaph in the Taj Mahal. While writers used floral imagery to metaphorically describe the flourishing of the Mughal empire under Shah Jahan's rule, artists used floral imagery to reinforce these symbolic associations. The success of this joint venture between poets and architects suggests an audience steeped in Persianate literary culture, equipped to

FIGURE 5.9
Artist unknown, facing folios
(*Naqqar Khane* and *Diwan-i ʿAmm,
Delhi*), c. 1815. Opaque watercolor
and gold on paper, 15.5 × 9 in.
(39.4 × 22.8 cm) (single folio).
British Library, London. © The
British Library Board, Add. 20735.

perceive the resonances and interconnections between the imagery deployed in both architecture and poetry.[23] Membership in such a developed literary culture was characteristic of the early modern Islamic and Indian courts, from the Ottomans and Safavids to the Mughals and Rajputs.

The audience for the 1815 ʿAmal-i Ṣāliḥ was, of course, not the Persianate literary elite who populated the Mughal court of Shah Jahan, but a British government official (who was the "custodian" of Mirza Jahangir, Akbar II's errant—and imprisoned—son).[24] In devising this image-based language, the creators of the manuscript were able to address a diverse audience of Indians and Britons. Again, the manuscript was ultimately presented to the British government. Many Britons living in nineteenth-century India could read Persian, Urdu, Sanskrit, and other Indian languages; they employed translators and language teachers, and some could actually claim membership in the developed scholarly and literary culture characteristic of early modern India.[25] But in the case of this manuscript, those not educated in Persian could engage with the visual narrative offered by the architectural depictions.

Accordingly, the architectural representations in the 1815 manuscript render monumental and recognizable buildings in bold color and line, visualizing the historic rather than the poetic. For the reader of Persian, the paintings would correspond less to Kanbo's poetic descriptions, and more to the selected textual passages with concrete information about the structures, such as their size and building materials, or passages that recalled events from the ceremonial life of the palace-fortress. For instance, a description of the Diwan-i ʿAmm emphasizes the placement of the hall within the palace complex, its building materials and parts, and the role it played in daily court ceremonial:

> To the west of the Imtiyaz Mahal there is an iwan [pavilion] overlooking the garden of that building. It is of red sandstone, but made white by Multani stone. It has received an elegant polish, like the brightness of the morning, on shell-plaster applied by skillful workmen. Near the ceiling is the jharoka of the Khass-o ʿAmm [Hall of Public Audience], which is the place of the people's prostration. . . . It is built of pure marble . . . 4 gaz by 3 gaz, and is supported by four columns. Behind the jharoka there may be seen a niche, 7 by 2 1/2 gaz, which is famed for its various colored stones inlaid into the wall, and which, through the skill of excellent artists, has been adorned with rare pictures, and a railing of pure gold on three sides. This auspicious place is honored by the emperor, who takes his seat in it early every day. In front of this, there is a magnificent and lofty hall, supported by forty columns, and measuring 67 [gaz] by 24 [gaz].[26]

Kanbo emphasizes the monumentality of the structure by providing its dimensions and information about its layout, and conveys the importance of the building by informing us that the emperor takes his seat in the hall's jharoka throne every day. Although the original seventeenth-century text has remained the same, the omnipresent poetic metaphors are underemphasized in the visual depictions. The textual information highlighted by the paintings includes information about monumental dimensions, expensive materials, and historic relevance.

With this particular emphasis, the architectural depiction celebrates a building type with powerful historical associations. The audience halls in the Mughal palace-fortresses of Delhi, Agra, and Lahore all followed a similar plan: they were all multi-pillared, rectangular, flat-roofed pavilions, realized on a monumental scale (fig. 5.10). Both the Diwan-i ʿAmm, or public audience hall, and the Diwan-i Khass, or private audience hall, adhered to this basic typology, though it was more elaborately realized in the larger space of the Diwan-i ʿAmm. Across the palaces of the three capitals, there were some variations in ornament, proportion, and scale, but the multi-pillared audience hall functioned as the center of court ceremonial in each of these spaces.[27] They also invoked the *chihil sutūn,* or "forty-pillared" assembly halls of Iran, from the ancient hall at Persepolis to Timurid spaces recorded in the sources to the more contemporary Safavid Chihil Sutun in Isfahan (fig. 5.11).[28] As Ebba Koch has argued, the typology of the multi-pillared hall had strong associations with Iranian notions of divine kingship, and with the figure of Solomon in particular.[29] These multiple associations were made tangible first through the construction of multi-column wood timber audience halls, which were ultimately replaced by audience halls realized in stone.[30]

In other words, the depiction of the hall of public audience in the *ʿAmal-i Ṣāliḥ* not only referenced the standing structure, but also a rich history that preceded it and that spoke of the Mughals' dynastic connections to Iran and their claims to universal and divine kingship. It was the decision to favor monumental form over poetic detail that allowed the Mughals to visually signify their illustrious, imperial past and to use visual signs to order the narration of that history. These depictions of seventeenth-century Mughal architecture represent a rejection of its poetic conception. By doing so, they exemplify a clear preference for the historical weight of the built environment, signaling an awareness of Mughal architectural legacies. This significant rupture makes clear the growing historicism of the age and its clear linkage to the concrete design of built form and its conception.

FIGURE 5.10

Diwan-i ʿAmm, Red Fort of Agra, c. 1637.

FIGURE 5.11

Chihil Sutun, Isfahan, begun 1647.

With these goals in mind, it is obvious why Akbar II chose to illustrate this manuscript as a gift to Roberdean. He could have selected any one of a range of other existing texts about Shah Jahan's famed period of rule. Of all the Shah Jahan histories, the *ʿAmal-i Ṣāliḥ* provides the most extensive description of the buildings and urban fabric of Mughal Delhi as it was founded by Shah Jahan in 1639.[31] Other choices included the *Pādshāhnāma* of Qazwini, which chronicles the first ten years of Shah Jahan's reign and was compiled by the royal court historian Mirza Muhammad-Amin Qazwini. But because of its focus on the years 1627–37, it does not include architectural details about Shahjahanabad, the completion of which postdated this period.[32] Another option was a second *Pādshāhnāma*, which covers the first thirty years of the emperor's reign, and was cowritten by the court historians Abd al-Hamid Lahori and his student Muhammad Waris.[33] There were two other histories on the reign of Shah Jahan, works entitled *Shāhjahānnāma* (History of Shah Jahan). The first was composed by the emperor's *wāqiʿa-nawīs* (personal record keeper), Sadiq Khan, and narrates events until 1658 (the year of Shah Jahan's deposition from the throne and house arrest by his son, ʿAlamgir). The second *Shāhjahānnāma*, compiled by ʿInayat Khan, is an abridgment of the *Pādshāhnāma* of Lahori and Waris. In addition to these official prose histories, there are also multiple histories in verse: the *Ẓafarnāma-i Shāh Jahāni* of Muhammad Jan Qudsi Mashhadi, the *Pādshāhnāma* of Yahya Kashi, and the *Shāhjahānnāma* by Abu Talib Kalim of Hamadan and Kashan.[34] Finally, the writings of the Mughal state secretary Chandarbhan Brahman serve as an additional historical record.[35]

Again, this extensive catalogue underscores the point that the makers of the *ʿAmal-i Ṣāliḥ* had a rich repository of texts to choose from, as it was one of several histories of the reign of Shah Jahan. Moreover, all of these were imperially sanctioned narratives composed by court historians and state officials. The focus on this particular seventeenth-century narrative also suggests an active, architecture-focused—but also retrospective—choice, as there were a number of histories dating to the late eighteenth and nineteenth centuries, much closer to the time of the manuscript's commission.[36] The choice of the *ʿAmal-i Ṣāliḥ*, with its architectural accounting and emphasis on the seventeenth century, revealed the potential of architectural representation to shape historical narratives, a capacity that, as the following section demonstrates, would be mined in the decades to come.

THE *ʿAMAL-I ṢĀLIḤ* AND NINETEENTH-CENTURY ARCHITECTURAL HISTORY

In its potential to link architectural representation and textual narrative, the *ʿAmal-i Ṣāliḥ* anticipates later nineteenth-century projects that used architecture to organize the narrative structure and substance of the texts with which they were paired. In considering the Mughal manuscript in relation to these later works, I do not suggest a strict genealogy, whereby the *ʿAmal-i Ṣāliḥ* serves as an origin or paradigmatic template for the architectural histories that would emerge in subsequent decades. Instead, I contend that the manuscript must be located at a transitional point between the historicism evident in the architectural projects of the Mughal eighteenth century, and that which informed the textual geographies written in the nineteenth century. The textual geographies of this period were written in English, Persian, and Urdu, and emphasized the centrality of architecture in constructing histories of Delhi.[37]

One of the first, the *Sayr al-Manāzil,* describes buildings in the city and includes short passages concerning their historical significance.[38] Written between 1818 and 1821 by Sangin Beg, the work is composed in Persian and was originally dedicated to Charles Metcalfe, the British Resident at Delhi from 1813 to 1819.[39] While the manuscript includes a chronologically organized list of the monuments it describes, as a whole, the work is *not* structured chronologically, but rather geospatially. The author begins his account with the symbolic center of Shahjahanabad, the Red Fort. He then goes on to portray such major monuments as the Jamiʿ Masjid, before moving beyond the limits of the walled city to the districts south of it, including descriptions of the tomb of Humayun and the dargah of Nizam al-Din. He then moves to the outskirts of greater Delhi: the area around the Qutb Minar and dargah of Bakhtiyar Kaki.[40] Sangin Beg's focus is not on the Mughal monuments of the city, but rather, the collective structures that make up Delhi's urban fabric. To read the *Sayr al-Manāzil* is truly to take a tour of the sites, one governed by movement across space, rather than to chart development along a linear chronology. A similar logic governs the architectural depictions in the *ʿAmal-i Ṣāliḥ,* which are ordered according to their placement in the city. For instance, just as the gateway of the Red Fort, the Naqqar Khana and the Diwan-i ʿAmm audience hall unfold in that very order, so too are they sequenced in the "space" of the manuscript.

The work likely served a commemorative function, documenting the monuments of Delhi just before Metcalfe's departure from the city to serve as the Resident at Hyderabad. Thomas Metcalfe, brother of Charles and a later British Resident at Delhi, commissioned a similar project in 1843. Entitled *Reminiscences of Imperial Dehlie* and often referenced as the *Dehlie Book,* this work of eighty-nine folios includes over 130 paintings, most of monuments and landscapes in and around Delhi.[41] Originally produced as individual landscapes and studies by the artist Mazhar ʿAli Khan, the images in the album were then bound together and accompanied by brief histories and personal impressions of the represented sites. In addition, Metcalfe's own residence is inserted into the pictorial and textual narrative of the city. The *Dehlie Book* thus reads as a personal memoir of the city (and in fact Metcalfe sent the album to his daughter Emily as she prepared for her first voyage from England to India).[42]

In this account of Delhi, the visual image is foregrounded. The paintings dominate the folios; in some instances, the text veers into the margin, or wraps around an image (fig. 5.12). It is thus architecture that conceptually and visually structures the narrative. In other words, the album is a *muraqqaʿ* in the Indo-Persian tradition, but one that ties together monuments and urban spaces through word and image.[43] Though the *Sayr al-Manāzil,* by contrast, is a textual narrative, it too is structured by the author's spatial perception of the city. While the latter was not illustrated, blank spaces werc left on some of

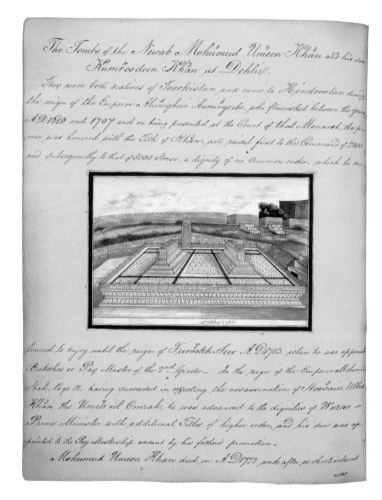

the folios for this very purpose, and it is Delhi's monuments—as they stand in space—that
organize the narrative.

Other types of urban narratives, which were not as architecture-centered, emerged
later in the nineteenth century, though even these drew upon existing Indo-Persian conventions of recounting place and space. One such work was the Persian-language *Mirʾat-i
Gītīnumā* (Mirror of the universe, 1850), written by ʿAbd al-Karim Mushtaq.[44] Although
the text, commissioned by Lord Hardinge, governor-general of India, was supposed to
be a history of the Qutb Minar and related monuments, the author instead composed a
universal geography, which included Delhi among its subjects.[45] In its scope, the *Mirʾat-i
Gītīnumā* was not unlike the *Bustān al-Siyāḥat* (Garden of voyaging, 1833–34), by the
Iranian author Zayn al-ʿAbidin Shirwani.[46] Shirwani writes of forty different real and
virtual cities, both those he had visited and those he had "only heard about but considered noteworthy."[47] His account begins with a history of Delhi; an overview of the city's
geographical characteristics, such as its situation on a large open plain; and references
to types of buildings, including "elegant mosques, fine Sufi hospices, attractive markets

with overflowing shops, delightful gardens and orchards, and countless tombs of saints and kings."[48] He makes a special mention of the Red Fort, which he says is built of stone "the colour of sumac berries."[49] His description finishes with an overview of the political powers that have held Delhi as a capital city, from the Ghurids to the Mughals, and praises the beauty and accomplishments of the residents of the city.[50] In their expansive and encyclopedic scope, these texts are written in the tradition of the *Haft Iqlim* (Seven climes) of Amin Ahmad Razi, the sixteenth- and seventeenth-century Safavid geographer and author.[51] They also incorporate elements of the shahrāshūb and tazkira genres, which focused on urban settings, as discussed in Chapter 2. Thus the "new" genre of urban history writing drew upon existing Indo-Persian genres and traditions.

It was not only Delhi that was the subject of urban portrayal in the nineteenth century. The architecture of two other former Mughal capitals, Agra and Lahore, also received attention. Like many of the texts under discussion, these resulted either from British patronage or encouragement. The *Tafrih al-ʿImārāt* (Account of the buildings, 1824), focusing on the architecture of Agra, was one such example.[52] Written in Persian and containing thirteen color drawings, the text was composed by Lalah Sil Chand, a student at Government College, and was commissioned by John Steven Lushington, a collector and magistrate at Agra.[53] In Lahore, Noor Ahmad Chishti published the *Tahqiqaat Chishti: Tarikh-e-Lahor ka Encyclopedia* (Chishti's inquiries: An encyclopedia of Lahore's history, 1867).[54] In this case, it was a British assistant commissioner, William Coldstream, who made the suggestion. While this later work was written in Urdu, it connected to the earlier Persian literary tradition embodied by the works discussed above, and was composed in "a literary Persianate Urdu."[55]

Many of these texts function as critical precursors or contemporaneous texts to the renowned *Āsār al-Sanādīd* of 1847, long thought to be the first history of the buildings of Delhi and one of the earliest architectural histories produced by an Indian scholar.[56] Written in Urdu by the renowned intellectual Sayyid Ahmad Khan, *Āsār al-Sanādīd* was revised and republished in 1854 by the same author.[57] The first edition was a six-hundred-page, four-volume work that included lithographed woodcuts illustrating the monuments discussed in the text, based on renderings by the artists Mirza Shah Rukh Beg and Fayz ʿAli Khan. Like the *Sayr al-Manāzil,* the 1847 *Āsār al-Sanādīd* is organized geospatially, with buildings grouped together not by type or date but by location; moreover, it also includes historical notes on Delhi. The work is divided into four parts: the first concentrates on what would today be considered the outskirts of Delhi; the second on the area of the Old Fort; the third on Shahjahanabad; and the fourth on the history, culture, and climate of the city.[58] The text thus subverts the primacy of the imperial center in the imagination of the reader. Extramural spaces that had grown more prominent in the eighteenth century—and been the site of Mughal patronage—now played a crucial role in the mental mapping of the city.

Though this ordering also broadly corresponds with the chronological development of the city, the result is a narrative that unfolds in spatial terms. This emphasis on architectural space is vividly conveyed through the incorporation of the roughly 130 lithographed illustrations. The artists of the renderings, Mirza Shah Rukh Beg and Fayz ʿAli Khan, were both included in a description in the fourth part of the *Āsār al-Sanādīd*.[59] Mirza Shah Rukh Beg, in particular, is believed to have been part of the community of artists in Delhi responsible for producing many of the architectural and topographical depictions that circulated at this time. He was the nephew of the painter Ghulam ʿAli Khan, who worked as both a Mughal court painter and for British patrons, including James Skinner.[60]

The *Āsār al-Sanādīd* is believed to be one of the first illustrated lithographed books in India.[61] Mughal painters had long played a central role in the reception of print culture in India, a phenomenon that can be witnessed as early as the sixteenth century, when Jesuit missionaries brought European prints and books to the courts of Akbar and Jahangir. Mughal artists, in turn, appropriated imagery and techniques from this European material.[62] Yael Rice has argued that Mughal artists were perfectly positioned to absorb the pictorial style and technologies represented by European prints, since they had long been exposed to and practiced a tradition of line-based art exemplified by calligraphy.[63] Indeed, the woodcuts in the *Āsār al-Sanādīd* demonstrate just such a skillful adaptation. The manuscript paintings in the *ʿAmal-i Ṣāliḥ*, and indeed the Company School architectural paintings circulating in the early nineteenth century, used saturated fields of color to render vivid portrayals of architectural monuments. In the lithographed woodcuts, such as the depiction of the Akbarabadi mosque, cross-hatching instead adds depth to the composition, as in the multiple portals leading to individual aisles (fig. 5.13). Line is also

used to convey other details, from the brickwork on the mosque's domes to its extensive courtyard and staircase, all with an appealing tactility. The resulting images are used to illustrate the text extensively, with images interspersed throughout the book alongside textual descriptions of the related monuments and spaces. Just as one visually encountered the Delhi of Shah Jahan and his Mughal descendants in the *'Amal-i Ṣāliḥ*, so too does one act as both reader and viewer when presented with the 1847 *Āsār al-Sanādīd*.

Given the focus on architecture in the textual and visual narrative, it is striking that the fourth section of the work does not concentrate on architecture, but on the history and people of Delhi. It begins with an account of the historic populations of Delhi, and goes on to discuss language and climate. The author finishes with a catalogue of the city's notables, from shaykhs, poets, and musicians to calligraphers, painters, and intellectuals.[64] This last section is significant for two major reasons. First, it connects directly to the Persian tazkira tradition (discussed in Chapter 2), whereby so-called "biographical dictionaries" of individuals (usually religious figures, poets, or viziers) transcended a purely biographical function to reveal much about the cultural milieu in which such figures operated.[65] Second, in this earlier edition of the *Āsār al-Sanādīd*, it is a narrative about architecture that provides the larger structure for a portrayal of the city and its inhabitants; and in turn, a description of the city's spaces is incomplete without an account of how those spaces are animated. Architectural, urban, and social and cultural histories are thus inextricably linked, and conveyed in a text- *and* image-based narrative.

This narrative logic is absent from the 1854 edition, which features substantial revisions and a reorganization of the work along chronological lines.[66] The 1854 version begins with tables listing, in chronological order, the individuals and dynasties that had historically ruled in the city. Sayyid Ahmad Khan also expanded the description of buildings, including more examples in his survey. But instead of the illustrative woodcuts that were printed in the 1847 edition, the 1854 version includes an appendix of building inscriptions and presents data about the buildings in tabular form. In addition, he painstakingly provides a detailed bibliography about the architecture he surveys.

Thus, the earlier 1847 *Āsār al-Sanādīd*—of which there are fewer, less easily located copies—takes an approach to architectural history that is based on a spatial and social experience of the urban setting. In the works, a history of buildings is tied to a history of people, a history of a lived space.[67] It emphasizes the idea of the city as a living and lived space, celebrating its inhabitants and its vibrancy (following the conventions of the shahrāshūb genre), or narrating the artistic, cultural, and socioreligious communities that formed the living fabric of the city (continuing the tazkira tradition).[68] The connection to Indo-Persian literary tradition is underscored by the very title of the work, which was taken from a poetic couplet by 'Urfi Shirazi, a poet at the court of Akbar:

> *Az naqsh o nigār-e dar o diwar-e shikasta*
> *āsār padīd ast sanādīd 'ajam rā*

The marks and decorations of ruined gates and walls
reveal traces of the princes of Iran.[69]

The Persianate form of the work is also conveyed by the title page of the published book, which lithographs the type of illuminated frontispiece that one would find in a Mughal manuscript.

But beyond this idea of the city as an animated space, the 1847 version of the text showed the potential of architecture and urban space to play a key role in organizing—versus merely enriching—broader historical narratives. Despite the obvious differences between this textual geography and the *ʿAmal-i Ṣāliḥ*, the architectural depictions in each of these works function similarly with respect to the project of history writing. In contrast, the 1854 *Āsār al-Sanādīd* is more closely aligned with the survey, documentation, and classification methods that gained currency in north India in the later nineteenth century, primarily through the growth of antiquarian societies such as the Archaeological Society of Delhi and the establishment of the Archaeological Survey of India in 1861.[70] Sayyid Ahmad Khan collaborated with the Delhi Archaeological Society as he revised the work, adapting it for publication. In the preface of the second version, he thanks, among others, A. A. Roberts, a collector and magistrate who also served as vice-president of the Archaeological Society of Delhi.[71] It was Roberts who urged Sayyid Ahmad Khan to revise the work in order that it might be published in English; Sayyid Ahmad Khan did so, gearing the new version toward the British antiquarian audience represented by the Archaeological Society.

In the process, he exposed a significant shift in modes of producing architectural knowledge in India, with the earlier mode exemplified by the *ʿAmal-i Ṣāliḥ*. In the 1854 version of the *Āsār al-Sanādīd,* Mughal architecture was evacuated of its constitutive capacity to structure and enact history; it moved squarely into the territory of historical subject, rather than historical agent. The *Āsār al-Sanādīd* is not a lone text, but rather a prime example of the approach espoused by nineteenth-century scholars, and a marker of the profound shift away from the mode of historicism evident in earlier Mughal buildings and their representations.

The shift was connected to broader changes within the genre of urban writing, discernible in writing on other cities, such as Lahore.[72] William Glover argues that Chishti's *Tahqiqaat Chishti: Tarikh-e-Lahor ka Encyclopedia,* discussed earlier, evinces an awareness of the criticisms leveled against the earlier version of the *Āsār al-Sanādīd.* As a result, the text is organized by building type, in a broadly chronological framework. Chishti begins the work with a history of Lahore from the ancient to contemporary periods, following it with his listing of monuments; he bases his account on manuscript and inscriptional sources. However, Chishti also incorporates information learned from personal conversations, often kept alive through oral tradition. He thus equally relies on a knowledge base that was "affective and embodied, deriving its authority and relevance through social relationships rather than scientific methodology."[73] Some decades later, Syad Muhammad Latif wrote the English language *Lahore: Its History, Architectural Remains, and Antiquities, with an Account of Its Modern Institutions, Inhabitants, Their Trade, Custom, &c.* (1892).[74] While he partially based the text on Chishti, Latif correlated the earlier text with additional manuscript sources, supplementing Chishti's "affective knowledge" with research sources and methodologies that would read as "objective," and that were borrowed from archaeology and architectural history as practiced by British colonial agents in South Asia.[75] It is this theme that we turn to now.

PRODUCING THE MUGHAL PAST

Much scholarship has focused on antiquarianism and archaeology as emerging fields of study in the nineteenth century, and in particular, the close interconnections between knowledge production and colonial strategies of control.[76] Those who have analyzed the shifts between the first and second versions of the *Āsār al-Sanādīd* have positioned the second version of this text as the starting point of a tradition of positivist architectural history, linked to the growth of British archaeology in India.[77] Indeed, Sayyid Ahmad Khan was inducted into the Archaeological Society of Delhi, and he had close contacts with its members. The *Āsār al-Sanādīd* received a positive scholarly reception from such individuals as Aloys Sprenger, the principal of the Delhi College, and Henry M. Elliot, the translator and scholar who would later become (in)famous for translating and editing Indian historical sources in the multivolume *The History of India as Told by Its Own Historians.*[78]

Alongside and connected to archaeology, architectural history was also becoming a crucial field of inquiry in nineteenth-century India. But it was not only Mughal architecture that was subject to new modes of theorization. One of the most striking examples of the "new" architectural history of the nineteenth century was Ram Raz's *Essay on the Architecture of the Hindus* (1834, published posthumously).[79] While not an academic by training, Ram Raz collected and translated *silpashastras* (the term "silpashastra" is usually translated as "architectural treatise," but, as a genre, encompasses a wider group of longstanding proscriptive texts for architecture in India).[80] Like Sayyid Ahmad Khan, Ram Raz had professional and scholarly ties to the English East India Company. He began his career as a clerk for the company, went on to a position at the East India Company College, and eventually became a judge and magistrate. Upon completing the *Essay*, he was elected to the Royal Asiatic Society, and his work drew widespread attention from figures such as the landscape painter William Daniell to the architect Sir John Soane.[81]

In his *Essay*, Ram Raz presented the idea that there was a coherent "ancient Hindu" architecture, and that it was comparable to Greek and Roman architecture. He developed a system of ordonnance for depicting and conveying architectural systems, one that he claimed was based on the shastras. He thus established a set of "Hindu orders," comparable to the Doric, Ionic, and Corinthian orders from the column-based system of classical

Greek orders. While the *Essay* and the *Āsār al-Sanādīd* differ in their format and mode of presentation, what the two works share is the idea of conceptualizing the Indian architectural past according to an epistemological framework that aligned with British interests and audiences. In conceptualizing Delhi's architectural past in this way, the revised, later *Āsār al-Sanādīd* departed from earlier modes of Indo-Persian historical narration. These two texts mark a shift in the sensibility of historicism that seemed to have been alive with the *'Amal-i Ṣāliḥ* and related efforts.

Central to the debate concerning the production of architectural and other types of cultural and historical knowledge has been the question of Indian "agency."[82] Thus far, this book has gone further than ascribing agency to individual Indian scholars, exploring instead how the idea of historicism permeated Mughal architectural culture during this period. In the textual geographies of the nineteenth century, Mughal architecture is folded into a broader architectural history of Delhi: the Mughal past is historicized in relation to, and together with, a more distant past. But in nineteenth-century Delhi the Mughal past was the recent past, a past that had been conceptualized in relation to a notion of architectural history that had circulated in Mughal north India since the late seventeenth century.

❖ ❖ ❖

Rather than restrictively defining architectural history as a mode of knowledge production that was brought to India by British scholars, I embrace architectural histories that were produced locally, in the visual and spatial realms, as well as that of the linguistic. This language would be appropriate for a literary elite steeped in Persianate culture, where the pictorial and the textual were already intertwined. It would also be suitable for British audiences growing ever more familiar with images of Mughal architecture through the genre of Company Painting. As discussed in Chapter 4, this artistic genre comprises ethnographic painting, studies of flora and fauna, customs and manners albums, and architectural representations. But as I have shown, there was much more at play in the representation of Mughal monuments than a taste for the faraway or a souvenir of the exotic. Undoubtedly, the paintings in the *'Amal-i Ṣāliḥ* had currency because of the popularity of Company Painting. But examining their inclusion in an imperial manuscript, and their relationship to textual history, reveals the larger historical stakes of these paintings.

What was at issue in the manuscript paintings of the *'Amal-i Ṣāliḥ* was the legacy of the Mughal past, and its construction in the nineteenth-century present. As the Mughals undertook the task of representing themselves to new audiences, they took a decidedly retrospective approach, turning to the architectural achievements of their predecessors to counter the losses of the present. In the process, Mughal architecture emerged as both a historical and historicized entity, linking a sense of self to a past that was not fixed or static, but instead carefully and purposely framed. For the Mughal artists and patrons of the early 1800s, the pursuits of claiming the past and constructing narratives of the past were linked to each other, and to the project of architectural representation.

Conclusion

From Historicization to Abstraction

This book has centered on the fundamental question of how the *concept* of Mughal architecture emerged over the course of the long eighteenth century. It has considered the constitution of Mughal architecture both as an architectural style and historical category, and the specific aesthetic, political, and cultural dimensions of this process. The writing of Mughal architectural history is typically thought to be the product of the British antiquarians, archaeologists, and historians who surveyed, documented, and classified Indian architecture in the nineteenth century. But before the establishment of the Archaeological Survey of India or the publication of James Fergusson's *History of Indian and Eastern Architecture,* a notion of architectural history circulated among the architects, patrons, and audiences of the late Mughal empire. Over the course of the Mughal eighteenth century, architecture played a multidimensional role in the formation of historical subjectivity: monuments both served as subjects of inquiry, while also providing a structural and conceptual logic for the construction of historical imagination, perception, and narrative.

The architectural style that we think of as "Mughal" began to take historical and aesthetic shape in the late seventeenth century. Architects and patrons joined forces to produce a standardized architectural style that served as an indisputable marker of Mughal imperial identity. They turned to a recently established imperial style, visible in such monuments as the Taj Mahal, and adapted it by adjusting building proportions and rendering spatial surfaces with greater dimensionality. The resulting Mughal style was both innovative and historically rooted, and served as the dynasty's signature architectural idiom over the next century and a half. In the early decades of the eighteenth century, it proliferated across the Mughal capital at Delhi across a variety of building types, from madrasas to imperial tombs. Simultaneously, Mughal monuments from the past, such as the Jami' Masjid of Shah Jahan, were quoted in smaller building projects sponsored by the nobility and the urban elite. Through the combined forces of reflexivity and recursivity, a recognizable Mughal style, as well as specific Mughal monuments, were historicized. This process was one that unfolded publicly and visibly, as many of these new building projects were located at highly trafficked spaces, such as Sufi shrines or major urban thoroughfares. Beginning in the mid-eighteenth century, Mughal visual codes were appropriated and reinforced even more emphatically. A prime case in point is the funerary complex of

Safdar Jang, prime vizier of the Mughal empire and nawab of Awadh. With its revival of an imperial architectural tradition, identified by a monumental domed mausoleum set within elaborate funerary gardens in a chahār bāgh, the tomb of Safdar Jang posits the Awadhi dynasty as the inheritors of the imperial Mughal tradition.

Issues of historicization and codification continued to loom large in the later eighteenth century, when Mughal monuments were represented on paper, in the form of architectural studies and in imperial manuscripts. The *Palais Indiens* collection of architectural renderings, commissioned by Jean-Baptiste Gentil and produced by an Indian artist in Faizabad, demonstrate how the Mughals' architectural legacy was manipulated and historicized at this time. In this collection, seventeenth-century architecture is described in the visual language of eighteenth-century monuments, especially those sponsored by the Awadhi nawabs. To do so, the artists presented the architectural monument as a distinct subject of depiction and historical inquiry, revealing the potential not only of built architecture, but also its representation on paper, to play a role in the perception of the past and the construction of historical narrative.

In the early decades of the nineteenth century, architectural representation would play an even larger role in the formation of Mughal histories. For the first time, architectural depiction would emerge as a distinctive genre in imperial Mughal manuscripts. In the *ʿAmal-i Ṣāliḥ*, a set of depictions of Mughal monuments feature prominently in the object's visual program. These are oriented in such a way that they can be "read" both in relation to, and as distinct from, the text, offering a visual history of architecture that complements and stands independent from the textual description of the same buildings. This important imperial manuscript vividly displays how architecture was used both to convey history and to structure historical narrative. Later in the nineteenth century, printed textual geographies, written in Persian and Urdu, included architectural representations among their pages. Like the paintings in the *ʿAmal-i Ṣāliḥ*, these accounts of Delhi and its history were not organized according to a strict linear chronology. Instead, the structure of these works was based on the spatial ordering of the city. In other words, by the mid-nineteenth century, the act of conceptualizing Delhi's past was inseparable from the act of considering its architectural and urban spaces, especially Mughal imperial zones.

Thus while it did not take a textual form or follow the principles of positivism espoused by later architectural historians, the architectural culture of the eighteenth-century Mughal empire, comprising both built architecture and two-dimensional architectural representations, did offer a vision of Mughal architectural history. In recent years, scholars have eloquently illuminated the modes of historicism that circulated in early modern South Asia prior to the advent of European colonialism.[1] While most scholarly attention has been directed to an exciting range of textual sources, the visual, material, and spatial spheres were just as integral to the formation of historical knowledge and narratives in the late Mughal empire. Mughal architects, artists, and patrons not only referenced the past in their projects, they also framed that past for reception by contemporary

FIGURE 6.1
Royal Pavilion, Brighton, 1803–32.

audiences, constituting a historical subjectivity that centered around Mughal architecture.

Ironically, the historical specificity and reflexivity that characterized eighteenth-century Mughal architectural culture eventually gave way to an abstracted history in the later nineteenth century, when the Mughal architectural language first codified and historicized in the long eighteenth century developed into a supra-dynamic idiom associated more generally with rulership and luxury. Architects from London to Lucknow developed distinctive reinterpretations of the Mughal visual idiom, simultaneously referencing and abstracting aspects of Mughal architecture. In Britain, John Nash and Humphry Repton built the Royal Pavilion at Brighton, sponsored by George IV of England while he was Prince Regent (1803–32; fig. 6.1). Between 1815 and 1823, the architects renovated an existing palace, adding a cast-iron superstructure of bulbous domes and chhatrī-topped minarets as well as a façade of cusped arches.[2] These forms, once identified strictly as Mughal, had become generalized enough that the Brighton Pavilion was described as incorporating an "Indian" style: in his 1808 essay accompanying proposed designs for the Brighton Pavilion, Repton remarks on the introduction of "Indian" architecture into the palaces and houses of England.[3]

In India, buildings were constructed in a European Neoclassical style or in the newly developing "Indo-Saracenic" idiom. The Murshidabad palace of 1837 in Bengal features a Neoclassical façade in the Doric order, and was built by Duncan McLeod of the Bengal Engineers. While it was meant to house the nawabs of Bengal, the palace was paid for and built under the direction of the British, who had suzerainty over the province.[4] Later British-sponsored projects in India were constructed in the Indo-Saracenic style, which fused elements of Indian and Gothic revival architecture.[5] This mode was exemplified by Mayo College, built in the 1870s in Ajmer, Rajasthan (fig. 6.2).[6] The brainchild

FIGURE 6.2

Mayo College, Ajmer, 1870s.

of Lord Mayo, the viceroy of India (1869–72), the college was conceived of as a boarding school for the princes of Rajasthan. It includes Mughal and Rajput architectural features, such as chhatris, jalis, and cusped arches, woven together in a multilevel composition crowned by a prominent clock tower.

In contrast to the "Indianizing" trend in Britain and the deployment of new hybrid styles in India, at the Mughal center there was a revival of forms coded explicitly as Mughal. The nineteenth-century Mughal emperors fashioned their own distinctive responses to the architectural idiom of the previous centuries. This was the case when Akbar II (r. 1806–37) and Bahadur Shah II (r. 1837–58) inhabited the Zafar Mahal, the palace introduced at the start of this book, which exhibited clear visual associations with the Mughal past. The façade of the Zafar Mahal featured a monumental gateway reminiscent of earlier Mughal forts and palaces, as well as an extensive use of red sandstone and white marble, which were signature Mughal building materials (fig. 6.3). That the visual program of the Zafar Mahal strongly signified Mughal-ness is clear when it is compared with other nineteenth-century projects in India.

Given its visual contrast with contemporary projects, which conspicuously drew on European architectural forms, the Zafar Mahal invokes the Mughal visual idiom that had been current in seventeenth- and early eighteenth-century India. While Britain increased its political and economic power in the subcontinent during the nineteenth century, particularly after the annexation of Delhi in 1803, the Mughal emperors continued to maintain a carefully constructed symbolic authority, staged primarily in Delhi. This process involved the ongoing manipulation of symbolic forms and recoding of space, issues explored in this book in the context of the long eighteenth century. The Zafar Mahal palace is situated on a site adjoining the dargah of Bakhtiyar Kaki, its spatial layout and the choice of site speaking to the significant alterations in the Mughal socioreligious order and urban reconfigurations analyzed in Chapter 2. Additionally, the use of Mughal architectural forms associated with fortress-palaces commissioned at the height of Mughal

FIGURE 6.3
Zafar Mahal, Delhi, c. 1806–58.

political power, in the seventeenth century, suggests a process of appropriation similar to that which characterized art and architectural projects in the later eighteenth century, from the funerary complex of Safdar Jang to the *Palais Indiens* and the 1815 *ʿAmal-i Ṣāliḥ*. Like these other examples, the Zafar Mahal does not merely reference architecture from the past. It casts "Mughal architecture" as a distinctive stylistic and historical category, one that proved to be flexible and dynamic, capable of framing the past and generating new meanings for the present.

NOTES

Introduction

1. Crinson, *Empire Building;* Dadlani, "'Palais Indiens' Collection of 1774."

2. Fergusson, *History of Indian and Eastern Architecture.*

3. This subject is treated extensively in Crinson, *Empire Building.* On the formation of interpretive paradigms in the nineteenth century, see the introduction to Juneja, *Architecture in Medieval India.*

4. Havell, *Indian Architecture.*

5. Brown, *Indian Architecture,* 112.

6. Goetz, "Qudsia Bagh at Delhi." Goetz also insists that the ornamentalism in the Qudsiyya Bagh complex indicates a "Hinduisation" of architecture in the late Mughal era, which he explains as the result of the expansion of the empire and the "Hindu origin" and "Hindu spirit" of Qudsiyya Begum, a Hindu convert and courtesan who eventually married the emperor Muhammad Shah (r. 1719–48).

7. This lacuna is highlighted in the bibliographic essay in Asher, *Architecture of Mughal India,* 354–55.

8. Key studies along these lines include Asher, *Architecture of Mughal India;* Begley, "Myth of the Taj Mahal"; Brand, "Orthodoxy, Innovation, and Revival"; Lisa Golombek, "From Tamerlane to the Taj Mahal," in *Essays in Islamic Art and Architecture: In Honor of Katharina Otto-Dorn,* ed. Abbas Daneshvari (Malibu: Undena, 1981), 43–50; Koch, *Mughal Architecture;* Neeru Misra, *The Garden Tomb of Humayun: An Abode in Paradise* (New Delhi: Aryan, 2003); D. Fairchild Ruggles, "Humayun's Tomb and Garden: Typologies and Visual Order," in Petruccioli, *Gardens in the Time of the Great Muslim Empires,* 173–86; and Wescoat and Wolschke-Bulmahn, *Mughal Gardens.*

9. See works by Catherine Asher: "Architecture of Murshidabad"; "Later Mughals and Mughal Successor States"; and "Piety, Religion, and the Old Social Order."

10. Kavuri-Bauer, *Monumental Matters.*

11. Blake, *Shahjahanabad.*

12. Gupta, *Delhi Between Two Empires;* and Hosagrahar, *Indigenous Modernities.*

13. Ehlers and Krafft, *Shāhjahānābād, Old Delhi.*

14. These include Chenoy, *Shahjahanabad, a City of Delhi;* Frykenberg, *Delhi Through the Ages;* and Kumar, *Present in Delhi's Pasts.* Two exceptions from the Frykenberg volume are Bayly, "Delhi and Other Cities"; and Chandra, "Cultural and Political Role of Delhi."

15. Alam, *Crisis of Empire;* C. A. Bayly, *Rulers, Townsmen, and Bazaars: North Indian Society in the Age of British Expansion, 1770–1870* (Cambridge: Cambridge University Press, 1983).

16. For an excellent discussion of the debates in the study of eighteenth-century India, see Travers, "Eighteenth Century in Indian History."

17. Bruijn and Busch, *Culture and Circulation;* Busch, "Hidden in Plain View"; Busch, *Poetry of Kings;* Dudney, "Desire for Meaning"; Hakala, *Negotiating Languages;* Kia, "Adab as Literary Form and Social Conduct"; Pauwels, "Cosmopolitan Soirées"; S. Sharma, "City of Beauties"; S. Sharma, "If There Is a Paradise on Earth.'"

18. Dalrymple and Sharma, *Princes and Painters;* Losty, *Sita Ram's Painted Views of India;* Roy, "Origins of the Late Mughal Painting Tradition"; Roy, "Revival of the Mughal Painting Tradition"; Roy, "Some Unexpected Sources for Paintings."

19. This particular recent trend has been placed in historiographical perspective in N. Eaton, "'Enchanted Traps?'" Also see N. Eaton, *Colour,*

Art and Empire; N. Eaton, *Mimesis Across Empires;* and Jasanoff, *Edge of Empire.*

20. The exhibition catalogues are Dalrymple and Sharma, *Princes and Painters;* and Gude and Markel, *India's Fabled City.* While its focus was not exclusively the eighteenth century, see Losty and Roy, *Mughal India.*

21. Avcıoğlu, *"Turquerie";* Avcıoğlu and Flood, *Globalizing Cultures;* Bleichmar and Martin, *Objects in Motion;* Leibsohn and Peterson, *Seeing Across Cultures;* Saurma-Jeltsch and Eisenbeiss, *Power of Things.* The theme of mobility has also been a concern in early modern art historical studies outside of the eighteenth century. For a key example, see David Young Kim, *The Traveling Artist in the Italian Renaissance: Geography, Mobility, and Style* (New Haven, CT: Yale University Press, 2014).

22. Hamadeh, *City's Pleasures;* Rüstem, "Architecture for a New Age."

23. Khera, "Marginal, Mobile, Multilayered"; Khera, "Picturing India's 'Land of Kings'"; Roy, "Origins of the Late Mughal Painting Tradition"; Roy, "Revival of the Mughal Painting Tradition"; Roy, "Some Unexpected Sources for Paintings"; Sachdev and Tillotson, *Building Jaipur;* Y. Sharma, "In the Company of the Mughal Court."

24. Khera, in particular, discusses the importance of assessing the "translocal" in addition to the transcultural in Khera, "Marginal, Mobile, Multilayered."

25. The challenges facing the field of eighteenth-century art history were the subject of a CAA roundtable held by *Journal 18.* See Michael Yonan, "Eighteenth-Century Perspectives: On the *Journal 18* and Frick Roundtable," *Journal 18* (April 2017), http://www.journal18.org/1702. Yonan writes of "a real danger that accompanies the field's expansion. Along with bigger numbers and increased visibility may come pressure to standardize our approaches, canonize objects, fine-tune methodologies, and create a unified conception of what the eighteenth century offers the larger art-historical community of which it is a part."

26. Alam and Subrahmanyam, *Mughal State;* Richards, *Mughal Empire.*

27. The reason for the success of these rebellions has been theorized and debated by numerous historians. The case of the Sikhs was most notably analyzed in Alam, *Crisis of Empire.* For a succinct discussion of the dissolution of the Mughal empire in comparative perspective with the Ottomans and Safavids, see Dale, *Muslim Empires,* 256–70.

28. Richards, *Mughal Empire,* 253–63. For the case of Awadh especially, see Alam, *Crisis of Empire.*

29. Cole, *Roots of North Indian Shīʿism,* 50; Barnett, *North India Between Empires,* 21–22.

30. Llewellyn-Jones, *Fatal Friendship.*

31. Leonard, "Hyderabad Political System."

32. Travers, *Ideology and Empire,* 3–5.

33. Stern, *Company-State.*

34. Marsh, *India in the French Imagination,* chap. 1. Wellington, *French East India Companies.*

35. Jasanoff, *Edge of Empire,* 17–23.

36. In 1719, for instance, before the accession of Muhammad Shah (r. 1719–48), two imperial candidates were installed on the throne for a short number of months. Richards, *Mughal Empire,* 273.

37. For a full description of these events, see Cheema, *Forgotten Mughals.*

38. On the relationship between Sufism and Indian political history, see Ernst, *Eternal Garden.*

39. Cole, *Roots of North Indian Shīʿism,* 22–27; Richards, *Mughal Empire,* 171–77.

40. Cole, *Roots of North Indian Shīʿism,* 23.

41. Asher, *Architecture of Mughal India;* Brand, "Orthodoxy, Innovation, and Revival"; Koch, *Complete Taj Mahal;* Koch, *Mughal Architecture.*

42. Evers and Thoenes, *Architectural Theory;* Hart and Hicks, *Paper Palaces;* Necipoğlu, *Age of Sinan;* Payne, *Architectural Treatise;* Sinan, *Sinan's Autobiographies: Five Sixteenth-Century Texts,* Studies and Sources in Islamic Art and Architecture, vol. 11 (Leiden: Brill, 2006).

43. Ali, *Invoking the Past;* Aquil and Chatterjee, *History in the Vernacular;* Chakrabarty, *Provincializing Europe;* K. Chatterjee, *Cultures of History;* K. Chatterjee, "History as Self-Representation"; Guha, "Speaking Historically"; Pollock, *Forms of Knowledge;* Rao, Shulman, and Subrahmanyam, *Textures of Time;* Subrahmanyam, "Hearing Voices"; Subrahmanyam, "On World Historians."

44. For a discussion of alphabetic versus other texts and literacies, see Cummins and Rappaport, *Beyond the Lettered City.*

45. Roxburgh, *Prefacing the Image.*

46. Lippit, *Painting of the Realm.*

47. Minor, *Piranesi's Lost Words.*

48. Moxey, *Visual Time.* See also Partha Mitter and Keith Moxey, "A 'Virtual Cosmopolis': Partha

Mitter in Conversation with Keith Moxey," *Art Bulletin* 95, no. 3 (September 2013): 381–92.

49. Dadlani, "Transporting India."

50. This topic is discussed more extensively in Chap. 2.

51. S. Sharma, "City of Beauties; S. Sharma, "'If There Is a Paradise on Earth.'"

Chapter 1: Between Experimentation and Regulation

1. Exceptions to this trend in the art historical literature include Asher and Koch, whose surveys of Mughal architecture have called for further study of late seventeenth-century monuments. See Asher, *Architecture of Mughal India,* chap. 6; and Koch, *Mughal Architecture,* 125–31. On the problematic historiography of ʿAlamgir's reign in other fields, see Brown, "Did Aurangzeb Ban Music?" and Kinra, "Infantilizing Bābā Dārā." Also see Audrey Truschke, *Aurangzeb: The Life and Legacy of India's Most Controversial King* (Stanford: Stanford University Press, 2017), which was published after preparation of this book.

2. On Mughal gardens, including formative influences beyond the Timurids, see Wescoat, "Changing Cultural Space of Mughal Gardens." On the relationship between tents and pavilions, see O'Kane, "From Tents to Pavilions"; Roxburgh, "Ruy González de Clavijo's Narrative."

3. Asher, *Architecture of Mughal India,* esp. 169–71, 250–51; Koch, *Complete Taj Mahal,* 217–23; Koch, *Mughal Architecture,* esp. 93–96; Necipoğlu, "From International Timurid to Ottoman"; Necipoğlu, *Topkapı Scroll,* 113–15, 217–20.

4. The English definitions are standardized by Koch in *Mughal Architecture,* 137–42.

5. See Losensky, *Welcoming Fighānī,* esp. 12, 107–14, for an extended discussion of receptivity, istiqbāl, and related terms and concepts.

6. Ibid., 109.

7. Roxburgh explores the dynamics of this process in depth in *Persian Album,* esp. 137–44. As with poetry, intentionality is clearly discernible: models and copies would often be found on the same album page (140). Roxburgh also discusses a number of scholarly responses to the question of imitative practice, ranging from its description as "backward-looking" to discussions of copying as connected to establishing legitimacy.

8. Aitken, *Intelligence of Tradition.*

9. Asher makes a similar observation in her survey text, *Architecture of Mughal India,* 256.

10. Koch, "Baluster Column."

11. The vase motif was likely inspired by seventeenth century European paintings and engravings. Koch, *Complete Taj Mahal,* 219.

12. Asher points to this new "spatial tension" in the buildings from the period in *Architecture of Mughal India,* 256–57.

13. This was also the basis of the bungalow, on which see King, *Bungalow.*

14. Wescoat, "Changing Cultural Space of Mughal Gardens."

15. See Asher, *Architecture of Mughal India,* 43–47, 105–10, 172–74, 209–15; Brand, "Orthodoxy, Innovation, and Revival"; Koch, *Complete Taj Mahal;* and Koch, *Mughal Architecture,* 70–78, 97–102.

16. Koch, *Complete Taj Mahal,* 96–97.

17. Although ʿAlamgir's son, the prince Aʿzam Shah, was responsible for overseeing the construction of the tomb, scholars have agreed that it was authorized and ultimately supervised by ʿAlamgir. See Asher, *Architecture of Mughal India,* 263; and Parodi, "Bibi-Ka Maqbara," 354.

18. See Koch, *Complete Taj Mahal,* 158–59.

19. Ibid., 217–24.

20. Parodi provides an extended descriptive comparison between elements of the Bibi ka Maqbara and select Bijapuri examples in "Bibi-Ka Maqbara." In this paragraph, I draw on her stylistic comparison. On earlier Deccani influences on Mughal architecture, see Andrews, "Trellis Tent and Bulbous Dome."

21. Ibid., 364.

22. Inayatullah Kashmiri Khān, *Kalimat-i Taiyibat,* trans. S. M. Azizuddin Husain as *Collection of Aurangzeb's Orders* (Delhi: Idar-i Adabiyat-i Delli, 1982), 27.

23. Saqi Mustaʿidd Khan, *Maāsir-i ʿAlamgīrī,* trans. Sarkar, 145–46.

24. The coalescing of Mughal and Deccani forms was especially meaningful given the program of expansion that ʿAlamgir undertook, annexing Bijapur, Golconda, and the Maratha lands. For a full description of this period of expansion, see Richards, *Mughal Empire,* 225–52. For the growth of Sufism in the Deccan, see Ernst, *Eternal Garden;* Green, *Indian Sufism;* and Nile Green, "Stories of Saints and Sultans: Remembering History at the Sufi Shrines of Aurangabad," *Modern Asian Studies* 38, no. 2 (May 2004): 419–46.

25. ʿAta Allah is named as the architect (*miʿmār*) in an inscription carved on the side of the brass door of the complex. The same inscription states that the building was the "work" of Haspat Rai, most likely the engineer (*bi ʿamal-i Haspat Rai*). An additional metal plate names Aqa Abu al-Qasim Beg as the supervisor (*darūgha*). For more on these inscriptions, see Z. Desai, *Arabic, Persian, and Urdu Inscriptions*, 33.

26. For more on this family of architects, see W. E. Begley, "'Ata Allah" and "Ustad Ahmad," in *Macmillan Encyclopedia of Architects*, ed. Adolf K. Placzek (New York: Free Press, 1982), 4; Begley and Desai, *Taj Mahal*, xli–xlix, 266–75; Chaghtai, "Family of Great Mughal Architects"; Sayyid Sulaiman Nadvi, "The Family of the Engineers Who Built the Taj Mahal and the Delhi Fort," *Bihar Research Society Journal* 34 (1948): 75–110; Necipoğlu, *Topkapı Scroll*, 155–58; Parodi, "Bibi-ka Maqbara," 376–78; and Qaisar, *Building Construction in Mughal India*, 5–15.

27. The bibliography on the War of Succession, and in particular the contest between Aurangzeb-ʿAlamgir and Dara Shikoh, is extensive. For instance, see Husain, *Structure of Politics*, 13–48; and Richards, *Mughal Empire*, 151–68.

28. Farooqi, *Mughal–Ottoman Relations*, 58.

29. Saqi Mustaʿidd Khan, *Maʾāsir-i ʿĀlamgīrī*, trans. Sarkar, 100.

30. Adapted from ibid., 50, 217.

31. Recent scholarship has demonstrated that little is actually known about the nature and extent of this ban, and its effects for musical activity. Brown, "Did Aurangzeb Ban Music?" Also see Delvoye, "Indo-Persian Literature."

32. Saqi Mustaʿidd Khan, *Maʾāsir-i ʿĀlamgīrī*, trans. Sarkar, 313.

33. Ibid., esp. 103–6. See also Husain, *Collection*, xv.

34. Husain, *Collection*, 108.

35. Saqi Mustaʿidd Khan, *Maʾāsir-i ʿĀlamgīrī*, trans. Sarkar, 200.

36. Ibid., 200.

37. The Arabic text is published as Shaykh Niẓām et al., *al-Fatāwá al-Hindīyah al-maʿrūfah bi-al-Fatāwá al-ʿĀlamkīrīyah* (Beirut: Manshūrāt Muḥammad ʿAlī Bayḍūn; Dār al-Kutub al-ʿIlmīyah, 2000). A partial English translation can be found in Baillie, *Digest of Moohummdan*. See Guenther, "Hanafi Fiqh in Mughal India," 209–30.

38. The *Fatāwá al-ʿĀlamgīriyya*, trans. in Baillie, *Digest of Moohummdan*, 619.

39. The fatwa is attributed to the Central Asian Hanafi jurist Fakhr al-Din Qadi Khan. Necipoğlu, "Qurʾanic Inscriptions," suggests that this fatwa might have influenced the exclusion of epigraphy from the mosque.

40. Haq, *Khafi Khan's History of ʿAlamgir*; Necipoğlu, "Qurʾanic Inscriptions," 97; and Saqi Mustaʿidd Khan, *Maʾāsir-i ʿĀlamgīrī*, trans. Sarkar, 13.

41. I am grateful to Nada Mamtouz for discussing this fatwa and its particular language of proscription with me.

42. Transcribed and translated in Chaghtai, *Badshahi Masjid*, 7.

43. Ibid.

44. Transcribed and translated in Hasan, *Monuments of Delhi*.

45. Begley, "Symbolic Role of Calligraphy," 11.

46. Ibid.

47. Ibid.

48. Blair, *Islamic Inscriptions*, 214; Hillenbrand, "Qurʾanic Epigraphy in Medieval Islamic Architecture," 173.

49. There are a total of three Mughal mosques designated "Moti Masjid": one in the Red Fort of Delhi (1658–63), another in the Red Fort of Agra (1653, discussed in this paragraph), and a third in Mehrauli, Delhi, dating to the early eighteenth century and discussed in the next chapter.

50. Begley, "Symbolic Role of Calligraphy," 8.

51. Latif, *Agra*, 188.

52. Begley, "Symbolic Role of Calligraphy"; Bokhari, "'Light' of the Timuria."

53. Transcribed and translated in Husain, *Historical Guide to the Agra Fort*, 58–61.

54. Begley explores these and other themes in earlier seventeenth-century mosques in "Symbolic Role of Calligraphy."

55. These have been documented and discussed at length by Begley, "Myth of the Taj Majhal"; and Koch, *Complete Taj Mahal*, 224–28.

56. Necipoğlu, "Qurʾanic Inscriptions."

57. Ibid., 89.

58. Ibid., 76–78, 89.

59. I have translated the architectural terms and description from the Persian edition of Saqi Mustaʿidd Khan, *Maʾāsir-i ʿĀlamgīrī*, ed. Agha Ahmad Ali, 29. My translation of the passage adapts that in Saqi Mustaʿidd Khan, *Maʾāsir-i ʿĀlamgīrī*, trans. Sarkar, 17. "Colored pietra dura" can refer to pietra dura in two colors—that is, black inlaid marble against a white marble ground—and does not exclusively refer to

multicolored pietra dura seen in the nearby palace pavilions of the Delhi Red Fort.

60. Saqi Musta'idd Khan, *Ma'āsir-i 'Ālamgīrī*, trans. Sarkar, 208.

61. The description of his daily activities is recorded in the *'Alamgīrnāma*, an excerpt of which is translated in Sarkar, *Studies in Aurangzib's Reign*, 64–70.

62. Koch, *Complete Taj Mahal*, 215–24.

63. Haji Muhammad Jan Qudsi, *Zafarnama-i Shah Jahan*, British Library, Pers. ms., Ethe 1552, fol. 129a, trans. and cited in Koch, *Complete Taj Mahal*, 224.

64. Muhammad Salih Kanbo, *'Amal-i Salih or Shah Jahan nama*, ed. Wahid Qurayshi (Lahore: Majlis-i Taraqqi-yi Adab, 1967–72), based on Ghulam Yazdani's edition (Calcutta: Asiatic Society, 1912–46), 3:24, trans. and cit. in Koch, *Complete Taj Mahal*, 224. For parallels that appeared earlier in Ottoman floral ornament and court poetry, see Gülru Necipoğlu, "L'idée de décor dans les régimes de visualité islamiques," in *Purs decors? Arts de l'Islam, regards du XIXe siècle. Collections des Arts Décoratifs*, ed. Rémi Labrusse (Paris, 2007), fns. 41, 42, 57.

65. Lahori, trans. and cit. in Koch, *Complete Taj Mahal*, 216.

66. The subject of painting during the reign of 'Alamgir is itself a vast topic that deserves its own dedicated study. For an introduction to the period, see Beach, *Mughal and Rajput Painting*, 157–73; Leach, *Paintings from India*.

67. Koch, "Hierarchical Principles of Shah-Jahani Painting," 131–43.

68. Leach, *Mughal and Other Indian Paintings*, cats. 4.8, 4.12.

69. Beach, *Mughal and Rajput Painting*, 172–73.

Chapter 2: The Urban Culture of Mughal Delhi

1. Asher, *Architecture of Mughal India*, 191–204; Blake, *Shahjahanabad;* Koch, *Mughal Architecture*, 106–14; Necipoğlu, "Framing the Gaze," 312–17.

2. Babur and 'Alamgir were the exceptions to this trend.

3. On the economic conditions of the Mughal empire during this period, see Chandra, *Parties and Politics*, 29–39.

4. These were Bahadur Shah (r. 1707–12), Jahandar Shah (r. 1712–13), and Farrukh Siyar (r. 1713–19). This period of instability is detailed in Richards, *Mughal Empire*, 253–73.

5. On the artistic climate in Delhi during the reign of Muhammad Shah, see Dalrymple and Sharma, *Princes and Painters*. For a fuller discussion of events surrounding the Nadir Shah invasion, see Alam, *Crisis of Empire*, 50–53; and Chandra, *Parties and Politics*, 280–92. Because of the extent of the massacre and the monumental losses to the imperial treasury, which was essentially drained, the Nadir Shah attack has been portrayed in understandably catastrophic terms. At the same time, historians have also pointed out that the city appears to have continued to function, with the city's economy quickly recovering and cultural activity resuming. See Chandra, "Cultural and Political Role of Delhi," 106–18.

6. Tavernier, *Travels in India*, 96–101.

7. Koch, "Shah Jahan's Visits to Delhi Prior to 1648."

8. Aquil, "Hazrat-i-Dehli," 23–48. Schimmel, *Islam in the Indian Subcontinent*, 14, 24–25, 37. The location of the shrine in Mehrauli, in the vicinity of the Qutb Minar complex, makes sense given that this was the religious center of the Delhi Sultanate during the reign of Sultan Iltutmish (r. 1210–36), when Bakhtiyar Kaki had come to Delhi. An episode from the Lodi period demonstrates the shrine's importance to this dynasty. Before defending Delhi against Husain Sharqi of Jaunpur, the Lodi Sultan Buhlul (r. 1451–89) is said to have gone to the tomb of Bakhtiyar Kaki and prayed all night, standing.

9. Asher, *Architecture of Mughal India*, 293.

10. Ibid., 56–58, 174–78; Koch, *Mughal Architecture*, 64–66, 120–21.

11. The dome covering the grave and marble balustrade surrounding it are nineteenth-century additions; until then, the grave remained uncovered and unadorned. Hasan, *Monuments of Delhi*, 3:49.

12. Although often referred to as the Moti Masjid of Bahadur Shah, there are no inscriptions or other textual evidence to support this conclusion. Asher attributes the mosque to Bahadur Shah on the basis of Hasan in *Architecture of Mughal India*, 294. The entry in Hasan, meanwhile, states that Sayyid Ahmad Khān, in the 1854 *Āsār al-ṣanādīd*, claims that the mosque was built by Bahadur Shah in c. 1709 (2:32). Nath's translation of *Āsār al-sanādīd* corroborates this; see Nath, *Monuments of Delhi*, 65. However, it remains unclear on what basis Sayyid Ahmad Khān assigned this particular date and patron to the mosque. In light of the fact that Bahadur Shah

never entered Delhi, and also in consideration of shifting patterns of patronage, it is possible that a member of the imperial family or a deputy of Bahadur Shah was responsible for the mosque.

13. Stephen, *Archaeology and Monumental Remains*, 103.

14. The Mughal historian Lahori, for instance, describing the architecture of the period, wrote that "sky-touching mansions of marble were built which reflect like the mirror of Alexander and are pure like the heart of spiritual persons." Quoted in Koch, *Complete Taj Mahal*, 216.

15. Adapted from Hasan, *Monuments of Delhi*, 3:46.

16. Asher raises this point with reference to patronage at the dargah in *Architecture of Mughal India*, 293, also citing Matsuo Ara, *Dargahs in Medieval India* (Tokyo: Tokyo Daigaku Toyo Bunka Kenkyujp, 1977), 179–80.

17. Asher, *Architecture of Mughal India*, 295.

18. Keshani details the development of the Nizam al-Din dargah through the Sultanate and Mughal periods in "Building Nizamuddin." For a discussion of the earliest building activity at the site, see esp. ibid., 48–50. See also Schimmel, *Islam in the Indian Subcontinent*, 27–29.

19. Developments during this period are discussed in detail in Keshani, "Building Nizamuddin," 164–74; and the tomb of Atgah Khan is the subject of Welch, "Emperor's Grief."

20. For more on the tomb of Humayun, see Asher, *Architecture of Mughal India*, 43–47; Brand, "Orthodoxy, Innovation, and Revival"; Koch, *Mughal Architecture*, 43–44; Neeru Misra, *Garden Tomb of Humayun: An Abode in Paradise* (New Delhi: Aryan, 2003); and D. Fairchild Ruggles, "Humayun's Tomb and Garden: Typologies and Visual Order," in Petruccioli, *Gardens in the Time of the Great Muslim Empires*, 173–86.

21. On Jahan Ara, see Afshan Bokhari, "Gendered 'Landscapes': Jahanara Begum's Patronage, Piety, and Self-Representation in 17th-Century Mughal India" (Ph.D. diss., University of Vienna, 2009); and Bokhari, "'Light' of the Timuria."

22. This experience was enhanced in the nineteenth century, when Mirza Jahangir (d. 1821), the son of the emperor Akbar II, was buried in a similar enclosure. Three additional graves lie beside his: that of his brother, Mirza Babar, and two unnamed individuals. Zafar Hasan postulates that these two unmarked graves belong to members of the royal family in Hasan, *Guide to Niẓamu-d Dīn*, 17–18.

23. Hamadeh describes a similar "opening up," or *décloisonnement*, of cultural space and sensibilities in eighteenth-century Istanbul in *City's Pleasures*.

24. Johnson-Roehr, "Spatialization of Knowledge and Power," 6–9.

25. Ibid., 41.

26. Ibid., 15.

27. Ibid., 8.

28. Blake, *Shahjahanabad*.

29. Stephen Blake, "The Khanah Bagh in Mughal India: House Gardens in the Palaces and Mansions of the Great Men of Shahjahanabad," in Wescoat and Wolschke-Bulmahn, *Mughal Gardens*, 173.

30. Wescoat, "Changing Cultural Space of Mughal Gardens."

31. Goetz, "Qudsia Bagh at Delhi," 132–43.

32. Peck, *Delhi, a Thousand Years of Building*, 233.

33. For mosque patronage by Shah Jahan's wives, see Asher, *Architecture of Mughal India*, 201; and Blake, *Shahjahanabad*, 51–57, who also surveys mosques sponsored by other elite patrons.

34. Blake, *Shahjahanabad*, 56.

35. Asher, *Architecture of Mughal India*, 296–305; and Blake, *Shahjahanabad*, 51–55, 81–82. Mosques known as "Sunahri Masjid" were so-called because they at one time had gilt copper domes.

36. Alternative translations in Stephen, *Archaeology and Monumental Remains*, 157; and Hasan, *Monuments of Delhi*, 1:183.

37. Stephen, *Archaeology and Monumental Remains*, 157.

38. Koch, "Madrasa of Ghaziu'd-Din Khan at Delhi."

39. This text is adapted from the *Risalah-i Salar Jang*, British Library, Asian and African Collections, Add. 26237. This title was first given to the work in 1926, when it was edited by Mirza Muzaffar Hussain. See Dargah Quli Khan, *Muraqqaʿ-i Delhi*, trans. Shekar and Chenoy, xviii. This work includes an English translation of the *Muraqqaʿ*. The text was twice published in Persian with an accompanying Urdu translation. See Dargah Quli Khan, *Muraqqaʿ-i Delhi*, ed. Anṣārī; and Dargah Quli Khan, *Muraqqaʿ-i Delhi*, ed. Anjum.

40. For example, see Barlow and Subramanian, "Music and Society in North India"; Brown, "If Music Be the Food of Love," 64–71.

41. See, for example, Brown, "If Music Be the Food of Love." Alam and Subrahmanyam have proposed that the *Muraqqaʿ* was possibly being

excerpted from a larger work narrating contemporary political events of the time; see Alam and Subrahmanyam, "Discovering the Familiar," 140.

42. For example, see Alam and Subrahmanyam's *Indo-Persian Travels* and their "Discovering the Familiar."

43. Fisher, "From India to England and Back." Cole addresses Indo-Persian writers encountering Great Britain and British-controlled India in "Invisible Occidentalism." On Iranian depictions of India in the early nineteenth century, see Cole, "Mirror of the World." For travelers from Qajar Iran writing about voyages to Europe, see Ringer, "Quest for the Secret," 146–61; and Sohrabi, *Taken for Wonder.*

44. See Kia, "Contours of Persianate Community," esp. chap. 4, in which Kia discusses the self-reflexive aspect of tazkira literature in eighteenth-century India.

45. Hermansen and Lawrence, "Indo-Persian Tazkiras," esp. 256–64.

46. S. Sharma, "City of Beauties," 73–74; S. Sharma, "'If There Is a Paradise on Earth.'"

47. S. Sharma, "City of Beauties," 74–76.

48. Dargah Quli Khan, *Muraqqaʿ*, 79, 83. Citations in this section refer to the published Persian text edited by Anjum (see n39). Translations are mine.

49. On the Qadam Sharif shrine, see Welch, "Shrine of the Holy Footprint in Delhi." On the broader context for such shrines, see Hasan, "Footprint of the Prophet."

50. Dargah Quli Khan, *Muraqqaʿ*, 51.

51. Ibid., 54.

52. Ibid., 55.

53. Ibid., 52, 54–55.

54. Ibid., 53, 54.

55. Ibid., 55–56. Pakhāwaj was the name of a celebrated Indian musician; here, the term refers possibly to music performed in his style, or an instrument he popularized. "*Mur chang*"might refer to a type of harp. See the entry in Francis Steingass, *A Comprehensive Persian-English Dictionary* (London: Routledge, 1892).

56. Dargah Quli Khan, *Muraqqaʿ*, 54–55.

57. Bayly discusses the economic vibrancy of the Delhi markets in "Delhi and Other Cities."

58. Dargah Quli Khan, *Muraqqaʿ*, 61.

59. Ibid., 61–62.

60. On public space, entertainment, and consumerism, see Vanessa Schwartz, *Spectacular Realities: Early Mass Culture in Fin-de-Siècle Paris* (Berkeley: University of California Press, 1998); and Lisa Tiersten, *Marianne in the Market: Envisioning Consumer Society in Fin-de-Siècle France* (Berkeley: University of California Press, 2001).

61. Dargah Quli Khan, *Muraqqaʿ*, 60–61.

62. Ibid., 71–73.

63. Ibid., 66.

64. Ibid., 90, 91, 94, 100, 101.

65. Ibid., 58.

66. Ibid., 92.

67. Ibid., 94, 98.

68. Ibid., 73.

69. Ibid., 104.

70. Ibid., 70.

71. Two examples are the crowds in attendance at the Qadamgah of ʿAli during Muharram and at the weekly assemblies at the dargah of Nizam al-Din; ibid., 52–55.

72. Ibid., 54.

73. Ibid., 95.

74. Ibid., 109–10.

75. Little is currently known about women in Mughal India outside the imperial family circle or ranks of nobility, and it is only relatively recently that scholars have focused on elite women in Mughal India. Studies include Bokhari, "Gendered 'Landscapes'"; Bokhari, "'Light' of the Timuria"; Ellison Banks Findly, *Nur Jahan: Empress of Mughal India* (New York: Oxford University Press, 1993); Hambly, *Women in the Medieval Islamic World;* Lal, *Domesticity and Power;* and Ruggles, *Women, Patronage, and Self-Representation.* Ghosh examines women across different strata of society in the context of late eighteenth-century northern India, specifically those who cohabited with European men, in *Sex and the Family in Colonial India.* Also see Durba Ghosh, "Making and Unmaking Loyal Subjects: Pensioning Widows and Educating Orphans in Early Colonial India," *Journal of Imperial and Commonwealth History* 31, no. 1 (2003): 1–28.

76. Dargah Quli Khan, *Muraqqaʿ*, 70–71.

77. Ibid., 91.

78. Ibid., 86–89.

79. On the *Muraqqaʿ* as a source for music history, see Barlow and Subramanian, "Music and Society in North India"; Brown, "Dargah Quli Khan's Strange Vision"; and Chenoy and Shekhar, *Muraqqaʿ-i Delhi*, xxxiii.

80. Tavernier, *Travels in India*, 96–101.

Chapter 3. "The Last Flicker in the Lamp of Mughal Architecture"

1. Zafar Hasan uses this phrase to describe the mosque in the funerary complex, which is in the same style of the tomb. Hasan, *Monuments of Delhi*, 2:192.

2. Ibid., 191.

3. Heber, *Narrative of a Journey*, 2:309.

4. Asher and Koch point to the mausoleum of Safdar Jang as an example of the "late" Mughal idiom. Both cite the extensive use of stucco, an emphasis on ornament, and the incorporation of pointed domes and chhatris; they also point out that the tomb follows the precedents set by previous imperial Mughal mausolea. Asher, *Architecture of Mughal India*, 306; Koch, *Mughal Architecture*, 132.

5. The nawabs had effectively become vassals of the British by this time, and the formal declaration of independence from the Mughal empire was at British urging. For a full discussion of relationships between Awadh and the British, see Barnett, *North India Between Empires;* and Fisher, *Clash of Cultures.*

6. One example is the poet Mir. See Russell and Khurshidul Islam, *Three Mughal Poets*, 21. On the artistic patronage and collecting network in Awadh, see N. Eaton, *Mimesis Across Empires;* Jasanoff, *Edge of Empire.*

7. For a comparison of the Delhi and Lucknow schools of poetry, see Petievich, *Assembly of Rivals.* For a discussion of painting in the period, see Archer and Falk, *Indian Miniatures;* Beach, *Mughal and Rajput Painting*, 220–23; and J. P. Losty, "Towards a New Naturalism: Portraiture in Murshidabad and Avadh, 1750–80," in Schmitz, *After the Great Mughals*, 34–55. Tandan surveys Awadhi architecture in *Architecture of Lucknow and Oudh.*

8. Richards, *Mughal Empire*, 253–81.

9. Alam, *Crisis of Empire*, 204–42; Barnett, *North India Between Empires;* and Fisher, *Clash of Cultures.*

10. Muhammad Faiz Bakhsh, *Tarikh-i Bakhsh*, c. 1786. Translated as Muhammad Faiz Bakhsh, *Memoirs of Faizabad*, 2:48.

11. Visual connections between the tombs of Safdar Jang and Humayun are pointed to in Asher, *Architecture of Mughal India*, 306. Koch relates the tomb to the longer Mughal tomb tradition in *Mughal Architecture*, 132.

12. In her survey of Mughal architecture, Asher points to the connection between Safdar Jang's tomb and the later architectural idiom developed in Awadh, both in terms of style and the Awadhi adaptation of Mughal customs and ceremonial; Asher, *Architecture of Mughal India*, 306.

13. The tradition of Mughal mausolea set within funerary gardens is surveyed in Asher, *Architecture of Mughal India;* and Koch, *Mughal Architecture.* It is treated in comparative perspective in Brand, "Orthodoxy, Innovation, and Revival." Koch contextualizes the plan of the Taj Mahal and its garden in relationship to this tradition in *Complete Taj Mahal*, 24–27.

14. These practices continued until 1775. Barnett, *North India Between Empires*, 95.

15. The inscription ends with a chronogram. Hasan, *Monuments of Delhi*, 2:190.

16. Asher, *Architecture of Mughal India*, 130–33; Koch, *Mughal Architecture*, 74–75.

17. On the art and architecture of the Deccani dynasties of India, see Haidar and Sardar, *Sultans of the South;* Hutton, *Art of the Court of Bijapur;* Merklinger, *Indian Islamic Architecture;* and Michell and Zebrowski, *Architecture and Art.*

18. Farhat, "Islamic Piety and Dynastic Legitimacy."

19. Das, "Lucknow's Imambaras and Karbalas," 100–102.

20. For more on the Ottoman and Safavid "regimes of visuality," see Necipoğlu, "L'idée de décor."

21. Koch, *Complete Taj Mahal*, 26.

22. Alfred Schinz, *The Magic Square: Cities in Ancient China* (Stuttgart: Axel Menges, 1996), 294–95. Cited in Koch, *Complete Taj Mahal*, 26.

23. See Babaie, *Isfahan and Its Palaces*, 31; and Koch, *Complete Taj Mahal*, 26. Both authors note that the palace was completed by Uzun Hasan's son, Yaʿqub (r. 1478–90).

24. For the longer narrative, see Charles Grey, trans., *A Narrative of Italian Travels in Persia, in the 15th and 16th Centuries* (New York: Franklin, 1960). Cited in Babaie, *Isfahan and Its Palaces*, 59n1.

25. Babaie, *Isfahan and Its Palaces*, 32–33, and chap. 5, esp. 198–206.

26. Koch, *Complete Taj Mahal*, 26, 264n32.

27. Begley, "Mirak Mirza Ghiyas," 2:194–95.

28. Hussein Keshani has described the vaulting system in Safdar Jang's tomb in close detail, and I draw on his analysis here. Keshani, "Architecture of Ritual," 176–78.

29. See Chap. 1.

30. Stephen, *Archaeology and Monumental Remains*, 161; Hasan, *Monuments of Delhi*, 2:192.

31. J. Sharma, "British Treatment of Historic Gardens."

32. Hasan, *Monuments of Delhi*, 2:192.

33. See Chap. 1.

34. Cole, *Roots of North Indian Shīʿism*.

35. Ibid., 42–44. Cole argues that Burhan al-Mulk's motivations were financial rather than ideological. This policy was not universally applied, and the Sunni institutions were not replaced with Shiʿi ones.

36. Ibid., 50–60.

37. Das and Llewellyn-Jones, *Murshidabad*.

38. Cole, *Roots of North Indian Shīʿism*, 38–42.

39. Atgah Khan, the foster-father of Akbar, was interred in a tomb in the dargah in 1566. ʿAziz Koka, a noble at the court of Jahangir, had in 1624 built a hypostyle marble mausoleum adjoining the dargah, known as the Chausath Kambah (literally "sixty-four pillars"). Both Shah Jahan's daughter Jahan Ara and the Mughal emperor Muhammad Shah (r. 1719–39) had been buried at the precinct in finely wrought marble jali enclosures. The dargah also features numerous other buildings from the earlier Sultanate period, including the burial enclosure of Amir Khusraw (d. 1325). See Chap. 2 and Keshani, "Building Nizamuddin."

40. For Qudsiyya Begum's building program, see Goetz, "Qudsia Bagh at Delhi"; and Hasan, *Monuments of Delhi*, 2:195–96, 295–96. The gateway inscription is transcribed and translated in Hasan, *Monuments of Delhi*, 2:195: "Muhammad the friend of God said, 'I am a city of learning, and ʿAli is its gateway.' In the auspicious reign of Ahmad Shah Bahadur, the king and champion of faith, the building of the fort, the *Majliskhāna* (sufi congregation house), the mosque and the tank, was completed in one year, according to the orders of Her Highness Nawab Qudsiya Sahiba Zamaniya, under the supervision of Nawab Bahadur Jawid Khan Sahib, and under the control of the humble ʿAli Khan. 1164 (1750–1 CE)."

41. Findly, "Women's Wealth and Styles of Giving," 91–122.

42. Recent studies on architectural patronage by Mughal and other women in the Islamic world include Bokhari, "Gendered 'Landscapes'"; Bokhari, "'Light' of the Timuria"; Ellison Banks Findly, *Nur Jahan: Empress of Mughal India* (New York: Oxford University Press, 1993); Hambly, *Women in the Medieval Islamic World*; and Ruggles, *Women, Patronage, and Self-Representation*.

43. This serves as a parallel to Jahan Ara's directed program of patronage as related to her Chishti affiliations. See Bokhari, "'Light' of the Timuria."

44. On the issue of domed versus platform tombs, see the discussion of the "built tomb controversy" in Koch, *Complete Taj Mahal*, 85–88.

45. Hasan, *Monuments of Delhi*, 2:211.

46. The full text of the inscription reads: "He is living who will never die. / Alas! That the virtuous woman of angelic nature and auspicious birth repaired from this abode of ashes whose foundation is grief. / What a friend and namesake of the daughter of the Prophet (Muhammad)! May she be forgiven for the sake of the soul of Fatima Zahra! / She was devoted of heart to the kindred of ʿAli who is of high rank, and was enamored of the names of the venerated Imams. / She was the daughter of Najaf Khan, the Mir Bakhshi of India; may God grant her a place in the abode of the pure! / I breathed a sigh, and the chronogram was known: "'May ʿAli and Fatima be her intercessors on the Day of Judgment!' 1236 (1820–1 AD)." Ibid., 213.

47. For more on the imambara and related Shiʿi rituals, see Peter Chelkowski, "Monumental Grief: The Bara Imambara," in Llewellyn-Jones, *Lucknow: City of Illusion*, 101–33; and Keshani, "Architecture and the Twelver Shiʿi Tradition."

48. Keshani, "Architecture and the Twelver Shiʿi Tradition," 238n81.

49. Earlier, pre-Mughal examples include the Bara Gumbad mosque (Delhi, 1494) and the Moth-ki Masjid (Delhi, 1510), both sponsored by the Lodi dynasty.

50. Sail vaulting is discussed in Keshani, "Architecture and the Twelver Shiʿi Tradition," 238–42.

51. Though Kifayat Allah is often named, the architect of the Bara Imambara complex is not definitively known. See ibid., 233–34.

52. Abū Ṭālib Khān, *History of Asafuʾd Daulah*. The description quoted in this paragraph is on 73–74.

53. In fact, Abū Ṭālib seems torn between expressing wonder and criticism; for instance, he complains that the objects in the interior of the building provided challenges for the upkeep of the building and took up space that could have been used by the public. See Keshani, "Architecture and Twelver Shiʿi Tradition," 244.

54. 'Abd al-Latif Shushtari, *Tuhfat al-Alam*, 1802, British Library Add. 23533. This excerpt is translated in Keshani, "Architecture of Ritual," app. C.

55. The literature on the Picturesque, a concept developed primarily in late eighteenth-century England, is vast and includes studies such as the seminal writings of Gilpin, *Three Essays*, to more recent considerations of the topic, such as James Ackerman, "The Photographic Picturesque," *Artibus and Historiae* 24, no. 48 (2003): 73–94.

56. E. C. Archer, *Tours in Upper India*, 123–24.

57. Cavenagh, *Reminiscences of an Indian Official*, 10.

58. Mundy, *Pen and Pencil Sketches*, 45.

59. Russell, *My Diary in India*, 79.

60. Roberts, *Scenes and Characteristics of Hindostan*, 2:237.

61. Rousselet, *L'inde des rajahs: Voyage dans l'Inde centrale* (Paris: Hachette, 1875). Translated and quoted in Lafont and Lafont, *French and Delhi*, 137–38.

62. Peck, *Delhi: A Thousand Years of Building*, 130.

63. Losty, *Sita Ram's Painted Views of India*.

Chapter 4. Codifying Mughal Architecture on Paper

1. The majority of this collection (twenty-four folios) is housed in the Bibliothèque nationale de France (BnF), Paris. The *Palais Indiens* collection is included in Roselyne Hurel's extensive catalogue of Indian paintings in the Prints and Photographs Department at the BnF, *Miniatures and Peintures Indiennes*, 202, 222–23, and 228–30; and in Francis Richard's introduction to the Gentil materials at the BnF, "Jean Baptiste Gentil Collectionneur de Manuscrits Persans," 91–110. In addition, three of the folios are published in Lafont, *Chitra*; and an exhibition in Delhi featured facsimiles of selected folios: see Jean-Marie Lafont et al., *Lost Palaces of Delhi* (Delhi: EurIndia and Art Heritage Gallery, 2006). Also see Tandan's chapter on Gentil in *Architecture of Lucknow and Oudh*. In addition, three folios in the Victoria & Albert Museum, London, were most likely part of the original group. Their connection is discernible because of stylistic similarities but also because of a largely unexamined eighteenth-century catalogue kept in the BnF, which includes the titles of all of the *Palais Indiens* paintings in Paris, and three additional titles: *Sérail et jardin du palais du grand mogol à dely*, *Palais de darachetto àgra*, and *Tombeau de saftardjangue*. The first two titles match the inscriptions on two of the studies in London, and are recorded accordingly in the V&A's catalogues: Archer and Parlett, *Company Paintings*, 132; and Victoria & Albert Museum, *Art of India*. They are also included in Lafont, *Chitra*, 130. A third painting bearing a close stylistic similarity to the *Palais Indiens* images, catalogued by the V&A as "An unidentified Muslim building," is of the mausoleum of Safdar Jang and must be the "Tombeau de saftardjangue" from the eighteenth-century catalogue.

2. See Lafont, *Lost Palaces of Delhi*, 4.

3. For a general overview of this material, see Aitken, *Intelligence of Tradition in Rajput Court Painting*; Beach, *Mughal and Rajput Painting;* and Wright, *Muraqqa': Imperial Mughal Albums.*

4. Okada, *Indian Miniatures*, 148–65, 216–25; and Wright, *Muraqqa': Imperial Mughal Albums.*

5. Chester Beatty Library, In 34.5. Losty points to this as "One of the very few earlier Mughal paintings where it is possible to recognize an extant Mughal building"; see Losty, "Delineating Delhi," 15. He also points out that the building's presence in the painting is anachronistic: the event being depicted took place in 1606, while the tomb was completed in 1613.

6. On the *Pādshāhnāma*, see Beach, Koch, and Thackston, *King of the World.* On the pictorial logic of the paintings from this manuscript, see Koch, "Hierarchical Principles of Shah-Jahani Painting." While Koch discusses accurate architectural representation as a specific feature of the *Pādshāhnāma*, Beach considers the *Pādshāhnāma* as exemplary of broader trends in Shah Jahani and Mughal painting; see Beach, *Mughal and Rajput Painting*, 131–32, 166–67. In addressing the painting *Vishnu with Lakshmi and Attendant Ladies*, by Ruknuddin, he asserts that its "Mughal affiliation" is evident through visual characteristics such as "the specificness of its architecture" (167).

7. Koch, "Hierarchical Principles of Shah-Jahani Painting," 137–40.

8. This map and its dating are discussed in Koch, *Complete Taj Mahal*, 34; and Gole, *Indian Maps and Plans*, 201.

9. My thanks to Ebba Koch for sharing this plan with me. She has attributed it to the eighteenth century; see Koch, *Complete Taj Mahal*, 49, 76.

10. For an analysis of examples in comparative perspective with early modern Ottoman architectural plans, see Necipoğlu, "Plans and Models";

see also her comparative chapter on plans and scrolls in *Topkapi Scroll*. See also Lewcock, "Architects, Craftsmen, and Builders," 112–43.

11. Necipoğlu, "Plans and Models," esp. 225–31.

12. Ibid., 231.

13. Ibid., 233.

14. For a discussion of modular planning in Mughal architecture, see Koch, *Mughal Architecture*, 110.

15. For contrasting views on potential European influences on the planning of Jaipur, and implications for graphic plans, see Gole, *Indian Maps and Plans*, 44; Nilsson, *European Architecture in India*, 193–95; and Sachdev and Tillotson, *Building Jaipur*, 11–31, 43–46.

16. Wescoat, "Changing Cultural Space of Mughal Gardens."

17. The painting is also cited in this context in Necipoğlu, "Plans and Models"; Qaisar, *Building Construction in Mughal India*, 15; and Smart, "Graphic Evidence," 22–23.

18. Qaisar, *Building Construction in Mughal India*, 14.

19. Ibid.

20. For a full discussion of the status of architects and the professionalization of architecture in the Mughal empire, see ibid., 34–42.

21. The plans discussed in this section are published in Gole, *Indian Maps and Plans*. In addition to documenting each of them, Gole provides a brief overview of their textual inscriptions and discusses their dating.

22. The plan is currently held at the Jaigarh Fort Museum, where I was granted limited access. No cataloguing information is available.

23. Gole, *Indian Maps and Plans*.

24. This is explained by Tillotson, *Rajput Palaces*, n20. The three architectural paintings are Sawai Man Singh II Museum, Jaipur, Lib. 77, Lib. 78, Lib. 83, as cited in ibid.

25. Lafont, *Chitra*, 24.

26. As elsewhere in this book, historical place-names are used in this section, befitting the eighteenth-century context under discussion. The largest collection of these is housed in the Archives nationales d'outre-mer, Archives de France, Aix-en-Provence. See Rinckenbach, *Archives du dépôt*. For an additional introduction to this material, see Lafont, *Chitra*.

27. This is not to reify Indian painting practices, but simply to point out that there were precedents for an effective selective adaptation of European pictorial modes. On the Jesuit missions to India, see Bailey, *Art on the Jesuit Missions*, 112–43.

28. Archer and Parlett, *Company Paintings*, 117–18.

29. McInerney, "Mughal Painting During the Reign of Muhammad Shah," 12–33; Roy, "Origins of the Late Mughal Painting Tradition."

30. Dadlani, "Transporting India," esp. 754–58.

31. The inscription reads, "pierre rouge incrustée en marbre blanc et noir: la dessus des Dômes en marbre blanc."

32. For a full description of the Gentil collection in the BnF, see Richard, "Jean-Baptiste Gentil," 102–9. Archer briefly discusses the scope of Gentil's commissions in Archer and Parlett, *Company Paintings*, 117–18. For his interest in Mughal and other historical texts, see Dadlani, "Transporting India."

33. See nn29–30.

34. For the atlas, see Gole, *Maps of Mughal India*. On the *Gentil Album*, see Dadlani, "Transporting India." The manuscripts referenced here are, in order: *Empire Mogol divisé en 21 soubahs ou gouvernements tiré de différens écrivains du pais en Faisabad en MDCCLXX*, 1770, British Library, India Office Library Collection, Add. Or. 4039; *Abrégé historique des Souverains de l'Indoustan ou Empire Mogol*, 1772, BnF, Manuscrits occidentaux, fr. 24219; and *Recueil de toutes sortes de dessins sur les Usages et coutumes des Peuples de l'Indoustan ou Empire Mogol*, 1774, V&A, Asian Collection, IS 25–1980.

35. These are published in Susan Gole, "Three Maps of Shahjahanabad," *South Asian Studies* 4 (1988): 13–27. They are also discussed in Losty, "Delineating Delhi"; and in Y. Sharma, "From Miniatures to Monuments."

36. While the Chandni Chowk plan contains multilingual labels, the Faiz Bazaar plan is labeled exclusively in Persian.

37. The entry records *2 rues de Dely* (Two streets of Delhi), listed alongside other paintings that eventually entered the V&A collection, such as the *Tombeau de saftardjangue*, and labeled as entry number ten. Paper analysis I conducted on the street plans reveals that they bear labels with the number ten, which were subsequently covered during mounting. (I am grateful to Nick Barnard at the V&A for facilitating this process.) For other interpretations of these plans, see Mildred Archer, who points to stylistic similarities between the plans and Joseph Tieffenthaler's *Historique et géographique de l'Inde* (Berlin: Spener, 1786) and dates them to 1774, in Archer and Parlett, *Company Paintings*, 132. Gole differs, dating the plans to

c. 1750, based on their inclusion of buildings that were destroyed in the late 1750s; see Gole, "Three Maps of Shahjahanabad," 25. This dating is problematic, since the plans could have been produced after the buildings were destroyed, using earlier visual or textual records. See also Falk and Archer, *Indian Miniatures*, 121, for visual connections between this plan and a similar one of the Red Fort by the artist Nidhamal. Lafont also mentions the plans in conjunction with the *Palais Indiens* album; see Lafont, *Chitra*, 130.

38. Gentil, *Mémoires sur l'Indoustan*, 240–41.

39. "Ce prince, charmé de l'ouverture de cette négo-ciation, voulant me mettre à même de traiter, d'égal à égal, avec les deux seigneurs Indiens, qui étaient à la tête des Anglais, me donna tous les titres qu'un grand de l'inde peut porter, m'appel-lant *Rafioudoulah, Nazemdjenk, Bahadour, Tadbir-oul-Moulouk*." Ibid., 244.

40. BnF, Manuscrits occidentaux, *Histoire des pieces de Monnoyes qui ont été frappés dans l'Indoustan*, fr. 25287, fols. 115–22. On Juliana, see Zaman, "Visions of Juliana."

41. BnF, *Histoire des pieces*, fol. 121. The palace was reportedly later sold to Safdar Jang by Juliana's descendants at an undervalued price; see Lafont, *Chitra*, 11.

42. The passage reads "si cette femme étois homme, je la ferois Vizir."

43. Razia, a ruler of the Delhi Sultanate (r. 1236–40), was the daughter and successor of Shams al-Din Iltutmish; Nur Jahan, the "favorite wife" of the Mughal emperor Jahangir, is often perceived as a co-ruler rather than consort; Jahanara was the daughter of Shah Jahan and a noted patron of architecture; and the legendary Begum Sumru was a Kashmiri-born dancer and courtesan who married a German named Walter Reinhardt, converted to Catholicism, and later led an independent army. She maintained residences in Sardhana and Delhi.

44. Losty, "Delineating Delhi."

45. Published in Tillotson, "Painting and Understanding Mughal Architecture," fig. 3.

46. For an expanded discussion of contemporary and subsequent Rajput renderings of place and space in the context of Udaipur, see Khera, "Picturing India's 'Land of Kings.'"

47. Quilley, "Picturing the History of India," in Quilley and Bonehill, *William Hodges*, 137–86.

48. Quilley, "Picturing the History of India," 139. Tillotson compares Hodges's depiction of architecture with Indian modes of architectural representation in Tillotson, "Painting and Understanding Mughal Architecture," 59–79; and Tillotson, "Hodges and Indian Architecture," in Quilley and Bonehill, *William Hodges*, 49–60. The original Hodges editions were William Hodges, *Select Views in India;* and Hodges, *Travels in India*.

49. M. Archer, *Early Views of India;* Shaffer, *Adapting the Eye*.

50. *Antiquities of India* was a project begun by Wales, but left unfinished at the time of his death. Charles Ware Malet, the British resident at Poona, commissioned Thomas Daniell to complete the publication; see Shaffer, *Adapting the Eye*, 6–7.

51. Quilley, "William Hodges, Artist of Empire," in Quilley and Bonehill, *William Hodges*, 1–8.

52. These themes are explored at length in Quilley and Bonehill, *William Hodges*, particularly in the essay by Quilley, "William Hodges, Artist of Empire," 1–8; Natasha Eaton, "Hodges's Visual Genealogy for Colonial India, 1780–95," 35–42; and Beth Fowkes Tobin, "The Artist's 'I' in Hodges's *Travels in India*," 43–48.

53. M. Archer, *Company Drawings;* Archer and Parlett, *Company Paintings*.

54. This has been a larger problem in the historiography of Indian painting. Recent scholarship has started to address this issue. See, for example, Guy and Britschgi, *Wonder of the Age*. Like its related exhibition at the Metropolitan Museum of Art in 2011, this catalogue aimed to highlight individual artistic biography and production, rather than dynastic or geographic periodization.

55. See, for example, Dalrymple and Sharma's introduction to *Princes and Painters*, 1–16.

56. The classic study on cartography in British India is Edney, *Mapping an Empire*. For a more recent study on this topic, see Raj, *Relocating Modern Science*, chap. 2. For a relevant study on visual knowledge and the project of empire in the Spanish imperial context, see Bleichmar, *Visible Empire*.

57. Archer and Parlett, *Company Paintings*, 134, 136. The paintings are IS 11–1964, V&A, London, and AL 4202, V&A, London.

58. Archer and Parlett, *Company Paintings*, 136.

59. Ibid., 114.

60. For more on Polier, including a translation of a section of his Persian correspondence, see Alam and Alavi, *European Experience*.

61. This material has been published in Gadebusch, "Celestial Gardens."

62. Alam and Alavi, *European Experience*, 77–80.

63. Archer and Parlett, *Company Paintings*, 215–27.

64. Losty, "Delineating Delhi."

65. Y. Sharma, "In the Company of the Mughal Court."

66. The emperor was effectively exiled in eastern India in the 1760s.

67. Y. Sharma, "From Miniatures to Monuments."

68. Kavuri-Bauer, *Monumental Matters*, chap. 1, esp. 34.

69. Dadlani, "Transporting India."

70. Lafont has asserted that earlier, French-commissioned art should not be assimilated into the later category of "Company School" painting; see Lafont, *Chitra*, 11.

71. See especially Gadebusch, "Celestial Gardens," 72–75.

72. Gentil, *Mémoires*, 421. These testimonials are referenced in an appendix to Gentil's memoirs, compiled by his son. Regarding the director of the Cabinet des Estampes, Gentil's son simply names a "M. Joly." This could refer either to Hugues-Adrien Joly, director from 1750 to 1792, or his son and successor, Adrien-Jacques Joly, director from 1792 to 1829.

73. Besides Duperron's translation of and commentary on the *Zend Avesta* (Paris: N. M. Tilliard, 1771), he published a treatise on Islamic law, *Législation orientale* (Amsterdam: Chez Marc-Michel Rey, 1778); an account of the history and geography of northern India, *Des recherches historiques et chronologiques sur l'Inde, et la description du cours du Gange et du Gagra*, published as part of Jean Bernoulli's edited volume on the history and geography of India, *Description historique et géographique de l'Inde* (Berlin: C. S. Spender, 1786–89); and a Latin translation of the *Upanishads* (Strasbourg: Levrault, 1801).

74. Archives nationales de France, C/2 174, ff. 107–10. For more on this exchange, see Martin, "Tipu Sultan's Ambassadors."

75. Hunt, Jacob, and Mijnhardt, *Bernard Picart;* Hunt, Jacob, and Mijnhardt, *Book That Changed Europe.*

76. For a brief discussion of these plans, see Lafont and Lafont, *French and Delhi*, 75–76, 83.

77. Another example that predates the *Palais Indiens* is the *Elevation of the Thousand Pillared Hall, Madura,* which has been dated to c. 1750 and includes an inscription dedicated to Charles Robert Godehu, a French commander who served as governor-general of French India from 1754 to 1755. AL 1760, Victoria & Albert Museum. See Archer and Parlett, *Company Paintings,* 41.

Chapter 5. Mughal Architecture Between Manuscript and Print Culture

1. The manuscript is catalogued in Losty, *Art of the Book in India;* and in Titley, *Miniatures from Persian Manuscripts,* 281. Losty also discusses the manuscript in relation to other manuscripts presented as diplomatic gifts in "Delineating Delhi," 37, and its paintings as inaugurating "the picturesque style of Delhi artists" that would develop in the nineteenth century, in "Depicting Delhi," 56.

2. For a full description of these events, see Cheema, *Forgotten Mughals.*

3. Wright, *Muraqqa': Imperial Mughal Albums,* 25–31.

4. Lentz and Lowry, *Timur and the Princely Vision,* 100–103.

5. For the Timurid genealogical portrait, see ibid., fig. 37, 102.

6. Necipoğlu, "Word and Image."

7. As Necipoğlu discusses, in the Safavid case, there was a greater emphasis on hagiography and the dynasty's spiritual origins with the Shaykh Safi al-Din of Ardabil; ibid., 5. On the impact of this source of legitimacy on Safavid architecture, see Kishwar Rizvi, *Safavid Dynastic Shrine.*

8. Losty, "Delineating Delhi," 37, 54.

9. Royal Collection Trust, RCIN 1005025. Reproduced in Beach, Koch, and Thackston, *King of the World.*

10. Koch, "Hierarchical Principles of Shah-Jahani Painting."

11. BL, Asian and African Collections, Add. 20735, fol. 371.

12. BL, Asian and African Collections, Add. 20735, fols. 609–10.

13. BL, Asian and African Collections, Add. 20735, fols. 23, 253–54, 521–22.

14. Beach, Koch, and Thackston, *King of the World.*

15. Losty, *Art of the Book,* 153.

16. BL, Asian and African Collections, Or. 2157.

17. Losty, *Art of the Book,* 153.

18. BL, Asian and African Collections, Or. 182.

19. On the relationship between knowledge circulation and books in the late Mughal period, see Green, "Uses of Books in a Late Mughal Takiyya."

20. See Charles Rieu, *Catalogue of the Persian Manuscripts in the British Museum* (London:

British Museum, 1879–83), 1:285, on the authorship and artists involved in the production of the text and the connection to painted works.

21. Yuthika Sharma explains that there was a proliferation of genealogies produced for Zafar during this period. See Dalrymple and Sharma, *Princes and Painters,* 46, 51n22. Offering a different interpretation than mine, Sharma delineates these and other genealogies as "alternative narratives to other sociocultural and urban histories of Delhi that were being commissioned outside the Mughal court," whereas I see them as closely related.

22. For a discussion of Persianate audiences and the description of Mughal landscape architecture in poetry, see Wheeler Thackston, "Mughal Gardens in Persian Poetry," in Wescoat and Wolschke-Bulmahn, *Mughal Gardens,* 233–58.

23. Alam, "Culture and Politics of Persian in Precolonial Hindustan."

24. Losty, "Delineating Delhi," 37.

25. On the instruction of Persian and changes in Persianate literary culture, see Fisher, "Teaching Persian."

26. Adapted from a translation by Gordon Sanderson, "Shah Jahan's Fort, Delhi," in *Archaeological Survey of India Annual Report, 1911–12,* ed. John Marshall (Calcutta: Superintendent Government Printing, 1915), 16.

27. On court ceremonial in the Diwan-i ʿAmm, see Necipoğlu, "Framing the Gaze."

28. Koch, "Diwan-i ʿAmm and Chihil Sutun." On the chihil sutun type in Safavid Iran, see Babaie, *Isfahan and Its Palaces.*

29. Koch, "Diwan-i ʿAmm and Chihil Sutun," 148–53.

30. Koch, "Wooden Audience Halls of Shah Jahan."

31. For a discussion of the Shah Jahan–era sources and their commentaries on architecture, see bibliographic essays in Asher, *Architecture of Mughal India,* esp. 347–48.

32. This was the text used for BL Add. 20734, the companion volume of the 1815 ʿAmal-i Ṣāliḥ.

33. Lahori wrote the history of the first two decades of the imperial reign, while Waris completed the history of the third decade. The vizier Saʿd Allah Khan and Fazil Khan ʿAlaʾ al-Mulk Tuni revised the text. See Wheeler Thackston's appendix in Beach, Koch, and Thackston, *King of the World,* 140.

34. Thackston describes the *Zafarnāma-i-Shāh-Jahāni* and *Shāhjahānnāma* of Kalim as unfinished in ibid.

35. Rajeev Kinra, *Writing Self, Writing Empire.*

36. Qademi, "Persian Chronicles," 407–16. Qademi ascribes the volume of history writing at this time to the formation of independent regional states and the East India Company. On histories pertaining to the Mughal empire, see ibid., 408–9.

37. Gupta explores the ways in which Delhi's history came to be linked to its monuments in "From Architecture to Archaeology."

38. The modern publication of this manuscript is Sangin Beg, *Sayr al-Manazil,* ed. Sharif Husain Qasimi (Delhi: Ghalib Institute, 1982).

39. BL, Asian and African Collections, Add. 24053. A second copy of the work was dedicated to William Fraser, BL, Asian and African collections, Or. 1762. See Rieu, *Catalogue of Persian Manuscripts,* 1:431. Naim discusses the manuscript and its dating in "Syed Ahmad and His Two Books."

40. On the structure of the text, see Naim, "Syed Ahmad and His Two Books."

41. British Library, Add. Or. 5475. Partially reproduced in Kaye, *Golden Calm.* The album also includes portraits of Bahadur Shah Zafar as well as a panoramic view of a Mughal procession.

42. Losty, "Depicting Delhi," 58; Losty, *Delhi 360°,* 10–11.

43. On a later iteration of this theme, see Patel, "Photographic Albums of Abbas Ali."

44. BL, Asian and African Collections, Or. 1891 and Or. 2033.

45. Lelyveld, "Qutb Minar," 152. Also see Fisher, "Britain in the Urdu Tongue," 122–46.

46. Zayn al-ʿAbidin Shirwani, *Bustan al-Siyahat* (Tehran: Kitabkhanah-i Sanaʾi, 1897), cited in Naim, "Syed Ahmad and His Two Books," 16.

47. Naim, "Syed Ahmad and His Two Books," 16.

48. Cited in ibid.

49. Cited in ibid., 17.

50. Ibid.

51. The *Haft Iqlim* also functioned as a tazkira, in which biographies of individuals were organized by region, or "clime."

52. BL, Asian and African Collections, Or. 1845 and Or. 6371.

53. Kavuri-Bauer, *Monumental Matters,* 96–97. Kavuri-Bauer argues that the text strikes a balance between "objective information," geared toward its British patron, and "local Muslim memory," whereby Agra is called Akbarabad and the ruined or destroyed palaces of the former Mughal nobility are included into the account.

54. Glover, *Making Lahore Modern*, 188–91.

55. Ibid., 189.

56. Sayyid Ahmad Khan, *Asar al-Sanadid*. Troll catalogues the various editions, reprints, and translations of the text in Troll, "Note," 137–38. On its status as the first architectural history of Delhi, see Nath, *Monuments of Delhi*, v. This work contains a partial translation of the *Āsār al-Sanādīd*. Lelyveld points to the way in which the *Sayir al-Manazil* anticipates the *Āsār al-Sanādīd* in Lelyveld, "Qutb Minar."

57. Sayyid Ahmad Khan, *Asar al-Sanadid: Tārīkh purānī*. Those who have commented on the differences between the two versions include Juneja, *Architecture in Medieval India*, 10–11; Lelyveld, "Qutb Minar"; Naim, "Syed Ahmad and His Two Books"; Troll, "Note"; and Nath, *Monuments of Delhi*, who describes the 1854 version as "tremendously improved" (v).

58. On the structure and content of the 1847 *Āsār al-Sanādīd*, see Naim, "Syed Ahmad and His Two Books," 4–7; Troll, "Note," 136–39.

59. Naim, "Syed Ahmad and His Two Books," 7.

60. Losty, "Depicting Delhi," 56.

61. Naim, "Syed Ahmad and His Two Books," 7.

62. Bailey, *Art on the Jesuit Missions*, 112–43.

63. Rice, "Brush and the Burin," 305–10. On a related note, Rice analyzes artistic interconnections between genres of calligraphy and painting in Rice, "Between the Brush and the Pen."

64. Naim, "Syed Ahmad and His Two Books," 6–7; Troll, "Note," 136.

65. Naim makes the connection to the tazkira tradition explicit in Naim, "Syed Ahmad and His Two Books," 6–7. He details nine categories of individual: Sufi masters (*masha'ikh*), Sufi mystics (*majazib*), physicians, religious scholars, preservers of the Qur'an (*haffaz*), poets, calligraphers, artists, and musicians.

66. Troll recounts these differences in Troll, "Note," 140; so does Naim, "Syed Ahmad and His Two Books," esp. 23–30.

67. Numerous scholars cited in this section make this point, including Glover, Gupta, Kavuri-Bauer, Lelyveld, and Naim.

68. Lelyveld, Naim, and Troll all reference the tazkira tradition, and Glover and Kavuri-Bauer both underscore the notion of the city as an inhabited space, in contrast to the archaeological approach taken in the later *Āsār* and other related examples.

69. The poem is translated in 'Abd-al-Ġanī, *History of Persian Language and Literature*, 119–25. The source of the couplet is identified by Naim, "Syed Ahmad and His Two Books," 1. See Lelyveld, *Qutb Minar*, 166n23.

70. For more on Syed Ahmad Khan's relationship to these scholarly societies, see Rajagopalan, "Nineteenth-Century Architectural Archive."

71. Naim, "Syed Ahmad and His Two Books," 29.

72. Glover, *Making Lahore Modern*, chap. 6. Glover extensively analyzes the two texts in this section, and I draw on his discussion.

73. Ibid., 190. After Bayly, *Empire and Information*, 55.

74. Syad Muhammad Latif, *Lahore, Lahore: Its History, Architectural Remains and Antiquities, with an Account of Its Modern Institutions, Inhabitants, Their Trade, Customs* (Lahore: New Imperial, 1892).

75. Glover, *Making Lahore Modern*, 193.

76. The classic study on this topic is Cohn, *Colonialism and Its Forms of Knowledge*. See especially his chapter on antiquarianism. Cohn's essay is placed in historiographical perspective by Ali and Sengupta, *Knowledge Production, Pedagogy, and Institutions*; and Pinch, "Same Difference in India and Europe." For recent treatments of this topic, see Desai and Rajagopalan, *Colonial Frames, Nationalist Histories*; Guha-Thakurta, *Monuments, Objects, Histories*.

77. These include Gupta, Lelyveld, Naim, and Rajagopalan.

78. Naim, "Syed Ahmad and His Two Books," 14. On Elliot, see Hodivala, *Studies in Indo-Muslim History*. See Gupta, "From Architecture to Archaeology," 58; and Lelyveld, *Qutb Minar*, 148–49, on the critical reception of the text by Sprenger, including Syed Ahmad Khan's disassociation from him.

79. Rām Rāz, *Essay on the Architecture of the Hindus*.

80. M. Desai, "Interpreting an Architectural Past."

81. Ibid., 473.

82. Ali and Sengupta, *Knowledge Production, Pedagogy, and Institutions*; Pinch, "Same Difference in India and Europe." See also Rajagopalan, "Nineteenth-Century Architectural Archive," in which she argues against "dichotomies such as European versus Indian," 29.

Conclusion

1. See the Introduction, esp. n43.

2. For more on the Brighton Pavilion, see Dinkel, *Royal Pavilion*; and Morley, *Making of the Royal Pavilion*; for the Brighton Pavilion and similar

examples, see Conner, *Oriental Architecture in the West,* chap. 9–11.

3. See Humphry Repton's "An inquiry into the changes in architecture, as it relates to palaces and houses in England, including the castle and abbey Gothic, the mixed styles of Gothic, the Grecian and modern styles; with some remarks on the introduction of Indian architecture," in Repton, *Designs for the Pavilion.*

4. BL, Oriental and India Office Collections, India Office Records, F/4/195/4426.

5. See T. Metcalf, *Imperial Vision,* esp. chaps. 3 and 4.

6. Ibid., 66–90.

SELECT BIBLIOGRAPHY

ARCHIVAL AND MANUSCRIPT SOURCES

Archives nationales de France, Archives nationales d'outre-mer
Série F
Série géographique Inde

Bibliothèque nationale de France, *Manuscrits*
LE FONDS FRANÇAIS (FR.) ET LES NOUVELLES
ACQUISITIONS FRANÇAISES (N.A.FR.)
Gentil letters, 1773, n.a.fr. 9366
Gentil, Jean-Baptiste. *Divinities of Hindustan*, 1774,
    fr. 24220
Gentil, Jean-Baptiste. *History of Indian Numismatics*,
    n.d., fr. 25287
Gentil, Jean-Baptiste. *History of the Sovereigns of
    Hindustan*, 1772, fr. 24219
List of manuscripts sent by Gentil, deposited in the
    Royal Library in 1777, n.a.fr. 5440
SUPPLÉMENT PERSAN (S. P.)
Anonymous. *Description of the Taj Mahal*, S. P. 295,
    G. 28

**British Library, Asia, Pacific and Africa
Collections (formerly Oriental and India
Office Collections)**
INDIA OFFICE RECORDS
Board's Collections, 1796–1858, IOR F/4
ORIENTAL MANUSCRIPTS
ʿAbd al-Hamid Lahori and Muhammad Waris.
    Pādshāhnāma, Add. 20734
Muhammad Fakhr al-Din Husain. *Mirāt al-Shaba
    Salatīn Asmān*, Or. 182
Muhammd Sālih Kanbo. *ʿAmal-i Ṣāliḥ*, Add. 20735
Sangīn Beg. *Sayr al-Manāzil*, Add. 19430
——. *Sayr al-Manāzil*, Add. 24053
PRIVATE PAPERS
Charles Theophilus Metcalfe Papers

Journal of Captain Charles Reynolds
Orme Papers
Ozias Humphry Papers
Warren Hastings Papers

Delhi State Archives
Deputy Commissioner's Papers (DC)

National Archives of India
Home Public Index and Consultations, 1830–1849

Royal Asiatic Society, Manuscripts
Hafiz Kallu Khan. *Inscriptions on Mosques*, RAS
    Persian 351
Muhammad Hasan Sahib. *A Description of the Public
    Buildings of Shahjahanabad and the Neighbouring
    Region, Mainly Concerned with the Inscriptions on
    Them*, RAS Persian 181
Sangin Beg. *Sayr al-Manāzil*, RAS Persian 351

PRINTED PRIMARY SOURCES
Abū Ṭālib Khān. *History of Asafuʾd Daulah, Nawab
    Wazir of Oudh Being a Translation of "Tafzihuʾl
    Ghafilin," a Contemporary Record of Events
    Connected with His Administrations*. Translated by
    William Hoey. Lucknow: Pustak Kendra, 1971.
Anand Ram Mukhlis. *Encyclopaedic Dictionary of
    Medieval India: Mirat-ul-istilah*. Translated by
    Tasneem Ahmad. Delhi: Sundeep Prakashan, 1993.
Archer, Edward Caulfield. *Tours in Upper India, and
    in Parts of the Himalayan Mountains*. London:
    R. Bentley, 1833.
Baillie, Neil B. E. *A Digest of Moohummdan [sic] Law;
    Compiled and Translated from Authorities in the
    Original Arabic*. Lahore: Premier Book House,
    1965.
Cavenagh, Orfeur. *Reminiscences of an Indian Official*.
    London: Allen, 1884.

Dargah Quli Khan. *Muraqqaʻ-e-Delhi: The Mughal Capital in Muhammad Shah's Time.* Translated by Chander Shekar and Shama Mitra Chenoy. Delhi: Deputy, 1989.

———. *Muraqqaʻ-i Dihlī.* Edited by Nūrulḥasan Anṣārī. Delhi: Shuʻbah-i Urdu, Dihlī Yūnīvarsiṭī, 1982.

———. *Muraqqaʻ-i Dihli: Fārsi matan aur Urdu tarjamah.* Edited by Khalīq Anjum. New Delhi: Taqsimkar Anjuman-i Taraqqī-yi Urdū, Hind, 1993.

Forbes, James. *Oriental Memoirs.* London: White, Cochrane, 1813.

Francklin, William. *The History of the Reign of Shah-Aulum.* London: Cooper and Graham, 1798.

Gentil, Jean-Baptiste Joseph. *Mémoires sur l'Indoustan, ou Empire Mogol.* Paris: Petit, 1822.

Ghulām Ḥusayn Khān Ṭabāṭabāʼī. *The Siyar-ul-Mutakherin, A History of the Mahomedan Power in India During the Last Century.* Revised from the translation of Haji Mustafa and collated with the Persian original. Edited by John Briggs. London: J. Murray, 1832.

Hamīd al-Dīn Khān. *Ahkām-i ʻĀlamgīrī: Anecdotes of Aurangzib and Historical Essays.* Translated by Jadunath Sarkar. Calcutta: M. C. Sarkar, 1912.

Haq, S. Moinul. *Khafi Khan's History of ʻAlamgir: Being an English Translation of the Relevant Portions of Muntakhab Al-Lubāb.* Karachi: Pakistan Historical Society, 1975.

Heber, Reginald. *Narrative of a Journey Through the Upper Provinces of India, from Calcutta to Bombay, 1824–1825.* London: J. Murray, 1828.

Hodges, William. *Select Views in India: Drawn on the Spot in the Years 1780, 1781, 1782 and 1783.* London: J. Edwards, 1786.

———. *Travels in India: During the Years 1780, 1781, 1782, and 1783.* London: J. Edwards, 1793.

Hoey, William. *A Monograph on Trade and Manufactures in Northern India.* Lucknow: American Methodist Mission, 1880.

ʻInāyat Allāh Khān Kashmīrī. *Kalimāt-i Tayyibat (Collection of Aurangzeb's Orders).* Edited by S. M. Azizuddin Husain. Delhi: Idārah-i Adabiyāt-i Delli, 1982.

ʻInāyat Khān. *The Shāh Jahān Nāma.* Translated by W. E. Begley and Ziyaud-Din A. Desai. Delhi: Oxford University Press, 1990.

Irwin, H. C. *The Garden of India, or, Chapters on Oudh History and Affairs.* London: W. H. Allen, 1880.

Khān, Sayyid Aḥmad. *Āsār al-ṣanādīd.* Delhi: Maṭbaʻ Sayyid al-Akhbār, 1847.

———. *Āsār al-ṣanādīd: Tārīkh purānī aur naʼī ʻAmaldārou aur purānī aur naʼī ʻumdah ʻimāraton ke bābat zilaʼah Dihlī.* Delhi: W. Demonte, 1854.

Law de Lauriston, Jean. *Mémoires sur quelques affaires de l'Empire Mogol, 1756–1761.* Paris: E. Champion, 1913.

Manucci, Niccolao. *Storia Do Mogor, 1653–1708.* Translated by William Irvine. London: J. Murray, 1907.

Modave, Louis Laurent de Féderbe, Comte de. *Voyage en Inde du comte de Modave, 1773–1776 (Nouveaux mémoires sur l'état actuel du Bengale et de l'Indoustan).* Edited by Jean Deloche. Paris: École Française d'Extrême-Orient, 1971.

Muhammad Faiz Bakhsh. *Memoirs of Faizabad.* 2 vols. Edited by Hamid Qureshi. Translated by William Hoey. Lucknow: New Royal, 1888.

Muhammad Salih Kanbo. *Amal-i-Ṣāliḥ, or, Shāh Jahān Nāmah of Muḥammad Ṣāliḥ Kambo: A Complete History of the Emperor Shāh Jahān.* Edited by Ghulam Yazdani. 3 vols. Calcutta: Baptist Mission, 1912–30.

Nugent, Lady Maria. *A Journal from the Year 1811 till the Year 1815, Including a Voyage to, and Residence in, India.* London, 1839.

Rām Rāz. *Essay on the Architecture of the Hindus.* London: Published for the Royal Asiatic Society of Great Britain and Ireland by J. W. Parker, 1834.

Repton, Humphry. *Designs for the Pavilion at Brighton.* London: Printed for J. C. Stadley, 1808.

Roberts, Emma. *Scenes and Characteristics of Hindostan, with Sketches of Anglo-Indian Society.* 2 vols. London: W. H. Allen, 1837.

Russell, William Howard. *My Diary in India, in the Year 1858–9.* London: Routledge, Warne, 1860.

Sangin Beg. *Sayr al-Manāzil.* Delhi: Ghalib Institute, 1982.

Saqi Mustaʻidd Khan. *Maʼāsir-i ʻĀlamgīrī.* Edited by Agha Ahmad ʻAli. Calcutta: Baptist Mission, 1870.

———. *Maʼāsir-i ʻĀlamgīrī: A History of the Emperor Aurangzib-ʻAlamgir.* Translated by Jadunath Sarkar. Calcutta: Royal Asiatic Society of Bengal, 1947.

Tavernier, Jean-Baptiste. *Travels in India.* Translated by V. Ball. London: Macmillan, 1889.

Tieffenthaller, Joseph. *Description historique et géographique de l'Inde.* Edited by Jean Bernoulli. Berlin: Spener, 1791.

SECONDARY SOURCES

Aitken, Molly Emma. *The Intelligence of Tradition in Rajput Court Painting.* New Haven, CT: Yale University Press, 2010.

Alam, Muzaffar. *The Crisis of Empire in Mughal North India: Awadh and the Punjab, 1707–48.* New Delhi: Oxford University Press, 1986.

———. "The Culture and Politics of Persian in Precolonial Hindustan." In *Literary Cultures in*

History: Reconstructions from South Asia (1), edited by Sheldon Pollock, 131–98. Berkeley: University of California Press, 2003.

Alam, Muzaffar, and Seema Alavi. *A European Experience of the Mughal Orient: The I͞jāz-I Arsalān͞i (Persian Letters 1773–1779) of Antoine-Louis Henri Polier*. New Delhi: Oxford University Press, 2001.

Alam, Muzaffar, and Sanjay Subrahmanyam. "Discovering the Familiar: Notes on the Travel-Account of Anand Ram Mukhlis, 1745." *South Asia Research* 16, no. 2 (1996): 131–54.

——. *Indo-Persian Travels in the Age of Discoveries, 1400–1800*. Cambridge: Cambridge University Press, 2007.

——. *The Mughal State, 1526–1750*. New Delhi: Oxford University Press, 1998.

Alavi, Seema, ed. *The Eighteenth Century in India*. New Delhi: Oxford University Press, 2002.

Alfieri, Bianca. *Islamic Architecture of the Subcontinent*. London: Laurence King, 2000.

Ali, Daud, ed. *Invoking the Past: The Uses of History in South Asia*. New Delhi: Oxford University Press, 1999.

Ali, Daud, Ronald B. Inden, and Jonathan S. Walters. *Querying the Medieval: Texts and the History of Practices in South Asia*. Oxford: Oxford University Press, 2000.

Ali, Daud, and Indra Sengupta, eds. *Knowledge Production, Pedagogy, and Institutions in Colonial India*. New York: Palgrave Macmillan, 2011.

Allan, James W. *The Art and Architecture of Twelver Shi'ism: Iraq, Iran and the Indian Sub-Continent*. London: Azimuth, 2012.

Alvi, Sajida Sultana. *Perspectives in Mughal India: Rulers, Historians, "Ulama" and Sufis*. Karachi: Oxford University Press, 2012.

Aquil, Raziuddin. "Hazrat-i-Dehli: The Making of the Chishti Sufi Centre and the Stronghold of Islam." *South Asia Research* 28, no. 1 (2008): 23–48.

Aquil, Raziuddin, and Partha Chatterjee, eds. *History in the Vernacular*. Delhi: Permanent Black, 2008.

Ara, Matsuo. *Dargahs in Medieval India*. Tokyo: Tokyo University Press, 1977.

Archer, Mildred. *Between Battles: The Album of Colonel James Skinner*. London: Al-Falak and Scorpion, 1982.

——. *Company Drawings in the India Office Library*. London: British Library, 1972.

——. *Early Views of India: The Picturesque Journeys of Thomas and William Daniell, 1786–1794: The Complete Aquatints*. New York: Thames and Hudson, 1980.

Archer, Mildred, and Graham Parlett. *Company Paintings: Indian Paintings of the British Period*. London: Victoria & Albert Museum, 1992.

Asher, Catherine B. *Architecture of Mughal India*. New York: Cambridge University Press, 1992.

——. "The Architecture of Murshidabad: Regional Revival and Islamic Continuity." In *Islam and Indian Regions*, edited by Anna L. Dallapiccola and Stephanie Zingel-Avé Lallemant, 61–74. Stuttgart: Steiner, 1993.

——. "The Later Mughals and Mughal Successor States: Architecture in Oudh, Murshidabad, and Rampur." In *Architecture in Victorian and Edwardian India*, edited by Christopher W. London, 85–98. Bombay: Marg, 1994.

——. "Piety, Religion, and the Old Social Order in the Architecture of the Later Mughals and Their Contemporaries." In *Rethinking Early Modern India*, edited by Richard B. Barnett, 193–209. New Delhi: Manohar, 2002.

——. "Sub-Imperial Palaces: Power and Authority in Mughal India." *Ars Orientalis* 23 (1993): 281–302.

Avcıoğlu, Nebahat. *"Turquerie" and the Politics of Representation, 1728–1876*. Farnham, UK: Ashgate, 2011.

Avcıoğlu, Nebahat, and Finbarr Barry Flood. *Globalizing Cultures: Art and Mobility in the Eighteenth Century*. Washington, D.C.: Smithsonian Museum of Art, 2011.

Azizuddin Husain, S. M. *Structure of Politics Under Aurangzeb, 1658–1707*. New Delhi: Kanishka, 2002.

Babaie, Sussan. *Isfahan and Its Palaces: Statecraft, Shi'ism and the Architecture of Conviviality in Early Modern Iran*. Edinburgh: Edinburgh University Press, 2008.

Bailey, Gauvin. *Art on the Jesuit Missions in Asia and Latin America, 1542–1773*. Toronto: University of Toronto Press, 1999.

Barlow, Jon, and Lakshmi Subramanian. "Music and Society in North India: From the Mughals to the Mutiny." *Economic and Political Weekly* 42, no. 19 (2007): 1779–87.

Barnett, Richard B. *North India Between Empires: Awadh, the Mughals, and the British, 1720–1801*. Berkeley: University of California Press, 1980.

——, ed. *Rethinking Early Modern India*. New Delhi: Manohar, 2002.

Bayly, C. A. "Delhi and Other Cities of North India During the 'Twilight.'" In *Delhi Through the Ages: Essays in Urban History, Culture, and Society*, edited by Robert E. Frykenberg, 121–36. New Delhi: Oxford University Press, 1986.

———. *Empire and Information: Intelligence Gathering and Social Communication in India, 1780–1870*. Cambridge: Cambridge University Press, 1996.

———. *Indian Society and the Making of the British Empire*. New Cambridge History of India. Cambridge: Cambridge University Press, 1988.

Beach, Milo Cleveland. *Mughal and Rajput Painting*. Cambridge: Cambridge University Press, 1992.

Beach, Milo Cleveland, Ebba Koch, and Wheeler M. Thackston. *King of the World: The Padshahnama: An Imperial Mughal Manuscript from the Royal Library, Windsor Castle*. London: Azimuth, 1997.

Begley, Wayne E. "Mirak Mirza Ghiyas." *Macmillan Encyclopedia of Architects*. Edited by Adolf K. Placzek. New York: Collier Macmillan, 1982.

———. "The Myth of the Taj Mahal and a New Theory of Its Symbolic Meaning." *Art Bulletin* 61, no. 1 (March 1979): 7–37.

———. "The Symbolic Role of Calligraphy on Three Imperial Mosques of Shah Jahan." In *Kalādarśana: American Studies in the Art of India*, edited by Joanna G. Williams, 7–18. Leiden: Brill, 1981.

Begley, W. E., and Z. A. Desai. *Monumental Islamic Calligraphy from India*. 1st edition. Villa Park, IL: Islamic Foundation, 1985.

———. *Taj Mahal: The Illumined Tomb. An Anthology of Seventeenth-Century Mughal and European Documentary Sources*. Cambridge, MA: Aga Khan Program for Islamic Architecture, 1989.

Bhatia, M. L. *Administrative History of Medieval India: A Study of Muslim Jurisprudence Under Aurangzeb*. New Delhi: Radha, 1992.

———. *The Ulama, Islamic Ethics, and Courts Under the Mughals: Aurangzeb Revisited*. New Delhi: Manak, 2006.

Blair, Sheila. *Islamic Inscriptions*. New York: New York University Press, 1998.

Blake, Stephen. *Shahjahanabad: The Sovereign City in Mughal India, 1639–1739*. Cambridge: Cambridge University Press, 1991.

Bleichmar, Daniela. *Visible Empire: Botanical Expeditions and Visual Culture in the Hispanic Enlightenment*. Chicago: University of Chicago Press, 2012.

Bleichmar, Daniela, and Meredith Martin, eds. *Objects in Motion in the Early Modern World*. Hoboken, NJ: Wiley, 2016.

Bokhari, Afshan. "Imperial Transgressions and Spiritual Investitures: A Begam's 'Ascension' in Seventeenth Century Mughal India." *Journal of Persianate Studies* 4, no. 1 (2011): 86–108.

———. "The 'Light' of the Timuria: Jahan Ara Begum's Patronage, Piety, and Poetry in 17th Century Mughal India." *Marg* 60, no. 1 (2008): 52–61.

Brand, Michael. "Orthodoxy, Innovation, and Revival: Considerations of the Past in Imperial Mughal Tomb Architecture." *Muqarnas* 10 (1993): 323–34.

Brown, Katherine Butler. "Dargah Quli Khan's Strange Vision: Mughals, Music, and the Muraqqaʿ-i Dehli." *Centre of South Asian Studies, University of Cambridge Occasional Paper* 4 (2003): 1–20.

———. "Did Aurangzeb Ban Music? Questions for the Historiography of His Reign." *Modern Asian Studies* 41 (2007): 77–120.

———. "If Music Be the Food of Love: Masculinity and Eroticism in the Mughal Mehfil." In *Love in South Asia: A Cultural History*, edited by Francesca Orsini, 64–71. Cambridge: Cambridge University Press, 2006.

Brown, Percy. *Indian Architecture*. Bombay: D. B. Taraporevala, 1942.

Bruijn, Thomas de, and Allison Busch. *Culture and Circulation: Literature in Motion in Early Modern India*. Leiden: Brill, 2014.

Busch, Allison. "Hidden in Plain View: Brajbhasha Poets at the Mughal Court." *Modern Asian Studies* 44, no. 2 (2010): 267–309.

———. *Poetry of Kings: The Classical Hindi Literature of Mughal India*. New York: Oxford University Press, 2011.

Chaghtai, M. Abdullah. *The Badshahi Masjid (Built by Aurangzeb in 1084/1674): History and Architecture*. Lahore: Kitab Khana-i-Nauras, 1972.

———. "A Family of Great Mughal Architects." *Islamic Culture* 11 (1973): 200–209.

Chakrabarty, Dipesh. *Provincializing Europe: Postcolonial Thought and Historical Difference*. Princeton, NJ: Princeton University Press, 2000.

Chandra, Satish. "Cultural and Political Role of Delhi, 1675–1725." In *Delhi Through the Ages: Essays in Urban History, Culture, and Society*, edited by Robert E. Frykenberg, 106–18. New Delhi: Oxford University Press, 1986.

———. *Parties and Politics at the Mughal Court, 1707–1740*. New Delhi: Oxford University Press, 2002.

Charlesworth, Michael. "India: The 1890 Album and the Canon of Mughal Architecture." In *Art and the Early Photographic Album*, edited by Stephen Bann, 237–59. Washington, D.C.: National Gallery of Art, 2011.

Chatterjee, Kumkum. *The Cultures of History in Early Modern India: Persianization and Mughal Culture in Bengal*. New Delhi: Oxford University Press, 2009.

——. "History as Self-Representation: The Recasting of a Political Tradition in Late Eighteenth-Century Eastern India." *Modern Asian Studies* 32, no. 4 (1998): 913–48.

Cheema, G. S. *The Forgotten Mughals: A History of the Later Emperors of the House of Babar, 1707–1857.* New Delhi: Manohar, 2002.

Chelkowski, Peter J. *Taziyeh, Ritual and Drama in Iran.* New York University Studies in Near Eastern Civilization. New York: New York University Press, 1979.

Chenoy, Shama Mitra. *Shahjahanabad, a City of Delhi, 1638–1857.* New Delhi: Munshiram Manoharlal, 1998.

Cohn, Bernard S. *Colonialism and Its Forms of Knowledge: The British in India.* Princeton, NJ: Princeton University Press, 1996.

Cole, J. R. I. "Invisible Occidentalism: Eighteenth-Century Indo-Persian Constructions of the West." *Iranian Studies* 25, nos. 3/4 (1992): 3–16.

——. "Mirror of the World: Iranian 'Orientalism' and Early 19th-century India." *Critique: Critical Middle Eastern Studies* 5, no. 8 (1996): 41–60.

——. *Roots of North Indian Shiʿism in Iran and Iraq: Religion and State in Awadh, 1722–1859.* Berkeley: University of California Press, 1988.

——. *Sacred Space and Holy War: The Politics, Culture and History of Shiʿite Islam.* London: Tauris, 2002.

Conner, Patrick. *Oriental Architecture in the West.* London: Thames and Hudson, 1979.

Crane, Howard, and Esra Akin, trans. and eds., and Gülru Necipoğlu, ed. *Sinan's Autobiographies: Five Sixteenth-Century Texts.* Leiden: Brill, 2006.

Crinson, Mark. *Empire Building: Orientalism and Victorian Architecture.* London: Routledge, 1996.

Cummins, Tom, and Joanne Rappaport. *Beyond the Lettered City: Indigenous Literacies in the Andes.* Durham, NC: Duke University Press, 2012.

Dadlani, Chanchal. "Innovation, Appropriation, and Representation:" In *Histories of Ornament: From Global to Local,* edited by Gülru Necipoğlu and Alina Payne, 178–189. Princeton, NJ: Princeton University Press, 2016.

——. "The 'Palais Indiens' Collection of 1774: Representing Mughal Architecture in Late Eighteenth-Century India." *Ars Orientalis* 39, no. 1 (2010): 175–97.

——. "Transporting India: The Gentil Album and Mughal Manuscript Culture." *Art History* 38, no. 4 (2015): 748–61.

Dale, Stephen Frederic. *The Muslim Empires of the Ottomans, Safavids, and Mughals.* Cambridge: Cambridge University Press, 2010.

Dalrymple, William, and Yuthika Sharma. *Princes and Painters in Mughal Delhi, 1707–1857.* New Haven, CT: Yale University Press, 2012.

Das, Neeta. *Architecture of Lucknow: Imambaras and Karbalas.* Dehli: B. R., 2008.

——. "Lucknow's Imambaras and Karbalas." In *Lucknow: Then and Now,* edited by Rosie Llewellyn-Jones, 90–103. Mumbai: Marg, 2003.

Das, Neeta, and Rosie Llewellyn-Jones, eds. *Murshidabad: Forgotten Capital of Bengal.* Mumbai: Marg, 2013.

Deleury, Guy, ed. *Les Indes Florissantes: Anthologie des Voyageurs Français, 1750–1820.* Paris: R. Laffont, 1991.

Delvoye, Françoise. "Indo-Persian Literature on Art-Music: Some Historical and Technical Aspects." In *Confluence of Cultures: French Contributions to Indo-Persian Studies,* edited by Françoise Delvoye, 93–130. New Delhi: Centre for Human Sciences; Tehran: Institut Français de Recherche en Iran, 1994.

Desai, Z. A. *Arabic, Persian, and Urdu Inscriptions of West India: A Topographical List.* New Delhi: Sundeep Prakashan, 1999.

Dinkel, John. *The Royal Pavilion, Brighton.* New York: Vendome, 1983.

Dudney, Arthur. *Delhi: Pages from a Forgotten History.* Delhi: Hay House, 2015.

——. "A Desire for Meaning: Ḵẖān-i Ārzū's Philology and the Place of India in the Eighteenth-Century Persianate World." Ph.D. diss., Columbia University, 2013.

——. "Sabk-e Hindi and the Crisis of Authority in Eighteenth-Century Indo-Persian." *Journal of Persianate Studies* 9, no. 1 (2016): 60–82.

Eaton, Natasha. *Colour, Art and Empire: Visual Culture and the Nomadism of Representation.* London: I. B. Taurus, 2013.

——. "'Enchanted Traps?' The Historiography of Art and Colonialism in Eighteenth-Century India." *Literature Compass* 9, no. 1 (2012): 15–33.

——. *Mimesis Across Empires: Artworks and Networks in India, 1765–1860.* Durham, NC: Duke University Press, 2013.

Eaton, Richard M., and Phillip B. Wagoner. *Power, Memory, Architecture: Contested Sites on India's Deccan Plateau, 1300–1600.* New York: Oxford University Press, 2014.

Edney, Matthew H. *Mapping an Empire: The Geographical Construction of British India, 1765–1843.* Chicago: University of Chicago Press, 1997.

Ehlers, Eckart, and Thomas Krafft. *Ṣẖāhjahānābād, Old Delhi: Tradition and Colonial Change.* Stuttgart: F. Steiner, 1993.

Ernst, Carl W. *Eternal Garden: Mysticism, History, and Politics at a South Asian Sufi Center.* Albany: State University of New York Press, 1992.

Ernst, Carl W., and Bruce B. Lawrence. *Sufi Martyrs of Love: Chishti Sufism in South Asia and Beyond.* New York: Palgrave Macmillan, 2002.

Evers, Bernd, and Christof Thoenes, eds. *Architectural Theory: From the Renaissance to the Present.* Cologne: Taschen, 2003.

Falāhī, Ziauddīn. "A Historical Survey of Arabic Fiqh Literature of Medieval India: An Analytical Study of Manuscripts." *Hamdard Islamicus* 28, no. 1 (January 2005): 53–64.

Falk, Toby, and Mildred Archer. *Indian Miniatures in the India Office Library.* London: Sotheby Parke Bernet, 1981.

Fanshawe, H. C. *Delhi Past and Present.* London: J. Murray, 1902.

Farhat, May. "Islamic Piety and Dynastic Legitimacy: The Case of the Shrine of ʿAlī B. Mūsá Al-Riḍā in Mashhad (10th–17th Century)." PhD diss., Harvard University, 2002.

Farooqi, Naimur Rahman. *Mughal–Ottoman Relations: A Study of Political and Diplomatic Relations Between Mughal India and the Ottoman Empire, 1556–1748.* Delhi: Idarah-i Adabiyat-i Delli, 1989.

Fergusson, James. *A History of Architecture in All Countries: From the Earliest Times to the Present Day.* London: J. Murray, 1873.

———. *History of Indian and Eastern Architecture.* London: J. Murray, 1876.

Findly, Ellison Banks. "Women's Wealth and Styles of Giving: Perspectives from Buddhist, Jain, and Mughal Sites." In *Women, Patronage, and Self-Representation in Islamic Societies,* edited by D. Fairchild Ruggles, 91–122. Albany: State University of New York Press, 2000.

Firmage, Edwin Brown, Bernard G. Weiss, and John W. Welch, eds. *Religion and Law: Biblical-Judaic and Islamic Perspectives.* Winona Lake, IN: Eisenbrauns, 1990.

Fisher, Michael. *A Clash of Cultures: Awadh, the British, and the Mughals.* Riverdale, MD: Riverdale, 1987.

———. *Counterflows to Colonialism: Indian Travelers and Settlers in Britain 1600–1857.* Delhi: Permanent Black, 2004.

———. "Britain in the Urdu Tongue." In *A Wilderness of Possibilities: Urdu Studies in Transnational Perspective,* edited by Kathryn Hansen, 122–46. New Delhi: Oxford University Press, 2005.

———. "From India to England and Back: Early Indian Travel Narratives for Indian Readers." *Huntington Library Quarterly* 70, no. 1 (2007): 153–72.

———. "Teaching Persian as an Imperial Language in India and in England During the Late 18th and Early 19th Centuries." In *Literacy in the Persianate World: Writing and the Social Order,* edited by Brian Spooner and William L. Hanaway, 328–58. Philadelphia: University of Pennsylvania Museum of Archaeology and Anthropology, 2012.

Frykenberg, Robert E., ed. *Delhi Through the Ages: Essays in Urban History, Culture, and Society.* New Delhi: Oxford University Press, 1986.

Gadebusch, Raffael. "Celestial Gardens: Mughal Miniatures from an Eighteenth-Century Album." *Orientations* 31 (2000): 69–74.

Ghosh, Durba. *Sex and the Family in Colonial India: The Making of Empire.* Cambridge: Cambridge University Press, 2006.

Glover, William J. *Making Lahore Modern: Constructing and Imagining a Colonial City.* Minneapolis: University of Minnesota Press, 2008.

Goetz, Hermann. "The Qudsia Bagh at Delhi: Key to Late Moghul Architecture." *Islamic Culture* 26, no. 1 (1952): 132–43.

Gole, Susan. *Indian Maps and Plans: From Earliest Times to the Advent of European Surveys.* New Delhi: Manohar, 1989.

———. *Maps of Mughal India: Drawn by Jean-Baptiste-Joseph Gentil, Agent for the French Government to the Court of Shuja-ud-daula at Faizabad, in 1770.* New Delhi: Manohar, 1988.

———. "Three Maps of Shahjahanabad." *South Asian Studies* 4 (1988): 13–27.

Green, Nile. "Auspicious Foundations: The Patronage of Sufi Institutions in the Late Mughal and Early Asaf Jah Deccan." *South Asian Studies* 20, no. 1 (2004): 71–98.

———. *Indian Sufism Since the Seventeenth Century: Saints, Books, and Empires in the Muslim Deccan.* Hoboken, NJ: Taylor and Francis, 2006.

———. *Making Space: Sufis and Settlers in Early Modern India.* New Delhi: Oxford University Press, 2012.

———. "The Uses of Books in a Late Mughal Takiyya: Persianate Knowledge Between Person and Paper." *Modern Asian Studies* 44, no. 2 (2009): 241–65.

Gude, Tushara Bindu, and Stephen Markel. *India's Fabled City: The Art of Courtly Lucknow.* Los Angeles: Los Angeles County Museum of Art, 2010.

Guenther, Alan M. "Hanafi Fiqh in Mughal India: The Fatāwá-I Al-Ālamgīrī." In *India's Islamic Traditions: 711–1750,* edited by Richard M. Eaton, 209–30. New Delhi: Oxford University Press, 2003.

Guha, Sumit. "Speaking Historically: The Changing Voices of Historical Narration in Western India, 1400–1900." *American Historical Review* 109, no. 4 (2004): 1084–1103.

Guha-Thakurta, Tapati. *Monuments, Objects, Histories: Institutions of Art in Colonial and Postcolonial India.* Cultures of History. New York: Columbia University Press, 2004.

Gupta, Manik Lal. *Sources of Mughal History, 1526 to 1740.* New Delhi: Atlantic, 1989.

Gupta, Narayani. *Delhi Between Two Empires, 1803–1931: Society, Government and Urban Growth.* New Delhi: Oxford University Press, 1981.

——. "From Architecture to Archaeology: The 'Monumentalising' of Delhi's History in the Nineteenth Century." In *Perspectives of Mutual Encounters in South Asian History, 1760–1860,* edited by Jamal Malik and Gail Minault, 49–64. Leiden: Brill, 2000.

Guy, John, and Jorrit Britschgi. *Wonder of the Age: Master Painters of India, 1100–1900.* New York: Metropolitan Museum of Art, 2011.

Habib, Irfan. *An Atlas of the Mughal Empire.* Aligarh: Centre of Advanced Study in History, Aligarh Muslim University, 1982.

Haidar, Navina Najat, and Marika Sardar, eds. *Sultans of the South: Arts of India's Deccan Courts, 1323–1687.* New York: Metropolitan Museum of Art, 2011.

Hakala, Walter. *Negotiating Languages: Urdu, Hindi, and the Definition of Modern South Asia.* New York: Columbia University Press, 2016.

——. "On Equal Terms: The Equivocal Origins of an Early Mughal Indo-Persian Vocabulary." *Journal of the Royal Asiatic Society* 25, no. 2 (2015): 209–27.

——. "A Sultan in the Realm of Passion: Coffee in Eighteenth-Century Delhi." *Eighteenth-Century Studies* 47, no. 4 (2014): 371–88.

Hallaq, Wael B. *An Introduction to Islamic Law.* Cambridge: Cambridge University Press, 2009.

Hamadeh, Shirine. *The City's Pleasures: Istanbul in the Eighteenth Century.* Seattle: University of Washington Press, 2008.

——. "Public Spaces and the Garden Culture of Istanbul in the Eighteenth Century." In *The Early Modern Ottomans: Remapping the Empire,* edited by Virginia Aksan and Daniel Goffman, 277–312. Cambridge: Cambridge University Press, 2007.

Hambly, Gavin. *Women in the Medieval Islamic World: Power, Patronage, and Piety.* New York: St. Martin's, 1998.

Hanaway, William, and Brian Spooner. *Literacy in the Persianate World: Writing and the Social Order.* Philadelphia: University of Pennsylvania Museum of Archaeology and Anthropology, 2012.

Hart, Vaughan, and Peter Hicks. *Paper Palaces: The Rise of the Renaissance Architectural Treatise.* New Haven, CT: Yale University Press, 1998.

Hasan, Perween. "The Footprint of the Prophet." *Muqarnas* 10 (1993): 335–43.

Hasan, Zafar. *A Guide to Nizamu-d Din.* Memoirs of the Archaeological Survey of India. Calcutta: Superintendent Government Printing, 1922.

——. *Monuments of Delhi: Lasting Splendour of the Great Mughals and Others.* Edited by J. A. Page. 1916. Reprint, New Delhi: Aryan, 1997.

Havell, E. B. *Indian Architecture: Its Psychology, Structure, and History from the First Muhammadan Invasion to the Present Day.* London: J. Murray, 1913.

Hermansen, Marcia, and Bruce Lawrence. "Indo-Persian Tazkiras as Memorative Communications." In *Beyond Turk and Hindu: Rethinking Religious Identities in Islamicate South Asia,* edited by David Gilmartin and Bruce Lawrence, 149–75. Gainesville: University Press of Florida, 2000.

Hill, Samuel Charles. *The Life of Claud Martin, Major-General in the Army of the Honourable East India Company.* Calcutta: Thacker, Spink, 1901.

Hillenbrand, Robert. "Qurʾanic Epigraphy in Medieval Islamic Architecture." *Revue des études Islamiques* 54 (1986): 171–81.

Hollister, John Norman. *The Shiʿa of India.* London: Luzac, 1953.

Hosagrahar, Jyoti. *Indigenous Modernities: Negotiating Architecture and Urbanism.* Architext. London: Routledge, 2005.

Howes, Jennifer. *Illustrating India: The Early Colonial Investigations of Colin Mackenzie (1784–1821).* New York: Oxford University Press, 2010.

Hunt, Lynn, Margaret C. Jacob, and W. W. Mijnhardt, eds. *Bernard Picart and the First Global Vision of Religion.* Los Angeles: Getty Research Institute, 2010.

——. *The Book That Changed Europe: Picart and Bernard's Religious Ceremonies of the World.* Cambridge, MA: Harvard University Press, 2010.

Hurel, Roselyne. *Miniatures et peintures indiennes: Collection du département des Estampes et de la photographie de la Bibliothèque nationale de France.* Vol. 1. Paris: Bibliothèque nationale de France, 2010.

Husain, Muhammad Ashraf. *An Historical Guide to the Agra Fort (Based on Contemporary Records).* Delhi: Manager of Publications, 1937.

Hussain, Jamila. *Islamic Law and Society: An Introduction.* Sydney: Federation, 1999.

Hutton, Deborah S. *Art of the Court of Bijapur.* Bloomington: Indiana University Press, 2006.

Irvine, William. *Later Mughals.* Calcutta: Sarkar, 1921.

Jalal, Talha. *Memoirs of the Badshahi Mosque: Notes on History and Architecture Based on Archives, Literature, and Archaic Images.* Karachi: Oxford University Press, 2013.

Jasanoff, Maya. *Edge of Empire: Lives, Culture, and Conquest in the East, 1750–1850.* New York: Knopf, 2005.

Johnson-Roehr, Susan N. "The Spatialization of Knowledge and Power at the Astronomical Observatories of Sawai Jai Singh II, C. 1721–1743 CE." Ph.D. diss., University of Illinois, 2011.

Jones, Justin. *Shi'a Islam in Colonial India: Religion, Community and Sectarianism.* Cambridge: Cambridge University Press, 2012.

Juneja, Monica. *Architecture in Medieval India: Forms, Contexts, Histories.* Delhi: Permanent Black, 2001.

Kafescioğlu, Çiğdem. *Constantinopolis/Istanbul: Cultural Encounter, Imperial Vision, and the Construction of the Ottoman Capital.* University Park: Pennsylvania State University Press, 2009.

Kaicker, Abhishek. "The Colonial Entombment of the Mughal Habitus: Delhi in the Eighteenth and Nineteenth Centuries." Master's thesis, University of British Columbia, 2006.

———. "Unquiet City: Making and Unmaking Politics in Mughal Delhi, 1707–39." Ph.D. diss., Columbia University, 2014.

Kavuri-Bauer, Santhi. *Monumental Matters: The Power, Subjectivity, and Space of India's Mughal Architecture.* Durham, NC: Duke University Press, 2011.

Kaye, M. M., ed. *The Golden Calm: An English Lady's Life in Moghul Delhi.* New York: Viking, 1980.

Keddie, Nikki, and Rudi Matthee, eds. *Iran and the Surrounding World: Interactions in Culture and Cultural Politics.* Seattle: University of Washington Press, 2002.

Keshani, Hussein. "The Architecture of Ritual: Eighteenth-Century Lucknow and the Making of the Great Imambarah Complex, a Forgotten World Monument." Ph.D. diss., University of Victoria, 2004.

———. "Architecture and the Twelver Shi'i Tradition: The Great Imambara Complex of Lucknow." *Muqarnas* 23 (2006): 219–50.

———. "Building Nizamuddin, a Delhi Sultanate Dargah and Its Surrounding Buildings." Master's thesis, University of Victoria, 2000.

———. "The Writing on the Walls: Selections from the Twelver Shi'i Epigraphs of Lucknow's Hussainabad Imambara." In *People of the Prophet's House: Artistic and Ritual Expressions of Shi'i Islam,* edited by Fahmida Suleman, 115–25. London: Azimuth, 2015.

Khera, Dipti. "Marginal, Mobile, Multilayered: Painted Invitation Letters as Bazaar Objects in Early Modern India." *Journal 18,* no. 1 (Spring 2016). http://www.journal18.org/527.

———. "Picturing India's 'Land of Kings' Between the Mughal and British Empires: Topographical Imaginings of Udaipur and Its Environs." Ph.D. diss., Columbia University, 2013.

Kia, Mana. "Accounting for Difference: A Comparative Look at the Autobiographical Travel Narratives of Hazin Lāhiji and Abd-al-Karim Kashmiri." *Journal of Persianate Studies* 2, no. 2 (2009): 210–36.

———. "Adab as Literary Form and Social Conduct: Reading the Gulistan in Late Mughal India." In *"No Tapping Around Philology": A Festschrift in Celebration and Honor of Wheeler McIntosh Thackston Jr.'s 70th Birthday,* edited by Alireza Korangy and Daniel Sheffield, 281–308. Wiesbaden: Harrassowitz, 2014.

———. "Contours of Persianate Community, 1722–1835." Ph.D. diss, Harvard University, 2011.

King, Anthony D. *The Bungalow: The Production of a Global Culture.* New York: Oxford University Press, 1995.

Kinra, Rajeev. "Infantilizing Bābā Dārā: The Cultural Memory of Dārā Shekuh and the Mughal Public Sphere." *Journal of Persianate Studies* 2, no. 2 (2009): 165–93.

———. *Writing Self, Writing Empire: Chandar Bhan Brahman and the Cultural World of the Indo-Persian State Secretary.* Berkeley: University of California Press, 2015.

Koch, Ebba. "The Baluster Column: A European Motif in Mughal Architecture and Its Meaning." *Journal of the Warburg and Courtauld Institutes* (1982): 251–62.

———. *The Complete Taj Mahal and the Riverfront Gardens of Agra.* London: Thames and Hudson, 2006.

———. "Diwan-i 'Amm and Chihil Sutun: The Audience Halls of Shah Jahan." *Muqarnas* 11 (1994): 143–65.

———. "The Hierarchical Principles of Shah-Jahani Painting." In *King of the World: The Padshahnama: An Imperial Mughal Manuscript from the Royal Library, Windsor Castle,* edited by Milo Cleveland

Beach, Ebba Koch, and Wheeler M. Thackston, 130–43. London: Azimuth and Thames and Hudson, 1997.

——. "The Madrasa of Ghaziu'd-Din Khan at Delhi." In *The Delhi College: Traditional Elites, the Colonial State, and Education Before 1857*, edited by Margrit Pernau, 35–59. New Delhi: Oxford University Press, 2006.

——. *Mughal Architecture: An Outline of Its History and Development, 1526–1858.* Munich: Prestel, 1991.

——. "Shah Jahan's Visits to Delhi Prior to 1648: New Evidence of Ritual Movement in Urban Mughal India." *Environmental Design* 9, no. 11 (1991): 18–29.

——. "The Symbolic Possession of the World: European Cartography in Mughal Allegory and History Painting." *Journal of the Economic and Social History of the Orient* 55 (2012): 547–80.

——. "The Wooden Audience Halls of Shah Jahan: Sources and Reconstruction." *Muqarnas* 30 (2013): 351–89.

Kostof, Spiro, ed. *The Architect: Chapters in the History of the Profession.* New York: Oxford University Press, 1986.

Kumar, Sunil. *The Present in Delhi's Pasts.* New Delhi: Three Essays, 2002.

Lafont, Jean Marie. *Chitra: Cities and Monuments of Eighteenth-Century India from French Archives.* New Delhi: Oxford University Press, 2001.

——. *Indika: Essays in Indo-French Relations, 1630–1976.* New Delhi: Centre de Sciences Humaines, 2000.

Lafont, Jean-Marie, and Rehana Lafont. *The French and Delhi: Agra, Aligarh, and Sardhana.* New Delhi: India Research, 2010.

Lal, Ruby. *Domesticity and Power in the Early Mughal World.* Cambridge: Cambridge University Press, 2005.

Latif, Syad Muhammad. *Agra: Historical and Descriptive.* 1896. Reprint, Lahore: Oriental, 1981.

Leach, Linda. *Mughal and Other Indian Paintings from the Chester Beatty Library.* 2 vols. London: Scorpion Cavendish, 1995.

——. *Paintings from India.* London: Nour Foundation in association with Azimuth Editions and Oxford University Press, 1998.

Leibsohn, Dana, and Jeanette Peterson, eds. *Seeing Across Cultures in the Early Modern World.* Farnham, UK: Ashgate, 2012.

Lelyveld, David. "The Qutb Minar in Sayyid Ahmad Khan's Asar Us-Sanadid." In *Knowledge Production, Pedagogy, and Institutions in Colonial India*, edited by Indra Sengupta and Daud Ali, 147–68. New York: Palgrave Macmillan, 2011.

Lentz, Thomas W., and Glenn D. Lowry. *Timur and the Princely Vision: Persian Art and Culture in the Fifteenth Century.* Los Angeles: Los Angeles County Museum of Art, 1989.

Leonard, Karen. "The Hyderabad Political System and Its Participants." *Journal of Asian Studies* 30, no. 3 (1971): 569–82.

Lewcock, R. "Architects, Craftsmen, and Builders: Materials and Techniques." In *Architecture of the Islamic World: Its History and Social Meaning*, edited by George Michell, 112–43. London: Thames and Hudson, 1978.

Lippit, Yukio. *Painting of the Realm: The Kano House of Painters in 17th-Century Japan.* Seattle: University of Washington Press, 2012.

Llewellyn-Jones, Rosie. *Engaging Scoundrels.* New York: Oxford University Press, 2000.

——. *A Fatal Friendship: The Nawabs, the British, and the City of Lucknow.* New Delhi: Oxford University Press, 1985.

——. *A Very Ingenious Man: Claude Martin in Early Colonial India.* New Delhi: Oxford University Press, 1992.

Llewellyn-Jones, Rosie, ed. *Lucknow: City of Illusion.* New York: Alkazi Collection of Photography, 2006.

——. *Lucknow, Then and Now.* Mumbai: Marg Publications on behalf of the National Centre for the Performing Arts, 2003.

Losensky, Paul. *Welcoming Fighānī: Imitation and Poetic Individuality in the Safavid-Mughal Ghazal.* Costa Mesa, CA: Mazda, 1998.

Losty, J. P. *The Art of the Book in India.* London: British Library, 1982.

——. *Delhi 360°: Mazhar Ali Khan's View from Lahore Gate.* New Delhi: Roli, 2012.

——. "Delineating Delhi: Images of the Mughal Capital." In *Delhi: Red Fort to Raisina*, edited by J. P. Losty and Pramod Kapoor, 14–87. New Delhi: Lustre, 2012.

——. "Depicting Delhi: Mazhar Ali Khan, Thomas Metcalfe, and the Topographical School of Delhi Artists." In *Princes and Painters in Mughal Delhi, 1707–1857*, edited by William Dalrymple and Yuthika Sharma, 53–60. New Haven, CT: Yale University Press, 2012.

——. *Sita Ram's Painted Views of India: Lord Hastings's Journey from Calcutta to the Punjab, 1814–15.* London: Thames and Hudson, 2015.

Losty, J. P., and Malini Roy. *Mughal India: Art, Culture, and Empire. Manuscripts and Paintings in the British Library.* London: British Library, 2012.

Madhuri Desai. "Interpreting an Architectural Past: Ram Raz and the Treatise in South Asia." *Journal of the Society of Architectural Historians* 71, no. 4 (2012): 462–87.

Marsh, Kate. *India in the French Imagination: Peripheral Voices, 1754–1815.* London: Pickering and Chatto, 2009.

Marshall, P. J. *East Indian Fortunes: The British in Bengal in the Eighteenth Century.* Oxford: Clarendon, 1976.

——, ed. *The Eighteenth Century in Indian History: Evolution or Revolution?* New Delhi: Oxford University Press, 2003.

Martin, Meredith. "Tipu Sultan's Ambassadors at Saint-Cloud: Indomania and Anglophobia in Pre-Revolutionary Paris." *West 86th: A Journal of Decorative Arts, Design History, and Material Culture* 21, no. 1 (2014): 37–68.

Mayer, L. A. *Islamic Architects and Their Works.* Geneva: A. Kundig, 1956.

McInerney, Terrence. "Mughal Painting During the Reign of Muhammad Shah." In *After the Great Mughals: Painting in Delhi and the Regional Courts in the 18th and 19th Centuries,* edited by Barbara Schmitz, 12–33. Mumbai: Performing Arts Mumbai, 2002.

Merklinger, Elizabeth Schotten. *Indian Islamic Architecture: The Deccan, 1347–1686.* Warminster, UK: Aris and Phillips, 1981.

Metcalf, Barbara. *Moral Conduct and Authority: The Place of Adab in South Asian Islam.* Berkeley: University of California Press, 1984.

Metcalf, Thomas R. *An Imperial Vision: Indian Architecture and Britain's Raj.* Berkeley: University of California Press, 1989.

Micallef, Roberta, and Sunil Sharma, eds. *On the Wonders of Land and Sea: Persianate Travel Writing.* Cambridge, MA: Harvard University Press, 2013.

Michell, George. *The Royal Palaces of India.* London: Thames and Hudson, 1994.

Michell, George, and Mark Zebrowski. *Architecture and Art of the Deccan Sultanates.* New York: Cambridge University Press, 1999.

Minor, Heather Hyde. *The Culture of Architecture in Enlightenment Rome.* University Park: Pennsylvania State University Press, 2010.

——. *Piranesi's Lost Words.* University Park: Pennsylvania State University Press, 2015.

Moin, A. Azfar. *The Millennial Sovereign: Sacred Kingship and Sainthood in Islam.* New York: Columbia University Press, 2012.

Morley, John. *The Making of the Royal Pavilion Brighton: Designs and Drawings.* London: Sotheby, 1984.

Moxey, Keith. *Visual Time: The Image in History.* Durham, NC: Duke University Press, 2013.

Mundy, Godfrey Charles. *Pen and Pencil Sketches, Being the Journal of a Tour in India.* London: J. Murray, 1832.

Murphy, Anne, ed. *Time, History and the Religious Imaginary in South Asia.* Florence: Taylor and Francis, 2012.

Naim, C. M. "Syed Ahmad and His Two Books Called 'Asar-al-Sanadid.'" *Modern Asian Studies* 45, no. 3 (2011): 669–708.

Narayana Rao, Velcheru, David Shulman, and Sanjay Subrahmanyam. *Textures of Time: Writing History in South India, 1600–1800.* Delhi: Permanent Black, 2001.

Nath, R. *History of Mughal Architecture.* New Delhi: Abhinav, 1982.

——. *Monuments of Delhi: Historical Study.* New Delhi: Indian Institute of Islamic Studies, Ambika Publication, 1979.

——. *Mysteries and Marvels of Mughal Architecture.* Gurgaon: Shubhi, 2009.

Necipoğlu, Gülru. *The Age of Sinan: Architectural Culture in the Ottoman Empire.* Princeton, NJ: Princeton University Press, 2005.

——. "Framing the Gaze in Ottoman, Safavid, and Mughal Palaces." *Ars Orientalis* 23 (1993): 303–42.

——. "From International Timurid to Ottoman: A Change of Taste in Sixteenth-Century Ceramic Tiles." *Muqarnas* 7 (1990): 136–70.

——. "Plans and Models in 15th- and 16th-Century Ottoman Architectural Practice." *Journal of the Society of Architectural Historians* (1986): 224–43.

——. "Qur'anic Inscriptions on Sinan's Imperial Mosques: A Comparison with Their Safavid and Mughal Counterparts." In *Word of God—Art of Man: The Qur'an and Its Creative Expressions,* edited by Fahmida Suleman, 69–104. Institute of Ismaili Studies Conference Proceedings. New York: Oxford University Press, 2007.

——. *The Topkapı Scroll: Geometry and Ornament in Islamic Architecture.* Santa Monica, CA: Getty Center for the History of Art and the Humanities, 1995.

——. "Word and Image: The Serial Portraits of Ottoman Sultans in Comparative Perspective." In *The Sultan's Portrait: Picturing the House of Osman,* edited by Ayşe Orbay, 22–61. Istanbul: İşbank, 2000.

Newman, Andrew J. *Twelver Shiism: Unity and Diversity in the Life of Islam, 632 to 1722.* New Edinburgh Islamic Surveys. Edinburgh: Edinburgh University Press, 2013.

Nilsson, Sten. *European Architecture in India, 1750–1850.* Translated by Elenore Zettersten and Agnes George. London: Faber, 1969.

O'Hanlon, Rosalind. "The Social Worth of Scribes." *Indian Economic and Social History Review* 47, no. 4 (2010): 563–95.

Okada, Amina. *Indian Miniatures of the Mughal Court.* New York: Abrams, 1992.

O'Kane, Bernard. "From Tents to Pavilions: Royal Mobility and Persian Palace Design." *Ars Orientalis* 23 (1993): 249–68.

Parodi, Laura E. "The Bibi-Ka Maqbara in Aurangabad: A Landmark of Mughal Power in the Deccan?" *East and West* 48, nos. 3–4 (1998): 349–83.

Patel, Alka. "The Photographic Albums of Abbas Ali as Continuations of the Mughal Muraqqaʿ Tradition." *Getty Research Journal* 7 (2015): 35–52.

Pauwels, Heidi. "Cosmopolitan Soirées in Eighteenth-Century North India: Reception of Early Urdu Poetry in Kishangarh." *South Asia Multidisciplinary Academic Journal* (2014). http://journals .openedition.org/samaj/3773.

Payne, Alina. *The Architectural Treatise in the Italian Renaissance: Architectural Invention, Ornament, and Literary Culture.* Cambridge: Cambridge University Press, 1999.

Peck, Amelia, and Amy Elizabeth Bogansky, eds. *Interwoven Globe: The Worldwide Textile Trade, 1500–1800.* New York: Metropolitan Museum of Art, 2013.

Peck, Lucy. *Delhi: A Thousand Years of Building.* New Delhi: Lotus, 2005.

Pernau, Margrit. *Ashraf into Middle Classes: Muslims in Nineteenth-Century Delhi.* New Delhi: Oxford University Press, 2013.

———. "Mapping Emotions, Constructing Feelings." *Journal of the Economic and Social History of the Orient* 58, no. 5 (November 23, 2015): 634–67.

———. "Space and Emotion: Building to Feel." *History Compass* 12, no. 7 (July 1, 2014): 541–49.

Petievich, Carla. *Assembly of Rivals: Delhi, Lucknow, and the Urdu Ghazal.* Delhi: Manohar, 1992.

———. "Poetry of the Declining Mughals: The Shahr Ashob." *Journal of South Asian Literature* 25, no. 1 (1990): 99–110.

Petruccioli, Attilio, ed. *Gardens in the Time of the Great Muslim Empires: Theory and Design.* Leiden: Brill, 1997.

Pinch, William R. "Same Difference in India and Europe." *History and Theory* 38, no. 3 (1999): 389–407.

Pollock, Sheldon, ed. *Forms of Knowledge in Early Modern Asia: Explorations in the Intellectual History of India and Tibet, 1500–1800.* Durham, NC: Duke University Press, 2011.

Qademi, Sharif Husain. "Persian Chronicles in the Nineteenth Century." In *The Making of Indo-Persian Culture: Indian and French Studies,* edited by Muzaffar Alam, Françoise Delvoye Nalini, and Marc Gaborieau, 407–16. New Delhi: Manohar, 2000.

Qaisar, Ahsan Jan. *Building Construction in Mughal India: The Evidence from Painting.* Delhi: Oxford University Press; Aligarh: Centre of Advanced Study in History, Aligarh Muslim University, 1988.

Quilley, Geoff, and John Bonehill, eds. *William Hodges, 1744–1797: The Art of Exploration.* New Haven, CT: Yale University Press for the National Maritime Museum, Greenwich, 2004.

Quraishi, Fatima. "*Asar-ul-Sanadid:* A Nineteenth-Century History of Delhi." *Journal of Art Historiography* 6 (June 2012). http:// arthistoriography.wordpress.com /number-6-june-20122.

Raj, Kapil. *Relocating Modern Science: Circulation and the Construction of Modern Knowledge in South Asia and Europe, 1650–1900.* London: Palgrave Macmillan, 2007.

Rajagopalan, Mrinalini. *Building Histories: The Archival and Affective Lives of Five Monuments in Modern Delhi.* Chicago: University of Chicago Press, 2016.

———. "A Nineteenth-Century Architectural Archive: Syed Ahmad Khan's *Āsār-us-Sanādīd.*" *International Journal of Islamic Architecture* 6, no. 1 (March 2017): 27–58.

Rajagopalan, Mrinalini, and Madhuri Desai, eds. *Colonial Frames, Nationalist Histories: Imperial Legacies, Architecture and Modernity.* London: Routledge, 2012.

Ray, Indrani. *The French East India Company and the Trade of the Indian Ocean: A Collection of Essays.* Edited by Lakshmi Subramanian. New Delhi: Munshiram Manoharlal, 1999.

Rice, Yael. "Between the Brush and the Pen: On the Intertwined Histories of Mughal Painting and Calligraphy." In *Envisioning Islamic Art and Architecture: Essays in Honor of Renata Holod,* edited by David J. Roxburgh, 148–74. Leiden: Brill, 2014.

———. "The Brush and the Burin: Mogul Encounters with European Engravings." In *Crossing Cultures: Conflict, Cultures, and Convergence: Proceedings of the 32nd Congress of the International Committee of the History of Art,* edited by Jaynie Anderson,

305–10. Carlton, Victoria: Miegunyah, Melbourne University Publishing, 2009.

Richard, Francis. "Jean-Baptiste Gentil collectionneur de manuscrits persans." *Extr. de dix-huitième siècle* 28 (1996): 91–110.

Richards, John F. "Early Modern India and World History." *Journal of World History* 8, no. 2 (1997): 197–209.

———. *The Mughal Empire.* Cambridge: Cambridge University Press, 1993.

Rinckenbach, Alexis. *Archives du dépôt des fortifications des colonies: Indes.* Aix-en-Provence: Centre des archives d'Outre-Mer, 1998.

Ringer, Monica. "The Quest for the Secret of Strength in Iranian Nineteenth-Century Travel Literature: Rethinking Tradition in the Safarnameh." In *Iran and the Surrounding World: Interactions in Culture and Cultural Politics,* edited by Nikki Keddie and Rudi Matthee, 146–61. Seattle: University of Washington Press, 2002.

Rizvi, Kishwar. *The Safavid Dynastic Shrine: Architecture, Religion and Power in Early Modern Iran.* London: Tauris, 2011.

Rizvi, Saiyid Athar Abbas. *A Socio-Intellectual History of the Isnā Asharī Shīʾis in India.* New Delhi: Munshiram Manoharlal; Marifat, 1986.

Roberts, Jennifer L. *Transporting Visions: The Movement of Images in Early America.* Berkeley: University of California Press, 2014.

Roxburgh, David J. *The Persian Album, 1400–1600: From Dispersal to Collection.* New Haven, CT: Yale University Press, 2005.

———. *Prefacing the Image.* Boston: Brill, 2001.

———. "Ruy González de Clavijo's Narrative of Courtly Life and Ceremony in Timur's Samarqand, 1404." In *The "Book" of Travels: Genre, Ethnology, and Pilgrimage, 1250–1700,* edited by Palmira Brummet, 113–58. Leiden: Brill, 2009.

Roy, Malini. "Origins of the Late Mughal Painting Tradition in Awadh." In *India's Fabled City: The Art of Courtly Lucknow,* edited by Stephen Markel and Tushara Bindu Gude, 165–86. Los Angeles: Los Angeles County Museum of Art, 2010.

———. "The Revival of the Mughal Painting Tradition During the Reign of Muhammad Shah." In *Princes and Painters in Mughal Delhi, 1707–1857,* edited by William Dalrymple and Yuthika Sharma, 17–24. New Haven, CT: Yale University Press, 2012.

———. "Some Unexpected Sources for Paintings by the Artist Mihr Chand (fl. c. 1759–86), Son of Ganga Ram." *South Asian Studies* 26, no. 1 (2010): 21–29.

Ruggles, D. Fairchild. *Women, Patronage, and Self-Representation in Islamic Societies.* Albany: State University of New York Press, 2000.

Russell, Ralph, and Khurshidul Islam. *Three Mughal Poets: Mir, Sauda, Mir Hasan.* Cambridge, MA: Harvard University Press, 1968.

Rüstem, Ünver. "Architecture for a New Age: Imperial Ottoman Mosques in Eighteenth-Century Istanbul." Ph.D. diss., Harvard University, 2013.

Sachdev, Vibhuti, and Giles Tillotson. *Building Jaipur: The Making of an Indian City.* London: Reaktion, 2002.

Sadiq, Mohammed. *A History of Urdu Literature.* 2nd edition. New Delhi: Oxford University Press, 1995.

Sarkar, Jadunath. *History of Aurangzib, Based on Original Sources.* Calcutta: M. C. Sarkar, 1919.

———. *Studies in Aurangzib's Reign.* Calcutta: M. C. Sarkar, 1933.

Saurma-Jeltsch, Lieselotte E., and Anja Eisenbeiss, eds. *The Power of Things and the Flow of Cultural Transformations.* Berlin: Deuscher Kunstverlag, 2010.

Schacht, J. "On the Title of the Fatāwā al-ʿĀlamgīriyya." In *Iran and Islam: In Memory of the Late Vladimir Minorsky,* edited by C. E. Bosworth, 475–78. Edinburgh: Edinburgh University Press, 1971.

Schimmel, Annemarie. *Islam in the Indian Subcontinent.* Leiden: Brill, 1980.

Schmitz, Barbara. *After the Great Mughals: Painting in Delhi and the Regional Courts in the 18th and 19th Centuries.* Mumbai: Performing Arts Mumbai, 2002.

Shaffer, Holly. *Adapting the Eye: An Archive of the British in India, 1770–1830.* New Haven, CT: Yale Center for British Art, 2011.

Sharar, Abdulḥalīm, and E. S. Harcourt. *Lucknow: The Last Phase of an Oriental Culture.* Boulder: Westview, 1976.

Sharma, Jyoti P. "The British Treatment of Historic Gardens in the Indian Subcontinent: The Transformation of Delhi's Nawab Safdarjung's Tomb Complex from a Funerary Garden into a Public Park." *Garden History* 35, no. 2 (2007): 210–28.

Sharma, Sunil. "The City of Beauties in Indo-Persian Poetic Landscape." *Comparative Studies of South Asia, Africa and the Middle East* 24, no. 2 (2004): 73–81.

———. "'If There is a Paradise on Earth, It Is Here': Urban Ethnography in Indo-Persian Poetic and Historical Texts." In *Forms of Knowledge in Early Modern Asia: Explorations in the Intellectual History of India and Tibet, 1500–1800,* edited by Sheldon

Pollock, 240–56. Durham, NC: Duke University Press, 2011.

———. "Representation of Social Types in Mughal Art and Literature: Ethnography or Trope?" In *Indo-Muslim Cultures in Transition*, edited by Karen Leonard and Alka Patel, 17–36. Leiden: Brill, 2011.

Sharma, Yuthika. "From Miniatures to Monuments: Picturing Shah Alam's Delhi 1771–1806." In *Indo-Muslim Cultures in Transition*, edited by Alka Patel and Karen Leonard, vol. 38, 111–38. Leiden: Brill, 2012.

———. "In the Company of the Mughal Court: Delhi Painter Ghulam Ali Khan." In *Princes and Painters in Mughal Delhi, 1707–1857*, edited by William Dalrymple and Yuthika Sharma, 41–52. New Haven, CT: Yale University Press, 2012.

Siddiqi, W. H. *Lucknow, the Historic City*. New Delhi: Sundeep Prakashan, 2000.

Singh, Upinder. *Discovery of Ancient India: Early Archaeologists and the Beginnings of Archaeology*. Delhi: Permanent Black, 2009.

Sinha, Surendra Nath. *The Mid-Gangetic Region in the Eighteenth Century, Some Observations of Joseph Tieffenthaler*. Allahabad: Shanti Prakashan, 1976.

Smart, E. S. "Graphic Evidence for Mughal Architectural Plans." *Art and Archaeology Research Papers* 6 (1974): 22–23.

Sohrabi, Naghmeh. *Taken for Wonder: Nineteenth-Century Travel Accounts from Iran to Europe*. New York: Oxford University Press, 2012.

Spear, Thomas George Percival. *Twilight of the Mughuls: Studies in Late Mughul Delhi*. Cambridge: Cambridge University Press, 1951.

Spear, Thomas George Percival, Narayani Gupta, and Laura Sykes. *Delhi: Its Monuments and History*. 3rd edition. New Delhi: Oxford University Press, 2009.

Srivastava, Ashirbadi Lal. *The First Two Nawabs of Awadh*. Agra: Shiva Lal Agarwala, 1954.

———. *Shuja-ud-Daulah*. Delhi: Agarwala, 1961.

Stephen, Carr. *Archaeology and Monumental Remains of Delhi*. Ludhiana: Mission, 1876.

Stern, Philip J. *The Company-State: Corporate Sovereignty and the Early Modern Foundations of the British Empire in India*. New York: Oxford University Press, 2011.

Subrahmanyam, Sanjay. "Hearing Voices: Vignettes of Early Modernity in South Asia, 1400–1750." *Daedalus* 127, no. 3 (1998): 75–104.

———. "On World Historians in the Sixteenth Century." *Representations* 91, no. 1 (2005): 26–57.

Tandan, Banmali. *The Architecture of Lucknow and Its Dependencies, 1722–1856: A Descriptive Inventory and an Analysis of Nawabi Types*. New Delhi: Vikas, 2001.

———. *The Architecture of Lucknow and Oudh, 1722–1856: Its Evolution in an Aesthetic and Social Context*. Cambridge: Zophorus, 2008.

Tavakoli-Targhi, Mohamad. *Refashioning Iran: Orientalism, Occidentalism, and Historiography*. Houndmills, UK: Palgrave, 2001.

Tillotson, Giles. *The Artificial Empire: The Indian Landscapes of William Hodges*. Richmond, UK: Curzon, 2000.

———. "Painting and Understanding Mughal Architecture." In *Paradigms of Indian Architecture: Space and Time in Representation and Design*, edited by Giles Tillotson, 59–79. Surrey, UK: Curzon, 1998.

———. *The Rajput Palaces: The Development of an Architectural Style, 1450–1750*. New Haven, CT: Yale University Press, 1987.

Titley, Norah M. *Miniatures from Persian Manuscripts: A Catalogue and Subject Index of Paintings from Persia, India, and Turkey in the British Library and the British Museum*. London: British Museum, 1977.

Tobin, Beth Fowkes. *Picturing Imperial Power: Colonial Subjects in Eighteenth-Century British Painting*. Durham, NC: Duke University Press, 1999.

Travers, Robert. "The Eighteenth Century in Indian History: A Review Essay." *Eighteenth-Century Studies* 40, no. 3 (2007): 492–508.

———. *Ideology and Empire in Eighteenth-Century India: The British in Bengal*. New York: Cambridge University Press, 2007.

Troll, Christian W. "A Note on an Early Topographical Work of Sayyid Aḥmad Khān: Āsār Al-Ṣanādīd." *Journal of the Royal Asiatic Society of Great Britain and Ireland* 2 (1972): 135–46.

Verma, Tripta. *Karkhanas Under the Mughals, from Akbar to Aurangzeb: A Study in Economic Development*. Delhi: Pragati, 1994.

Victoria & Albert Museum. *The Art of India: Paintings and Drawings in the Victoria & Albert Museum*. Surrey, UK: Emmett Microform, 1992.

Weiss, Bernard G. *The Spirit of Islamic Law*. Athens: University of Georgia Press, 1998.

Welch, Anthony. "The Emperor's Grief: Two Mughal Tombs." *Muqarnas* 25 (2008): 255–73.

———. "The Shrine of the Holy Footprint in Delhi." *Muqarnas* 14 (1997): 166–78.

Wellington, Donald C. *French East India Companies: A Historical Account and Record of Trade*. Lanham, MD: Hamilton, 2006.

Wescoat, James. "The Changing Cultural Space of Mughal Gardens." In *Companion to Asian Art and*

Architecture, edited by Rebecca M. Brown and Deborah S. Hutton, 201–29. Somerset, UK: Wiley, 2011.

Wescoat, James, and Joachim Wolschke-Bulmahn, eds. *Mughal Gardens: Sources, Places, Representations, and Prospects.* Washington, D.C.: Dumbarton Oaks Research Library and Collection, 1996.

Wright, Elaine, ed. *Muraqqaʿ: Imperial Mughal Albums from the Chester Beatty Library, Dublin.* Alexandria, VA: Art Services, 2008.

Zaman, Taymiya. "Visions of Juliana: A Portuguese Woman at the Court of the Mughals." *Journal of World History* 23, no. 4 (2012): 761–91.

INDEX

Italic page numbers refer to illustrations.

A

'Abd al-Hamid Lahori. *See* Lahori, 'Abd al-Hamid

'Abd al-Karim Mushtaq, *Mir'at al-Gitinumā* (Mirror of the universe, 1850), 168

'Abd al-Khaliq Varasta, 75

'Abd al-Latif Shushtari, 108

'Abd al-Rahim Khan-i Khanan, 90

Abu al-Fazl, 134

Abu al-Mansur Safdar Jang (r. 1739–54): as nawab of Awadh and prime vizier of Mughal empire, 18, 85, 91, 176; Shi'i identity of, 90–91, 102. *See also* Safdar Jang, funerary complex of, Delhi, 1753–54

Abu Talib Kalim, 166

Abu Talib Khan, 108, 188n53

'Adil Shahis of Bijapur (1490–1686), 91

Afghans, 11, 151

Agra: audience halls in, 165; *Map of Agra*, 119, *122*; and textual geographies, 169, 193n53. *See also specific buildings*

Ahmad Shah (r. 1748–54), 63, 65, 70, 90, 102

Ā'in-i Akbari (Institutes of Akbar), 134

Ajmer, 61, 65, 177

Akbar (r. 1556–1605): cenotaph of, 63; internment of, 65; and monumental tomb of Humayun, 59, 67; and Nizam al-Din dargah,

59, 67, 188n39; and tomb of Selim Chishti, 61, 141; tomb at Sikandra, *24*, *25*, 87, 99, 119, *120*, 138, 139, *139*, 189n5

Akbar II (r. 1806–37): commissioning of *'Amal-i Şāliḥ*, 151, 154, 166; and Shah Jahan, 150, 151, 154; and son, Mirza Jahangir, 164; and Zafar Mahal, 1, 67, 177

Akbarabadi Begum, 70

Akbarabadi Mahal, 70

Akbarabadi Masjid, Delhi, 70

Akbarnāma, 152

Alam, Muzaffar, 180n15

'Alamgir (r. 1658–1707): Badshahi Masjid sponsored by, 36; and Bibi ka Maqbara, 39, 44, 182n17; death of, 5; and Deccani architecture, 45; Goetz on, 5; grave of, 60, 72, 161; imperial architecture of, 52–53, 55, 124; and imperial regulation, 27, 46–52, 183n31; as patron of Moti Masjid, 22–23, 52, 94; piety of, 27, 52, 55; portrait of, 53, *54*; program of expansion, 182n24; and revision of recent history, 27; and War of Succession, 47, 53

Aliganj district, Delhi, 101, 102–3, 104, 110

'Ali Mardan Khan, 70

'Ali Riza al-'Abbasi, 52

'Amal-i Şāliḥ (c. 1815): and architectural representation, 150–51, 152, 154, 156, 157–58, 160, 161, 164–66, 167, 172, 174, 176, 179; audiences of, 150, 161, 164–66; *Diwan-i 'Amm, Red Fort, Delhi, 8*, 154, *155*;

Diwan-i 'Amm described in, 164, 165; Facing folios (*Naqqar Khane* and *Diwan-i 'Amm, Delhi*), 161, *162*, *163*; *The Funeral of Shah Jahan*, 157–58, *159*; *Gateway of the Red Fort, Delhi*, 154, *155*; and historicism, 151, 152, 154, 156, 165, 166–67, 172, 174, 176; image and text in, 152, 154, 156–58, 160–61, 164–66, 174, 176; and imperial authority, 151; *Jami' Masjid, Delhi*, 154, 156, *156*; *Naqqar Khane, Red Fort, Delhi*, 154, *155*; and nineteenth-century architectural history, 166–73, 174; and ornamental programs, 154, 161; on Shah Jahan, 123–24, 150, 152, 154, 157–58, 161, 166, 171; *Shah Jahan Before the Red Fort*, 157–58, *159*; woodcuts in, 170

'Amal-i Şāliḥ (c. 1830s), 160

Amanat Khan, 51

Amin Ahmad Razi, *Haft Iqlim* (Seven climes), 169

Amir Khusraw, 188n39

Anquetil-Duperron, Abraham Hyacinthe, 146, 192n73

antiquarianism, 152

Aqa Abu al-Qasim Beg, 183n25

Aqqoyunlus, Tabriz, 95

Archaeological Society of Delhi, 172, 173

Archaeological Survey of India, 13, 16, 99, 151, 152, 172, 175

Archer, Edward Caulfield, 108

Archer, Mildred, 140, 144

architects: networks of, 46, 99, 108; training of, 45–46, 53 architectural history, 173–74, 175, 176

architectural plans, 114, 122–25, 127–28

architectural representation: and *Amal-i Ṣāliḥ*, 150–51, 152, 154, 156, 157–58, 160, 161, 164–66, 172, 174, 176, 179; and Company Painting, 18, 138, 140–43, 144, 145, 146, 147, 170, 174, 191n54; and eighteenth-century Mughal architecture, 1–2, 4–8, 12; European representations of Indian architecture, 18–19, 114, 127–28, 130, 138–44; and historicization, 3–4, 12, 14, 15, 130–31, 133–37, 147, 150–51, 172, 174, 176–77; Koch on, 119, 189n6; and literary culture, 161, 164; and media, 4, 15; and Mughal painting, 119, 122, 130, 144, 150, 156, 158, 176; on paper, 2, 3, 18, 111, 147, 176; and plans, 122–23; and Rajput art, 119, 130, 138, 147; sociopolitical dimensions of, 144, 147; visual languages of, 114, 119, 122–25, 127–28, 130, 161. *See also Palais Indiens*

artist unknown: *Darbar of Akbar,* c. 1820, Delhi, *10*; *Detail of a Street Plan of Chandni Chowk in Delhi,* 135, *136–37*, 190–91n37; *Diwan-i ʿAmm, Red Fort, Delhi,* (c. 1815), *8*, 154, *155*; *Façade of a Delhi Palace* from the *Palais Indiens* (c. 1774), 118, *118–19*; *Façade of the Palace of Dara Shikoh in Agra* from the *Palais Indiens* (c. 1774), 128, *129*; Facing folios (*Naqqar Khane* and *Diwan-i ʿAmm, Delhi*),c. 1815, 161, *162, 163*; *The Funeral of Shah Jahan,*c. 1815, 157–58, *159*; *Gateway of the Red Fort, Delhi,* c. 1815, 154, *155*; *Gateway of the Red Fort of Delhi,* from the *Palais Indiens* (c. 1774), *3, 7,* 116, *117,* 131; *Gateway of the Taj Mahal,*c. 1820, 142–43, *142*; *Jahangir Receives a Prisoner* from the *Jahangirnāma* (c. 1618–20), 119, *120,* 189n5; *Jami Masjid in Delhi,* from the *Palais Indiens* (c. 1774), 116, *116*; *Map of Agra,* after 1722, 119, *122*;

Mausoleum of Safdar Jang, from the *Palais Indiens* (c. 1774), 116, *117*; *Plan of Amber Fort,* 125, *125*; *Plan of the Funerary Complex of Itimad al-Daula,* 18th century, 119, 122, *123*; *Plan of the Jami Masjid of Delhi* from the *Palais Indiens* (c. 1774), *118*, 119; *Plan of the Palace and Garden of Dara Shikoh in Agra* from the *Palais Indiens* (c. 1774), 128, *129*; *Portrait of ʿAlamgir,* c. 1700, 53, *54*; *Riverside Façade of the Red Fort of Delhi* from the *Palais Indiens* (c. 1774), 115, *115*; *Shah Jahan Before the Red Fort,* c. 1815, 157–58, *159*; *Tomb of Itimad al-Daula,* c. 1820, *4,* 18, 142, 143, *143*; *The Tomb of Selim Chishti,* c. 1820, 141–42, *141*; *Two Draftsmen at Work* from the *Boileau Album* (1785), *126,* 127

Āsār al-Sanādīd (Vestiges of the Past, 1847, revised 1854), 16, 19, 152, 169–72, *173,* 174, 184n12

Asaf al-Daula, 105, 108, 134

Asher, Catherine: on Bahadur Shah, 184n12; on funerary complex of Safdar Jang, 187n4; on Mughal architecture, 5, 182n1, 182n12, 187n12; on patronage at the dargah, 185n16

Asiatic Research Society, 152

ʿAta Allah Rashidi, 45–46, 99, 183n25

Atgah Khan, 67, 188n39

Aurangabad, India, 15, 17, 60. *See also* Bibi ka Maqbara, Aurangabad, 1660–61

Aurangzeb. *See* ʿAlamgir

Awadh: and allegiance to Mughals, 87, 89, 105; dynasty of, 85, 90, 101, 105, 110, 176; formal declaration of independence from Mughal empire, 85, 187n5; Gentil's role in Awadhi court, 135; and military alliance with Mughals against British forces, 85; provincial governors of, 2, 9, 18, 85, 91, 102, 104, 115, 176, 187n5; and Shiʿism, 12, 85, 102, 104, 188n35; and transregional contacts, 7

Awadhi architecture: building techniques of, 108; Gentil on, 134,

135; Goetz on, 5; and imperial architectural tradition, 18, 85, 86, 87, 89, 90, 91, 104, 105, 106, 110–11, 115, 133–34, 145, 147, 176, 187n12; and *Palais Indiens,* 114; visual idiom of, 105, 106, 107

Aʿzam Shah, 48, 182n17

ʿAziz Koka, 188n39

B

Babar ʿAli Khan, 160

Babur (r. 1526–30), 5, 14, 59, 60, 123

Bāburnāma (c. 1580), 123

Badshahi Masjid, Lahore, 1673–74: Bibi ka Maqbara compared to, 40, 45; and experimentation, 17, 100; inscriptions of, 49, 50, 51, 52; interior, *38,* 39; Jamiʿ Masjid compared to, 36, 39, 49–50, 51, 107; pīshtāq, 49, *50*; view of, 36, *37*

Bahadur Shah (r. 1707–12), 63, 65, 67, 68, 77–78, 135, 184n4, 184–85n12

Bahadur Shah Zafar (r. 1837–58): genealogies produced for, 160–61, 193n21; and Zafar Mahal, 1, 67, 178

Bakhtiyar Kaki dargah: and Bahadur Shah complex, 68, 77–78; burial enclosure of the nawabs of Loharu, 1802, 65, *65*; gateway of Farrukh Siyar, c. 1713–19, *62,* 63, 64–65, *64,* 77; and grave of Bakhtiyar Kaki, 61, 65, 184n8; literary representations of, 75, 76, 77–78; and patronage, 60, 61, 65; plan of, 60, *61*; renovations to, 18, 60; screen of Farrukh Siyar, c. 1713–19, 63, *63,* 64, *64,* 75, 77; in textual geographies, 167; and urban order, 59, 67; and Zafar Mahal, 67, 178

Benares, 125, 138

Bayly, C. A., 180n15

Bara Imambara (or Great Imambara) complex, Lucknow (1784–91): banglas of, 105, 108; funerary complex of Safdar Jang compared to, 105–6, 108; gateway, 105, *106,* 108; gateway, detail, 105–6, *107*; imambara of, 106, 108; mosque of, 106–8; ornamental program of, 105, 108, 134; ta'ziya in, 108

Beach, Milo Cleveland, 189n6

Begum Samru, 136, 191n43

Bengal, 9, 35, 85, 102, 177, 182n13

Bernard, Jean-Frédéric, 146

Bernier, François, travel narrative of, 16

Bibi ka Maqbara, Aurangabad, 1660–61: architectonic forms of, 44; and Bijapuri architecture, 44, 182n20; and experimentation, 17, 39, 40, 42, 43–44, 45, 100; façade, 40, *41*, 42; gateway, 40, *40*; gateway, inscription on door, 45, *45*; and imperial architectural tradition, 87, 89; interior, 44, *44*; Taj Mahal compared to, 39–40, 42–43, 46, 97; tomb of Safdar Jang compared to, 97, 99, 110; view of, *38*; walls of exterior vault, 40, *41*

Bibliothèque nationale de France (BnF), Paris, 145, 189n1

Bichitr, *Shah Jahan Receiving His Three Eldest Sons* from the *Pādshāhnāma* (c. 1656–57), 156–57, *157*

Bijapuri architecture, 44, 182n20

Bishindas, *Scene of a Garden Being Constructed,* from a *Bāburnama* (c. 1590), 123, *124*

Brajbhasha, 6

Britain: colonial historians of, 5; Delhi annexed by, 1, 6, 11, 151, 178; and Gentil's negotiations for Awadhi court, 135; transition from Mughal to British rule, 1, 2, 6, 151, 178; and transregional contacts, 7

Brown, Percy, 5

Browne, John, after William Hodges, *View of the Gateway of the Tomb of Akbar at Sikandra,* 139, *139*

Burhan al-Mulk Sa'adat Khan, 9, 12, 85, 102, 188n35

C

Calcutta, 127

Cavenagh, Orfeur, 108

chahār bāgh (four-fold) type: in Bishindas, *Scene of a Garden Being Constructed,* 123, *124*; and funerary complex of Safdar Jang, Delhi, 1753–54, 85, 86, 110; and garden plan, 23, 70; and tomb of Akbar, 138; and tomb of I'timad al-Daula, 90

Chakrabarty, Dipesh, 14

Chandarbhan, 166

Chandni Chowk. *See* Delhi

Chatterjee, Kumkum, 14

Chatterjee, Partha, 14

Chausath Kambah, 188n39

chihil sutūn, 165

Chihil Sutun, Isfahan, 165, *165*

Chiragh Delhi, dargah of, 75, 76

Chishti Sufi order: and Mughal empire, 11, 65, 102; sanctity of, 102; shrines of Sufi saints in extramural spaces of Delhi, 18, 58, 59–61, 63–65, 67–69, 70, 80

Chishti, Noor Ahmad, *Tahqiqaat Chishti: Tarikh-e-Lahor ka Encyclopedia* (Chishti's inquiries: An encyclopedia of Lahore's history, 1867), 169, 172–73

Chowk Sa'adullah Khan. *See* Delhi

circulation: transregional circulation of images, 15; circulation of images between India and Europe, 18–19; and transregional contacts, 7

Colbert, Jean-Baptiste, 11

Coldstream, William, 169

Cole, Juan, 188n35

Compagnie des Indes Orientales (CDIO). *See* French East India Company

Company Painting: and artistic agency, 144; as a category, 140–41; representations of Mughal architecture, 18, 138, 140–43, 144, 145, 146, 147, 170, 174, 191n54

Cunningham, Alexander, 13, 16, 151

D

Daniell, Thomas: and aquatint of Qudsiyya Bagh, 70; commissions of, 191n50; and Picturesque style, 138, 139, 145, 146, 147; *The Taje Mahale, at Agra,* 140, *140*

Daniell, William: and aquatint of Qudsiyya Bagh, 70; and Picturesque style, 138, 139, 145, 146, 147; and Ram Raz, 173; *The Taje Mahale, at Agra,* 140, *140*

Dara Shikoh, Mughal prince, 46, 47, 115, 128, 136, 158, 160

Dargah Quli Khan, *Muraqqa'-yi Dihlī,* 7, 18, 59, 73, 74–80, 81

Daulatabad, fortress of, 119, *121*

de Boigne papers, 147

Deccan: architecture of, 44–45, 52, 182n24; autonomy of, 85; and Iran, 11, 12; and Mughal visual idiom, 7; and Shi'ism, 11, 91

Delhi, India: Aliganj district, 101, 102–3, 104, 110; British annexation of, 1, 6, 11, 151, 178; British Residents of, 167; Chandni Chowk, 58, 70, 71, 72, 76, 77, 100, 135, *136*–37, 154, 190n36, 190–91n37; Chowk Sa'adullah Khan, 76, 77; expansion of imperial presence in, 60; Faiz Bazaar, 58, 70, 72, 135, *136*, 190n36; gardens of, 70, 76; histories of, 75, 167–74, 176; in literary texts, 3, 59, 73–80; maps of, 59, *60*, *101*; monuments of, 19; Mughal architecture of, 15, 17, 19, 23, 70, 73, 74–75, 77, 84, 91, 137, 151, 175, 176; as Mughal capital, 3, 4, 7, 11; Nadir Shah's invasion of, 58, 79, 184n5; public spaces of, 59, 73, 76, 77, 80; and religious architecture, 70–72, 75, 77, 100, 101; Shah Jahan as founder of, 154, 166; Shi'i shrines in, 18, 85, 101–4, 110; spatial organization of, 18, 58, 71, 72, 77, 78, 80, 85, 101; urban building projects, 69–73, 78, 80, 175; urban history of, 6, 7, 15, 17, 67, 86; urban image of, 18–19, 73–80; and urban subjectivity, 59, 80. *See also specific buildings*

Dhanraj, *Genealogical Chart of Jahangir,* 1610–23, 152, *153*

Diwan-i 'Amm. *See* Red Fort

Diwan-i Khass. *See* Red Fort

Diwān-i Muhandis, 46

Dumont, *Plan and Elevation of the Governor's Palace in Pondicherry*, 1755, 128, *128*

E

East India Company College, 173
Eaton, Natasha, 6
eighteenth century: characteristics of, 9, 11–12; long eighteenth century, 4, 12, 15, 175, 177, 178; and mobility, 7, 181n21; recasting of, 4–8; transitional nature of, 15
Elevation of the Thousand Pillared Hall, Madura, c. 1750, 192n77
Elliot, Henry M., 173
English East India Company, 7, 9, 11, 138, 140, 143, 147, 173

F

Faiz Bazaar. *See* Delhi
Faizabad, 6–7, 85
Fakhr al-Din Qadi Khan, 183n39
Fakhr al-Masajid, Pride of the Mosques, Delhi, 1728–29, 17–18, *17*, 71–72, *71*, 107
Fakhr al-Nisa, 71
Farrukh Siyar (r. 1713–19): gateway of, dargah of Bakhtiyar Kaki, Delhi, *62*, 63, 64–65, *64*, 77; and inscription, 64–65, 77; and instability, 184n4; screen of, dargah of Bakhtiyar Kaki, Delhi, 63, *63*, 64, *64*, 75, 77
Fatāwā al-ʿĀlamgīriyya (Fatwas of ʿAlamgir), and Mughal architecture, 16, 27, 48–49, 55, 183n39
Fatāwā al-Hindiyya (Fatwas of India), 27
Fatehpur Sikri, 61, 95
Fatehpuri Masjid, Delhi, 70
Fayz ʿAli Khan, 169, 170
Fergusson, James, 5, 13, 16, 151, 175
Fidai Khan Koka, 49
Fort William, Calcutta, *126*, 127
France, 7, 15, 18, 145–47
French East India Company (Compagnie des Indes Orientales, or CDIO), 7, 9, 11, 114, 127, 146
French Orientalism, 16, 145, 146

G

Gadebusch, Raffael, 145
Ganesh Pol, 125
Gentil, Jean-Baptiste: architectural studies commissioned by, 18, 114, 115–16, 125, 127, 130, 134, 147, 176; collection of, 134, 135, 145, 146; memoirs of, 134, 192n72; on Mughal architecture, 16, 137, 145; and Mughal history, 134–35, 145; and Polier, 142–43
Gentil Album, 134, 135
geographies: and illustrated geographies, 3; textual geographies, 15, 16, 19, 167, 169–73, 174, 176, 193n53, 194n65, 194n68
George IV (king of England), 177
Ghazi al-Din Khan: and madrasa of, 72
Ghulam ʿAli Khan, 6, 144, 160, 170
Ghulam Qadir, 11
Glover, William J., 172, 194n68
Godehu, Charles Robert, 192n77
Goetz, Hermann, 5, 180n6
Gole, Susan, 190n21, 190–91n37
Govardhan II, 130
Governor's Palace, Pondicherry, 128, *128*
Guha, Sumit, 14
Gur-i Amir (c. 1400–1404), 23, 39, 152

H

Hada Mahal, Fatehpur Sikri (1571–85), 95
Hadith, 52
Hakim Ahsan Ullah Khan, 160
Hamadeh, Shirine, 8, 185n23
Hanafi school of law, 48
Hardinge, Charles, 168
Hasan, Zafar, 84, 100, 184n12, 185n22, 187n1
Hasan Karahisari, 52
Haspat Rai, 183n25
Hastings, Warren, 138
Heber, Reginald, 84
historical subjectivity, and Mughal architecture, 12, 59, 65, 175, 177
historicization, of Mughal architecture, 1, 2–4, 5, 12–19, 29, 55, 65, 72, 73, 85, 101, 110, 111, 114, 130–31, 133–37, 144–45, 147, 150–51, 154, 174, 175, 179

history writing, 12–14, 169, 172, 175
Hodges, William: and Picturesque style, 138–39, 140, 144–45, 146, 147; *View of the Gateway of the Tomb of Akbar at Sikandra*, 139
Humayun (r. 1530–40, 1555–56): Fergusson on, 5; plan of tomb, *94*, 95; tomb of, 18, *24*, 59, 67, 87, 90, 91, 101, 102, 104, 109–10, 160, 167; tomb of Safdar Jang compared to, 97, 101, 104, 109–10
Hurel, Roselyne, 189n1

I

Iltutmish (r. 1201–36), 184n8
Imam al-Din Riyazi, 46
Imambara, 105–108, 134
ʿInayat Khan, 166
Indian architecture: and Company Painting, 138; European representations of, 18, 114, 116, 138–40, 144–45, 147; and landscape architecture, 39; and Picturesque style, 18, 114, 116, 138–40, 144–45, 147. *See also* Mughal architecture
India's Fabled City: The Art of Courtly Lucknow (Los Angeles County Museum of Art and Musée Guimet, 2010–11), 7
Indo-Persian manuscript culture, 16
Indo-Saracenic style, 177
innovation: and architectural practice, 23, 29, 36, 46, 99, 101, 110
inscriptions, 49–52
Iran, 11, 12, 23, 102, 165
Islamic art history, 8
istiqbāl, and Mughal architecture, 23, 27, 29, 32, 35–36, 39–40, 42–45, 46, 47, 100–101, 182n7
Iʿtimad al-Daula, tomb of, *4*, 18, 90, 119, 122, *123*, 142, 143, *143*

J

Jaffar Khan, 70
Jahan Ara, Mughal princess, 51, 68, 70, 102–3, 136, 188n39, 188n43, 191n43
Jahandar Shah (r. 1712–13), 184n4
Jahangir (r. 1605–27): Fergusson on, 5; and Iʿtimad al-Daula, 90, 142; in Mughal pictorial genealogies,

152, *153*; tomb of, Lahore, 1637, 87, 103

Jai Singh II, 69–70

Jaigarh Fort, 125, 190n22

Jaipur, 8, 69, 70

Jaipur City Palace Museum, 119

Jami' Masjid (1648), Agra, 50, 51

Jami' Masjid (1653), Delhi: in architectural studies, 72, 115, 143, 145; Badshahi Masjid compared to, 36, 39, 49–50, 51, 107; eastern gateway of, 76; Fakhr al-Masajid compared to, 17–18, 72; historicization of, 154; inscriptions of, 49–50, 51; *Jami' Masjid, Delhi,* c. 1815, 154, 156, *156; Jami Masjid in Delhi,* from the *Palais Indiens* (c. 1774), 116, *116; Plan of the Jami Masjid of Delhi* from the *Palais Indiens* (c. 1774), *118,* 119; Shah Jahan's sponsorship of, 70; and shift in urban order, 73; in textual geographies, 167; and urban building projects, 175; and Ustad Ahmad Lahori, 46; view of, 36, *37,* 72

Jantar Mantar, Delhi, c. 1725, 69–70

Jats, 9

Jesuit missions, 127–28, 170

Joly, Adrien-Jacques, 192n72

Joly, Hugues-Adrien, 192n72

K

Ka'ba, Mecca, 51

Kalimāt-i Ṭaiyabāt, 124

Kanbo, Muhammad Salih, 150, 164

Kavuri-Bauer, Santhi, 5–6, 144, 145, 193n53, 194n68

Keshani, Hussein, 185n18, 187n28

Khalil Sultan, 152

Khayr Allah, 46

Khera, Dipti, 8, 181n24

Khulasa'-i Rāz, 46

Khuldabad, 60, 161

Kifayat Allah, 188n51

Koch, Ebba: on architectural representation, 119, 189n6; on funerary complex of Safdar Jang, 187n4; on Mughal architecture, 5, 23, 182n1; on multi-pillared hall typology, 165

L

Lafitte de Brassier, Louis François Grégoire, *Plan of Fort William, Calcutta,* c. 1779, *126,* 127

Lafont, Jean-Marie, 147, 192n70

Lahore: audience halls in, 165; and textual geographies, 169, 172–73. *See also* Badshahi Masjid, Lahore, 1673–74

Lahori, 'Abd al-Hamid Lahori, 166, 185n14, 193n33

Lalah Sil Chand, *Tafrih al-'Imārāt* (Account of the buildings, 1824), 169, 193n53

Langlès, Louis-Mathieu, 146

Latif, Syad Muhammad, 173

Lelyveld, David, 194n68

Lippit, Yukio, 14

literary culture: and Delhi, 3, 59, 73–80, 186n71; imagery of, 161, 164; and lexicography, 6; and poetry, 3, 5, 15, 27, 53, 161, 164

Lodi dynasty, 184n8

Losensky, Paul, 27

Losty, J. P., 6, 144, 154, 189n5, 192n1

Louis XVI (king of France), 114, 125, 146

Lucknow, India, 6–7, 15, 85, 91. *See also* Bara Imambara (or Great Imambara) complex, Lucknow (1784–91)

Lushington, John Steven, 169

Lutf Allah Muhandis, 46

M

Ma'asir-i 'Ālamgīrī, 45, 47–48

McLeod, Duncan, 177

Makramat Khan, 46

Malet, Charles Ware, 191n50

mandalas, 95

Man Mandir, Benares, 125

Marathas, 9, 11, 151

Masjid-i Shah (1611–38), 51–52

Masjid-i Shaykh Lutfullah (1603–19), 51–52

Mayo, Richard Bourke, Lord, 178

Mayo College, Ajmer, 1870s, 177–78, *178*

Mazhar 'Ali Khan: Folio from the *Metcalfe Album (Reminiscences of Imperial Delhie),* 1844, 167, *168;*

Reminiscences of Imperial Dehlie, 167; as topographical painter, 6, 144

Metcalfe, Charles, 167

Metcalfe, Thomas, 167

Mihr Chand, 6, 130

Minor, Heather Hyde, 14

Mirak Mirza Ghiyas, tomb of Humayun, Delhi, 1562–71, *24,* 67, 95

Mir Musharraf, 78

Mirza Jahangir (son of Akbar II), 164, 185n22

Mirza Muhammad-Amin Qazwini, 166

Mirza Shah Rukh Beg: *Akbarabadi Mosque,* from *Āsār al-Sanādīd* (c. 1847), 170–71, *170;* as artist of renderings for *Āsār al-Sanādīd,* 169–70; and topographical painting, 144

mobility: and Mughal architectural culture, 8, 108; and global circulation of Mughal architecture, 18–19; and transregional contacts, 7, 181n21; and travel narratives, 74

Mohan Singh, 130

Mohsan Khan, 70

Motigny papers, 147

Moti Masjid, Mehrauli, Delhi, 1709: and Bahadur Shah, *62, 63,* 67, 68, 184–85n12; location of, 183n49

Moti Masjid, Red Fort of Agra, 1653, 51, 183n49

Moti Masjid ("Pearl Mosque"), Delhi, 1658–63: 'Alamgir as patron of, 22–23, 52, 94; arches of, 35; architectonic forms of, 35, 36; Badshahi Masjid compared to, 39; bangla pavilion, 35; bangla vault, 32, *33;* Bibi ka Maqbara compared to, 40, 45; capital, 29, *31;* cornice, detail, 36, *36;* courtyard wall, 35, *35;* dome, 32, *33,* 35; and experimentation, 17, 29, 32, 35, 36, 100; inscriptions of, 51; interior wall, detail, *30;* location of, 183n49; mihrab, 32, *34,* 35; minbar, 32, *34,* 35; Nagina Masjid compared to, 29, 35; plan of, *28*, 29; sculptural effects of, 94; vaulting and supports, 32, *32*; view of, *22*; visual qualities of, 22, 23

Mughal architecture: abstraction of, 19, 111, 146, 147, 175, 177; architectonic forms, 35, 36, 44, 55, 116, 147; and architectural plans, 123–24; and artistic merit, 17; and authority of Mughal empire, 9, 12; and Awadhi architecture, 18, 85, 86, 87, 89, 90, 91, 104, 105, 106, 110–11, 115, 133–34, 145, 147, 176, 187n12; and concept of the monumental, 2, 3, 5–6, 7, 23, 151, 161, 164–65, 175; and epigraphy, 51–52, 183n39; and essentialist interpretation, 5; and experimentation, 17, 23, 45–46, 55; and funerary complexes, 39, 51, 58, 59–60, 67; global consumption of, 18–19, 145–47; and historical subjectivity, 12, 59, 65, 175, 177; historicization of, 1, 2–4, 5, 12–19, 29, 55, 65, 72, 73, 85, 101, 110, 111, 114, 130–31, 133–37, 144–45, 147, 150–51, 154, 174, 175, 179; and imperial histories, 16, 19; and Islamicization, 5; and istiqbāl concept, 23, 27, 29, 32, 35–36, 39–40, 42–45, 46, 47, 100–101, 182n7; and landscape architecture, 39; in north India, 85, 86, 105–8; ornamental elements of, 116, 147, 161; and *Palais Indiens*, 114, 123; recasting eighteenth century, 4–8; reflexive style of, 13, 17, 18, 23, 59, 72, 81, 152, 154, 175, 177; and regulation, 17, 23, 27, 46–52, 55; and self-referentiality, 2, 3, 12; standardization of style, 17, 18, 23, 47, 53; Timurid roots of, 5, 12, 23, 39, 95; circulation of images in Europe, 15, 18–19; and urbanism, 1, 4, 6, 7, 15, 17, 19, 23, 70, 73; visual language of, 23, 27, 39, 53, 58, 73, 81, 84–85, 86, 91–92, 99, 110, 111, 175–76, 177. *See also* architectural representation

Mughal empire (1526–1858): architectural language of, 1, 7, 8, 15, 16–17, 18, 19, 23, 29, 46–47, 55, 73; authority of, 1, 9, 11, 12, 39, 58, 65, 87, 89, 90, 110, 144, 147, 151; autonomy of, 23; characteristics of eighteenth century, 9, 11–12; and decline narrative, 6, 84; emblematic architectural forms of, 1; European officers and visitors seeking audience with emperor, 9; genres of history writing of, 13–14; identity of, 1, 23, 39, 85, 86, 91, 105, 135, 137, 145, 150, 175; imperial histories, 15, 16; instability in, 58, 181n36, 184n4; legacy of, 2, 65, 73; pictorial genealogies of, 152, 154; and provinces, 9; rebellions against, 9, 85, 181n27; and Sunni-centered socioreligious order, 11–12, 18, 85–86, 102, 104, 188n35; transition from Mughal to British rule, 1, 2, 6, 151, 178

Mughal painting: and architectural representation, 119, 122, 130, 144, 150, 156, 158, 176; and European representational techniques, 127–28; genres of, 150, 156; and historicism, 3, 150; and portraiture, 53, 55, 119, 152, 160

Muhammad-Amin Qazwini, 166

Muhammad Fakhr al-Din Husain, 160

Muhammad Jan Qudsi Mashhadi, 166

Muhammad Salih Kanbo. *See* Kanbo, Muhammad Salih

Muhammad Shah (r. 1719–48): accession of, 58, 181n36; burial enclosure, dargah of Nizam al-Din, Delhi, 1748, *66*, 67–69, 161, 188n39; court of, 78, 79, 130; marriage to Qudsiyya Begum, 70, 102, 180n6; Sawai Jai Singh's astronomical text dedicated to, 69

Muhammad Waris. *See* Waris, Muhammad

Muharram, 79, 105

muhtasib, 77–78

Muʿin al-Din Chishti, 60, 61, 65

Mumtaz Mahal, 39, 60

Mundy, Godfrey, 108–9

Murad Bakhsh, 47

Muraqqaʿ-yi Dihlī: and Dargah Quli Khan, 7, 18, 59, 73, 74–80, 81; on music, 73, 74, 76, 77, 78–79, 186n55; on people of city, 76–77, 80; on poets, 73, 74, 75; on sacred spaces, 77, 80; on shrines of Delhi, 74, 75, 77, 78, 79, 80; and social hierarchy, 78–79; on urban culture, 16, 18, 73, 74–80; and urbanistic view of Delhi, 73–74

Murar, *The Siege of Daulatabad* from the *Pādshāhnāma* (c. 1635), 119, *121*

Murshidabad, Bengal, 102; and palace, 177

music: ʿAlamgir's regulation of, 48, 183n31; *Muraqqaʿ-yi Dihlī* on, 73, 74, 76, 77, 78–79, 186n55

N

Nadir Shah (r. 1736–47), 11, 58, 79, 184n5

Nagina Masjid, Agra, c. 1630, *28*, 29, 35

Naim, C. M., 194n65, 194n68

Najaf Khan, tomb of, 103, *104*

Naqqar Khana. *See* Red Fort, Delhi

Nash, John, 177

Nath, R., 184n12

nawabs of Loharu, burial enclosure, dargah of Bakhtiyar Kaki, Delhi, 1802, 65, *65*

Necipoğlu, Gülru, 189n10, 192n7

Neoclassical style, 139, 177

Nevasi Lal, 130

Nizam al-Din Auliya (d. 1325), 67, 102

Nizam al-Din dargah: and Akbar, 59, 67, 188n39; burial enclosure of Muhammad Shah, *66*, 67–69, 161, 188n39; grave of Nizam al-Din Auliya, 67, 68, 102, 185n18; literary representations of, 75, 76, 186n71; and patronage, 59–60, 78; plan of, 68, *68*; in textual geographies, 167; and tomb of Humayun, 101, 102, 104; view of, 68, *69*

Nizam al-Mulk Asaf Jah I, 9, 72, 73, 80
Nizam Shahis of Ahmadnagar (1496–1636), 91
Nur Allah, 46
Nur Jahan, 90, 102, 136, 142, 191n43

O

observatories, 58, 69, 70
Ottoman Baroque, 8
Ottoman empire (1299–1922): and architectural ornament, 91; and architectural plans, 122–23; and imperial portraiture, 152, 154; and inscriptional programs 51–52; and literary culture, 164

P

Pādshāhnāma: Bichitr, *Shah Jahan Receiving His Three Eldest Sons* (c. 1656–57), 156–57, *157*, 158; Murar, *The Siege of Daulatabad* (c. 1635), 119, *121*, 189n6; on Shah Jahan, 123–24, 156–59, 166
Palace of Dara Shikoh, 135, 136–37
Palace pavilions, Red Fort, Agra, c. 1630, *26*
Palais Indiens (c. 1774): audience of, 145–47; and codification of Mughal architectural past, 114–15, 116, 147; commemorative function of, 125, 127; and depiction of ornament, 130–31, 133, 134; *Façade of a Delhi Palace,* 118, *118–19; Façade of the Palace of Dara Shikoh in Agra,* 128, *129;* format of paintings, 115–16, 118–19, 127, 128, 154; *Gateway of the Red Fort of Delhi, 3,* 7, 116, *117,* 131; Gentil's commissioned architectural studies, 18, 114, 115–16, 125, 127, 130, 134, 147, 176; and gridded plans, 122, 125; and historical narrative, 130–31, 133–37, 144–45, 147, 176; idealization in, 143; inscriptions of, 116, 130, 190n31; *Jami Masjid in Delhi,* 116, *116;* Mausoleum of Safdar Jang, 116, *117;* pictorial conventions of, 145; *Plan of the Jami Masjid of Delhi, 118,* 119; *Plan of the Palace and Garden of Dara Shikoh in*

Agra, 128, *129; Riverside Façade of the Red Fort of Delhi, 115, 115;* subjective portrayals of, 131, 133; and textual glosses, 130; visual language of, 114, 116, 130, 176, 179
parchīn kārī, 52, 55
Parodi, Laura, 44, 182n20
patronage: in Awadhi provincial capitals, 85, 89; and bridging of past and present, 1; and cultural exchange, 6; and dargahs, 59–60, 61, 65, 67, 69, 78, 185n16; and Delhi building projects, 69, 70–73, 80, 169; and French and English East India Companies, 7; and imperial religiosity, 52–53, 55; and inscriptions, 49, 51; motivations of patrons, 15; and ornamental programs, 161; patterns of, 185n12; politics of, 5; and social hierarchy, 78, 80; and textual geographies, 169
Persian art, 14, 27
Persian language: and Britons living in India, 164; and shahrāshūb genre, 6; textual geographies in, 15, 16, 19, 167, 176
Persian poetry, 27
Picart, Bernard, 146
Picturesque style: and European representations of Indian architecture, 18, 114, 116, 138–40, 144–45, 146, 147; and tomb of Safdar Jang, 108, *109,* 110
pietra dura, 23, 42, 43, 52, 91, 105, 116, 131, 183n59
poetry, 3, 5, 15, 27, 53, 161, 164
Polier, Antoine, 143–44, 145
Pollock, Sheldon, 14
positivism, 151, 173, 176
Princes and Painters in Mughal Delhi: 1707–1857 (Asia Society, 2012), 7
Prophet Muhammad, 64, 79, 105
Purana Qila (Old Fort), 75

Q

Qadamgah of ʿAli (shrine of the footprint of ʿAli), 76, 102, 186n71
Qadam Sharif shrine, Delhi, 75, 79
Qademi, Sharif Husain, 193n36
Qudsiyya Bagh, Delhi, c.1748, 5, 70, 180n6

Qudsiyya Begum, 70, 71, 102–3, 180n6
Qutb Sahib Bakhtiyar Kaki (d. 1235), 59–60. *See also* Bakhtiyar Kaki dargah
Qutb Minar complex, 109, 167, 168, 184n8
Qutb Shahis of Golconda and Hyderabad (1496–1687), 91

R

Rabiʿa Daurani, 39, 44, 87
Rajasthan, 85
Rajput architecture, 5, 125, 139
Rajput art, 8, 27, 119, 130, 138, 147
Rajputs, 9, 164
Ram Raz, *Essay on the Architecture of the Hindus,* 173–74
Raushan al-Daula, 71, 100
Rawdon-Hastings, Francis, 110
Razia (r. 1236–40), 136, 191n43
Red Fort, Agra, c. 1630, 23, *26,* 165, *165*
Red Fort, Delhi (1639–48): in architectural studies, 115, 138, 143, 145; axes emanating from main entrances of, 58; base of jharoka throne, 29, *30;* capital, palace pavilion, 29, *31;* Delhi Gate of, 76; *Detail of a Street Plan of Chandni Chowk in Delhi, 135, 136–37,* 190–91n37; *Diwan-i ʿAmm,* 154, 164–65, 167; *Diwan-i ʿAmm, Red Fort, Delhi,* (c. 1815), 8, 154, *155;* Diwan-i Khass, 165; gateway of, 131, *131,* 138, 154, 167; *Gateway of the Red Fort, Delhi,* c. 1815, 154, *155; Gateway of the Red Fort of Delhi,* from the *Palais Indiens* (c. 1774), *3,* 7, 116, *117,* 131; historicization of, 154; and imperial architectural tradition, 91; Lahore Gate of, 76; limited access represented by, 58; and *Muraqqaʿ-yi Dihlī,* 75, 76, 80; Naqqar Khane, 154; *Naqqar Khane, Red Fort, Delhi,* c. 1815, 154, *155;* palace pavilions, 52, 99, 183–84n59; plan of, 138; and refinement of architectural forms, 46; *Riverside Façade of the Red Fort of Delhi* from the *Palais Indiens* (c. 1774), 115, *115; Shah Jahan Before*

the Red Fort, c. 1815, 157–58, *159*;
Shah Jahan's commissioning
of, 29, 53, 58; and shift in urban
order, 17, 58, 73, 75, 80; and shift
toward ornamental style, 36, 43;
in textual geographies, 167, 169;
and travel narratives, 59, 75
Reinhardt, Walter, 191n43
Reminiscences of Imperial Dehlie, 167
Repton, Humphry, 177
Rice, Yael, 170, 194n63
Richard, Francis, 189n1
Roberdean, J. T., 150, 158, 166
Roberts, A. A., 172
Roberts, Emma, 109
Rococo, 5
Rousselet, Louis, 109
Roxburgh, David, 14, 182n7
Roy, Malini, 6, 8
Royal Asiatic Society, 173
Royal Pavilion, Brighton, 1803–32,
177, *177*
Russell, William Howard, 109
Rüstem, Ünver, 8

S
Sadiq Khan, 166
Safavid empire (1501–1722): and
architectural ornament, 91;
and artistic genealogies, 14;
dissolution of, 12; and imitative
practice, 27; and inscriptional
programs, 51–52; and literary
culture, 164; palace architecture
of, 95; and Shiʿism, 11
Safdar Jang, funerary complex of,
Delhi, 1753–54: architectonic
forms, 89, 99; architectural studies of, 115; and bangla jharokas,
89, 95, 110; British travelers on,
108–10; cenotaph, *93*, 94, 106;
and chahār bāgh, 86; corner
tower, 86, *89*, 131, *133*; dome, 95,
96, 99; exterior vault, *92*; façades
of, 89; garden pavilion, 86, *88*;
gateway, 99; gateway, detail, 86,
86; and hasht bihisht plan, 95,
110; and imperial architectural
tradition, 18, 84, 85, 86–87,
89–92, 94–95, 97, 99–101, 104,
105, 106, 108, 110, 115, 133, 175–76,

179, 187n4; inscription of, 89–90,
90, 187n15; interior chamber,
upper zone, 95, *96*; interior
vaults, 92, *93*, 97, *99*; *Mausoleum
of Safdar Jang*, from the *Palais
Indiens* (c. 1774), 116, *117*; mosque,
86, *88*, 99–100, *100*; ornamental
program of, 86, 89, 91–92, 99,
108, 110; paintings of, 109–10;
and Picturesque style, 108, *109*,
110; plan of, 86, 87, *87*, *94*, 95,
99; sculptural relief on interior
vault, 97, *97*; and Shiʿi shrines in
Delhi, 18, 85, 101–4; side towers
of, 131; tomb of Humayun compared to, 97, 101, 104, 109–10;
and urban recoding, 101–2, 103,
104, 110; vaulting technology of,
94–95, 97, 106, 108, 110, 187n28;
views of, *2*, *7*, *84*, *132*
Sangin Beg, 167
Sanskrit, 164
Saqi Mustaʿidd Khan, 48
Sayr al-Manāzil (A Tour of the Sites,
1836), on urban history, 16, 19,
152, 167–68, 169
Sayyid Ahmad Khan, 169, 172, 173
Selim Chishti, tomb of, 61,
141–42, *141*
Seven Years' War, 11
Sèvres porcelain, 146
Shah ʿAlam II (r. 1759–1806), 11, 63,
65, 103, 144
Shahi Mardan dargah, Delhi, 71,
102, 103, 110
Shah Jahan (r. 1628–58): and
Akbar II, 150, 151, 154; ʿAlamgir's
deposing of, 27, 47, 53, 55, 166;
ʿAmal-i Ṣāliḥ on, 123–24, 150,
152, 154, 157–58, 161, 166, 171;
cenotaphs of Shah Jahan and
Mumtaz Mahal, 60, *93*; cenotaph surrounded by marble
lattice screen, 60, 158, 161; and
conceptions of space in Delhi,
58; court of, 164; and dargah of
Muʿin al-Din Chishti at Ajmer,
65; Fergusson on, 5; as founder
of Delhi, 154, 166; Goetz on,
5; imperial architecture of, 12,
13, 27, 29, 42, 49, 51, 53, 55, 107,

123–24, 154; imperial thrones
of, 161; Jami Masjid as imperial congregational mosque
of, 17–18, 36, 49; and Mughal
history writing, 14; *Pādshāhnāma*
on, 123–24, 156–59, 166; portraiture of, 53; urban order established by, 67
Shahjahanabad, Delhi: building
projects of, 80; city plans of,
134; completion of, 59; founding
of, 16; gardens of, 70; madrasa
of, 72; mosques of, 100, 107; as
Mughal capital, 6, 58, 67, 144;
palace-fortress of, 29; public
spaces of, 76; Safdar Jang and
descendants owning property
in, 99
Shāhjahānnāma (History of Shah
Jahan), 166
shahrāshūb genre: and literary
culture, 6; and *Muraqqaʿ-yi Dihlī*,
74; and nostalgia, 145; and textual geographies, 16, 169, 171
Shah Shujaʿ, 47
Shalimar Bagh, Lahore (1637–41), 99
Sharaf-al-Din ʿAli Yazdi, 152
Sharma, Yuthika, 6, 8, 140–41, 144,
145, 193n21
Shiʿism: and Delhi shrine district,
18, 85, 101–4, 110; identity of, 85;
and Mughal empire, 11–12, 85,
188n35; and Qudsiyya Begum,
102, 103
shrine of ʿAli, Najaf, 91
shrine of Husayn, Karbala, 91
shrine of Imam Riza, Mashhad, 91
Shujaʿ al-Daula (r. 1753–75), 105,
115, 135
Shujaʿat Khan, 71
Sikandra, 99, 119
Sikhs, 9, 181n27
Sinan, 14, 51
Sita Ram: as Picturesque artist, 6;
Tomb of Safdar Jang, *109*, 110
Skinner, James, 170
Soane, John, 173
South Asian art history, 8
souvenir paintings, 3, 18, 114, 143, 174
Sprenger, Aloys, 173
Subrahmanyam, Sanjay, 14

Sultanate period (1211–1526), 60,
  67, 184n8
Sunahri Masjid (Golden Mosque,
  1721–22), 71, 100
Sunni Islam: in Mughal empire,
  11–12, 18, 85–86, 102, 104, 188n35;
  schools of legal thought, 48

T

Taj Mahal (Mausoleum of Mumtaz
  Mahal), Agra, 1632–48: Bibi ka
  Maqbara compared to, 39–40,
  42–43, 46, 97; Daniells' *The Taje
  Mahale, at Agra*, 140, *140*; and
  epigraphy, 51; exterior dado,
  detail, 40, *42*; exterior spandrels,
  detail, 40, *43*; gateway of, 131,
  132; *Gateway of the Taj Mahal*,
  142–43, *142*; historicization of,
  154; and imperial architectural
  tradition, 87, 89, 175; and marble
  lattice screen, 60; and Mughal
  architecture, 12; and Mughal
  visual idiom, 7, 23; pietra dura,
  detail, *27*, 40; plan of, *94*, 95, 99;
  Shah Jahan as patron of, 49, 51,
  53, 161; tomb of I'timad al-Daula
  compared to, 90; tomb of Safdar
  Jang compared to, 97; and vase
  motif, 32, 182n11; views of, *13, 26*,
  99; visual language of, 23
Talkatora Karbala, Lucknow
  (1798), 91
taqlīd, 27
Taqrir al-Tahrir, 46
Tavernier, Jean-Baptiste, 16, 59, 80
ta'ziya, 105, 108
tazkiras (biographical dictionaries): and literary culture, 6; as
  multidimensional texts, 74; and
  textual geographies, 16, 169, 170,
  171, 194n65, 194n68
textual geographies, 15, 16, 19, 167,
  169–73, 174, 176, 193n53, 194n65,
  194n68
Tillotson, Giles, 8
Timur (r. 1370–1405), 152, 160
Timurid dynasty (1370–1507): and
  artistic genealogies, 14, 152, 154,
  160; and Mughal architecture, 5,
  12, 23, 39, 95
Tipu Sultan, 146

Todar Mal Baradari, 95
topographical painting, 6,
  119, 144
transregional contacts, 7, 15, 18–19
travel narratives, 3, 15, 16, 74
Travers, Robert, 180n16
Treaty of Paris of 1763, 11
Tripolia Gate, 115
Troll, Christian W., 194n68
Twelver Shi'ism, 11, 104, 105

U

Udaipur, 8
Ulugh Beg, 152
Ulūs-i arba'a-yi Chingīzī (The four
  Chingizid nations), 152
urbanism: and building projects
  in Delhi, 69–73, 78, 80, 175; and
  historical subjectivity, 59, 65; and
  Mughal architecture, 1, 4, 6, 7,
  15, 17, 19, 23, 70, 73; *Muraqqa'-yi
  Dihlī* on urban culture, 16, 18,
  73, 74–80; and Red Fort, Delhi,
  17, 58, 73, 75, 80; Sangin Beg on
  urban history, 16, 19, 152, 167–68,
  169; and tomb of Safdar Jang,
  101–2, 103, 104, 110; and urban
  spatial organization, 15, 17, 18,
  64–65, 67
Urdu: and Britons living in India,
  164; and shahrāshūb genre, 6;
  textual geographies in, 15, 16, 19,
  167, 169, 176
'Urfi Shirazi, 171–72
Ustad Ahmad Lahori: as architect of Shah Jahan, 45–46, 99;
  Mausoleum of Mumtaz Mahal
  (Taj Mahal), Agra, 1632–48, *13*,
  26, 99
Ustad Hamid, 46
Uzbek plans, 122–23
Uzun Hasan (r. 1453–78), 95

V

Velho, Juliana, 135–37
Velho, Thérèse, 135
Victoria & Albert Museum,
  London, 189n1

W

Wales, James, 139, 191n50
Waris, Muhammad, 166, 193n33

women: in changing social system,
  79, 186n75; royal Mughal women
  as patrons of architecture,
  102–3, 188n42

Y

Yahya Kashi, 166

Z

Zafar Mahal, Mehrauli, Delhi
  (c. 1806–58): and dargah of
  Bakhtiyar Kaki, 67, 178; and
  invocation of imperial past, 1, 2,
  178; plan of, *61*; view of, *xii*, *179*
Zafarnāma, 152
Zafarnāma-i Shāh Jahāni, 166
Zain al-Din, shrine in Khuldabad,
  Aurangabad, 60
Zayn al-'Abidin Shirwani, *Bustān
  al-Siyāḥat* (Garden of voyaging,
  1833–34), 168–69
Zinat al-Masjid, Delhi, 1707, 71
Zinat al-Nisa, Mughal princess, 71

ILLUSTRATION CREDITS

The photographers and the sources of visual material other than the owners indicated in the captions are as follows. Every effort has been made to supply complete and correct credits; if there are errors or omissions, please contact Yale University Press so that corrections can be made in any subsequent edition.

Aga Khan Museum, Toronto: fig. 5.1
Archives nationales d'outre-mer, Aix-en-Provence:
 figs. 4.14, 4.15
Bibliothèque nationale de France, Paris: figs. 0.4, 4.1–4.3,
 4.5, 4.6, 4.17
© The British Library Board, London: figs. 0.5, 0.6, 3.23,
 4.23, 4.24, 5.2–5.5, 5.7–5.9, 5.12, 5.13
Centre des Archives d'outre-mer, Aix-en-Provence:
 figs. 4.14, 4.15
Amos Chapple: fig. 1.21
Chester Beatty Library, Dublin: fig. 4.7
Maharaja Sawai Man Singh II Museum Trust, City Palace,
 Jaipur: figs. 4.9, 4.10, 4.12
Qadeem Musalman: fig. 1.23
Khizra Naseem: fig. 1.22
Ghumakkar Punit: fig. 1.24
Holly Shaffer: figs. 1.25, 1.27
Qmin: fig. 6.1
Royal Collection Trust/© Her Majesty Queen Elizabeth II
 2017: figs. 4.8, 5.6
© Zishan Sheikh: fig. 1.32
Anant Singh: fig. 1.25
Vetra: fig. 1.28
© Victoria and Albert Museum, London: figs. 0.4, 1.33, 4.4,
 4.11, 4.13, 4.16, 4.22, 4.25–4.27
Suzan Yalman: figs. 2.8, 2.10
Zenith210: fig. 5.1